Year-Round
BLOOMERS

www.jerrybaker.com

Year-Round BLOOMERS

Hundreds of *Super Secrets* for the Backyard Gardener

by Jerry Baker,
America's Master Gardener®

Published by American Master Products, Inc.

Published by American Master Products, Inc. / Jerry Baker

Executive Editor: Kim Adam Gasior
Managing Editor: Cheryl Winters Tetreau
Interior Design and Layout: Sandy Freeman
Cover Design: Kitty Pierce Mace
Illustration: Len Epstein and Elayne Sears
Copy Editor: Nanette Bendyna
Indexer: Nan Badgett

Publisher's Cataloging-in-Publication

Baker, Jerry.
    Jerry Baker's year-round bloomers : hundreds of
super secrets for the backyard gardener / author, Jerry
Baker ; editor, Kim Adam Gasior ; illustrator, Len
Epstein.
    p. cm.
    Includes index.
    ISBN 0–922433–54–2

    1. Gardening. 2. Plants, Ornamental.   I. Title.
II. Title: Year-round bloomers

SB453.B31745 2003   635.9
                                03–200541

Printed in the United States of America
2 4 6 8 10 9 7 5 3 hardcover

Introduction

Hey, folks—are you ready for a whole new way to look at gardening? Then you've come to the right place. I can't wait to introduce you to the exciting world of four-season gardening! No matter where you live—from the sunny South to the frigid North—it's possible to put together a bunch of ordinary plants to create *extraordinary* gardens that look as good in January as they do in June. I've rounded up some of the latest and greatest design ideas, mixed 'em together with the best of Grandma Putt's old-fashioned garden smarts, and put the whole kit and caboodle in one handy-dandy book: *Jerry Baker's Year-Round Bloomers*!

Here's an overview of what you'll find in the following pages, to help you on your way:

Part 1: "A Plan That's Pleasin' Season by Season" is packed with hints and how-to helpers for planning a beautiful year-round garden from the ground up.

Part 2: "Get Ready for a Spring Fling!" is the place to turn when you want to get the growing season off to an eye-popping start.

Part 3: "Fun in the Summer Sun!" helps turn up the heat, so your yard will burst forth with a bounty of blooms through the dog days.

Part 4: "Fall in Love with Autumn" is chock-full of terrific tips for celebrating the return of cooler weather with a rainbow of blooms, awesome autumn foliage, and more.

Part 5: "Wow! Wonderful Winter Bloomers" will help you turn your boring, off-season landscape into a winter wonderland that's positively bursting with color, foliage, and even fragrance!

So don't wait a minute longer—let me show you how to make the most of every square inch of your yard, all year long. Welcome to the wonderful world of year-round gardening!

Contents

PART 1

A PLAN THAT'S PLEASIN' SEASON BY SEASON

What would you give to have a yard that looks great every month of the year? No, it's not just wishful thinking—it's easier than you think! In fact, I can summarize the secret to successful year-round bloomers in three words: planning, planning, and planning. Well, okay—that's just one word, but you get the idea!

You see, four-season gardening takes a little more time up front, because you need to choose all of your plants carefully. Instead of sticking with the "same-old, same-olds" that bloom once and look boring the rest of the year, you'll discover plants that have more to offer: an extra-long flowering season, evergreen leaves, showy seedheads, and so on. These multi-season wonders can easily double, triple, or even quadruple the pleasure you get out of your yard year after year—*without* any extra effort on your part. And don't think you've got to do a lot of book research to get started; I've done all of the hard work for you. I've packed this section with my very best tips for planning the perfect four-season landscape. So c'mon—let's get growing!

CHAPTER 1

The Show Must Go On—and On!

C'mon, folks: Why settle for a yard that's pretty for only a few months, when you have to look at it every day of the year? If you fill your property with plants that pull their weight, you'll have a yard that works as hard as you do. In this chapter, I'll let you in on my super secrets for planning and planting the most magnificent multi-season landscape you've ever seen—*guaranteed!*

PLANNING

In this chapter, we're going to take a look at the down-and-dirty basics of planning a year-round yard from the ground up. Here are my top picks for creating a landscape that you'll always find pleasin', no matter what the season!

- Learn to look beyond blooms; plants have a lot of other interesting features, too
- Check out other people's yards and visit botanical gardens to get ideas
- Figure out which seasons your existing yard looks best in, then experiment as you fill in the gaps

- Make the most of *all* of your plant options; don't just stick with perennials, for example
- Be sure to include evergreen foliage for winter interest
- Where space is limited, look for dwarf varieties of four-season favorites
- Add a few plants with distinctive shapes as accent points
- Include lots of plants with colorful foliage for all-season interest

What's the first thing that catches your eye when you look at a pretty yard? Why—it's the bright blooms, of course! It's easy to have a beautiful backyard from mid-spring to midsummer, because that's when flowers are most abundant. But when you're ready for a landscape that looks great all year long, it's time to look beyond the obvious. Get ready to discover dozens of tips for turning a ho-hum, single-season bed into a fantastic, year-round attention-getter.

Explore Your Options

Now, don't assume that you have to give up on having lots of flowers—nothing could be further from the truth! The trick to four-season planning is using *all* of the interesting features that plants have to offer, including:

Beautiful berries. They come in an *amazing* array of colors—red, orange, yellow, blue, white—and even purple!

Lovely leaves. Remember to add some evergreen plants for winter color, too.

Striking seedheads. Many plants have seedheads that look great in wintertime—especially when they're frosted with a coating of snow or ice.

Spectacular stems. Shrubs are great choices—often having stems with bright colors, peeling bark, or curious twists and turns.

Don't Shop Early—Shop Often!

When you think about it, it's no surprise that many yards look their best in spring, then fizzle out by midsummer. That's because

forsythias, lilacs, and other inexpensive, flower-filled plants are an easy sell in spring, so garden centers load up on these old favorites to satisfy color-starved shoppers. But once the blooms fall, most of these plants look pretty boring for the rest of the year.

If you really want early color and you have plenty of room, go ahead and treat yourself to one or two of these single-season shrubs. But otherwise, I want you to be a smart shopper: Do your research before you head to the garden center, so you can pick out plants that have more to offer than just a few weeks of flowers. And shop once a month during the growing season to see what's new in bloom.

Walk for Success

Looking for ideas for your four-season garden? You can't do better than regular visits to a local botanical garden or arboretum! Grab a notebook and pencil, and then take a leisurely stroll around the grounds. When you see plants you find appealing, simply check their labels and make a note of their names. You'll know that the plants can grow in your area, since they are already thriving there!

Fill in the Blanks

Don't assume you have to start from scratch to make a great four-season garden! Simply take an inventory of the plants you already have—shrubs, trees, perennials, groundcovers, and so forth—then figure out what season (or seasons) each one looks best in. You'll want about a quarter of all your plants looking

BED BUILDER MIX

If you have a site that you'd like to fill with flowering beauties someday, it's never too soon to start the soil-building process. Scrape off the weeds and grass with a sharp spade, then add a dose of my super-duper Bed Builder Mix.

40 lbs. of bagged topsoil
10 lbs. of compost
5 lbs. of bonemeal
1 lb. of Epsom salts

Mix all of these ingredients in a wheelbarrow or garden cart, spread a 2- to 3-inch layer over the entire site, and then top the bed with mulch. Add the plants whenever you're ready!

good in each season, so take what you have and add other plants to fill in where things aren't well covered already. You may need just a few new additions to turn your existing yard into a real year-round showplace!

Talk About Flower Power!

Perennial plants don't just have a long life span—they can *bloom* for a long time, too! Instead of choosing the usual few-weeks-then-done classics like baby's breath (*Gypsophila paniculata*) and poppies (*Papaver*), look for perennials that'll bloom for months at a time— like coreopsis, catmints (*Nepeta*), and red valerian (*Centranthus ruber*), to name just a few. Keep your eye out, too, for new long-blooming or repeat-flowering cultivars, such as 'Autumn Snow' perennial candytuft (*Iberis sempervirens* 'Autumn Snow')—it shows off in both spring and fall!

Made to Be Broken

Everyone knows the number-one rule when planting beds and borders—short plants go in front, and taller plants go in back, right? Well, if you really want the best from your four-season garden, it's time to break that rule!

You see, the earliest-flowering perennials also tend to be the shortest in stature. So, if you put 'em all at the front of your garden, it'll look ho-hum boring for 11 months of the year. Instead, scatter the early risers throughout your beds and borders. That'll spread out the spring show.

Grandma Putt's
GREEN THUMB TIPS

Grandma loved to tell anyone who'd listen about the advantages of four-season gardening, but to be honest with you, she didn't always follow her own advice! Take this tip from her experience, and tailor your plantings to the seasons when you'll see them most. Around a pool, for instance, concentrate on summer color; outside the windows of your woodstove-warmed family room, a combination of evergreen foliage and bright berries will provide lots of winter interest.

Build Your Bed's "Bones"

Planning a year-round blooming yard is more than just selecting pretty flowers—it's about using everything you've got! Trees and shrubs, for instance, are a must for adding height and multi-season interest, while ground-covers are great for carpeting around their feet and keeping weeds to a minimum. When you plan good "bones" for your garden, and then fill in with flowers, you've got the recipe for a four-season showcase that's guaranteed to please!

It's Easy Being Green

I'll let you in on a little secret: The easiest way to turn an ordinary yard into a year-round landscape is to simply add evergreen foliage! Notice I didn't say only evergreen *trees*, like pines (*Pinus*) and spruces (*Picea*); I mean ever-green shrubs, perennials, and groundcovers, too. And really, "evergreen" means more than just the many shades of green; there are also plants that hold red, purple, blue, silver, black, tan, or multi-hued leaves all through the winter months. (For specific examples,

Ask Jerry

Q: *Help me out, Jerry: What's the difference between "evergreen" and "deciduous"—and what in heaven's name does the term "semi-evergreen" mean?*

A: Evergreen plants are the ones that hold on to their leaves or needles all year long, while deciduous trees and shrubs drop their leaves each fall and sprout new ones each spring. Semi-ever-green usually means that the plants hold on to their leaves well into winter; in cold climates, the leaves may last only until midwinter, while warmer temperatures help them stay almost until spring.

check out "Jerry's Best Bets for the Big Chill" on page 314.) Once you can count on a backdrop of colorful foliage all year long, it's a snap to add bright-blooming accents for stunning seasonal color!

Art at Work

Would you believe me if I said there's a way to get instant year-round interest without making any more work for yourself? It's true! All it takes is adding some kind of landscape accent— a concrete statue, a section of fencing, a piece of trellis, or some other object you find appeal-ing—to your favorite bed or border. Nestle the item among your flowers, or train a vine over it for the summer; then come fall, it'll reappear to brighten those dull winter days while your plants are taking a much-needed break.

Honey, I Shrunk the Shrubs!

Think you don't have room for shrubs in your yard? Trust me: If you've got enough room for flowers, you can grow shrubs, too! Check your local nursery or your favorite plant catalogs, and you'll be amazed at the number of new compact or dwarf shrubs that have come on

Grandma Putt's

GREEN THUMB TIPS

One of Grandma's favorite garden accents was a sun-dial she received as a wedding gift. I loved it, too, but when I bought one for my own garden from a mail-order catalog, I could never get it to keep time like hers! So what's the secret? Buy a locally made one, if possible, so the gnomon (the part that casts the shadow) is at the correct angle for your location. For more great tips, check out the Fre-quently Asked Questions (FAQ) page at www.sundials.org—the Web site of the North American Sundial Society.

the market recently. These pint-sized cuties are about half the size of their larger cousins—usually no more than 3 or 4 feet tall and wide, or about the size of a large clump of peonies or astilbes. Just about everyone has room for these!

8

Deck the Walls

Flowering vines are fantastic for seasonal color, but if you're going to plant them against your home, take a few precautions so they don't do more harm than good. I like to keep my vines on a lattice trellis that's stationed about 6 inches away from the exterior wall of my house. Besides keeping the wall clean and dry, this allows air to circulate behind the vine—and that'll go a long way toward stopping dastardly diseases in their tracks!

Winter Garden Smarts

When you're choosing plants to give your garden all-year interest, keep in mind the winter weather that is typical for your area. There's not much point in planting lots of evergreen groundcovers or planning on interesting perennial seedheads if you tend to get lots of snow every winter, since they'll be buried anyway! Or, if "green" winters are more common than white ones in your climate, look for plants with bright stems, leaves, or berries to keep the color comin' during those dull, dreary days.

MIX & FIX

FOUNDATION FOOD

High-visibility beds around the foundation of your house are perfect for four-season flowers, but the soil there is usually awful. Whip up the following tonic to fortify your beds and make 'em burst with blooms—with a minimum of work!

10 parts compost
3 parts bonemeal
2 parts bloodmeal
1 part kelp meal

Mix the ingredients in a garden cart or wheelbarrow. Spread a thin layer (about a half-inch or so) over the entire planting area, and lightly scratch it into the soil around the shrubs. Add a new layer each year. Top it with shredded bark or other mulch.

We gardeners love color—and lots of it! When you take your favorite flowers and mix 'em up with dependable four-season plants, you've got all the fixin's for a color-packed yard, no matter what time of year it is.

Take Your Garden's Temperature

Want to make your yard look like a million bucks? Use the same top-notch color tips that professional garden designers use:

➔ "Hot" colors—bright yellow, red, and orange—add excitement, and make beds and borders stand out at a distance.

➔ "Cool" colors, like blues, grays, and purples, create a soothing atmosphere and give the feeling of distance—ideal if your yard is on the small side.

➔ White, pale pinks, and light yellows usually act like hot colors because they catch your eye, even from a distance. They're super for brightening up shady spots, and they're perfect near a deck or patio where you relax on summer evenings, because they show up well in the pale moonlight.

Grandma Putt's

GREEN THUMB TIPS

Sure, Grandma loved flowers, but she taught me early on that leaves are just as important for making a long-lasting garden. So when you're planning your four-season showcase, search out plants with colorful foliage—red, orange, yellow, blue, purple, or silver—as well as green leaves that are marked with white, silver, cream, or gold. When you mix these in with the more common green-leaved flowers, their foliage adds zip that you can count on from earliest spring to the first freeze in fall. Talk about putting plants to work!

Keep It Simple

10

With so many thousands of possible plant combinations, how can you ever decide on the best ones for your year-round yard? Try this trick that the pros use: Choose a simple color scheme—two or three colors are best—for each bed, then stick to it!

Don't let anyone tell you which colors are "right" or "wrong"; it all depends on your own taste. If you like white and blue together, for instance, or pink and yellow, look for plants that have flowers, foliage, bark, or berries in those colors. That'll make plant shopping a snap, and it's a surefire way to create a great-looking garden!

Silver Is Gold

No matter what the season, you simply *can't* go wrong with silver foliage for sunny sites. Usually, the leaves themselves are green, but they look silvery or gray because of a covering of fine hairs that reflect the sunlight. Silvery plants—like lamb's ears (*Stachys byzantina*) and wormwoods (*Artemisia*)— are perfect for setting off brightly colored blooms, but they also look pretty with pastels. Best of all, most silver-leaved plants hold their foliage all through the winter, too, so they're the ideal companions for your evergreen shrubs, perennials, and groundcovers in the off-season!

MIX & FIX

RISE-'N'-SHINE CLEAN-UP TONIC

Want to start the growing season with a bang? This tonic will rouse your yard out of its slumber in spring, nailing any wayward bugs and thugs that spent the winter in your garden.

1 cup of Murphy's Oil Soap®
1 cup of tobacco tea*
1 cup of antiseptic mouthwash
¼ cup of Tabasco® sauce

Mix all of these ingredients in a 20 gallon hose-end sprayer, filling the balance of the sprayer jar with warm water. Apply to everything in your yard to the point of run-off.

*Place half a handful of chewing tobacco in an old nylon stocking, and soak it in a gallon of hot water until the mixture is dark brown.

Mother Knows Best

11

Take a tip from Mother Nature—spring is a terrific time for pastel colors in your year-round garden. The softer light of this season is kind to pale colors, so you can appreciate their delicate hues, even in sunny spots.

When the season swings toward summer, the sun gets more intense. Pastels look washed out, and pale petals may even get scorched by the sun. The lesson? Stick with bright colors for the dog days.

As the growing season winds down, anything goes. Softer colors, like lavender-blues, rusty oranges, and muted golds, are perfect for the gentle slide into winter. Or, go out in a blaze of glory with bright reds, glowing yellows, and peppy purples!

Get Potted

Feeling a little nervous about trying a new color combination? Well, then, give it a trial run in a container planting. A large pot or a wooden half-barrel is big enough to hold one or two small shrubs and several smaller perennials and annuals, so you can see how they look together. If you like the combination, move the plants to your in-ground garden in the fall; otherwise, experiment with different plants until you find a pairing that's picture-perfect.

DOUBLE-PUNCH GARLIC TEA

Thrips can really do a number on white- and pale-petaled flowers, causing discolored streaks and deformed blooms. Send 'em packing with a dose of this excellent elixir.

5 unpeeled cloves of garlic, coarsely chopped
2 cups of boiling water
½ cup of tobacco tea*
1 tsp. of instant tea granules
1 tsp. of baby shampoo

Place the chopped garlic in a heat-proof bowl, and pour the boiling water over it. Let it steep overnight. Strain through a coffee filter, mix it with the other ingredients in a hand-held sprayer, and thoroughly drench your plants.

*Place half a handful of chewing tobacco in an old nylon stocking, and soak it in a gallon of hot water until the mixture is dark brown.

MIX & FIX

Don't Ship Out—Shape Up!

People aren't the only ones who have habits—plants do, too! In this case, "habit" refers to their shape when you look at them from the side. Different habits work well in different areas, so it's worth paying attention to them when you're choosing plants for your four-season landscape.

Ask Jerry

Q: *I'd really like to add a great four-season tree to my garden, but I have a tiny yard. Any suggestions?*

A: You bet! Look for trees that are described as columnar or fastigiate, such as 'Princeton Sentry' ginkgo (Ginkgo biloba 'Princeton Sentry'). Their branches tend to grow up, rather than out, so they have a very narrow outline—perfect for those tight spots!

The Shape of Things to Come

Tree and shrub shapes tend to be most noticeable in wintertime, when the leaves are off of them (or they're set against a blanket of snow). Here's a quick rundown of the most common habits you'll run across:

Rounded. Think of a tree a child would draw: a straight, upright trunk topped with a globe-shaped mop of green on the top. Crabapples (*Malus*) and maples (*Acer*) are two trees that have this shape; many shrubs do, too, including hydrangeas and mugo pine (*Pinus mugo* var. *mugo*).

Weeping. Instead of growing upward or outward, the branches of weeping trees hang downward. Weeping willow (*Salix babylonica*) is the best-known example.

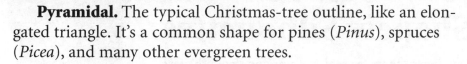
Pyramidal. The typical Christmas-tree outline, like an elongated triangle. It's a common shape for pines (*Pinus*), spruces (*Picea*), and many other evergreen trees.

Vase-shaped. These plants look like an upside-down triangle, or like a "V." Hybrid elms (*Ulmus*) usually have this shape.

Horizontal. The branches grow straight out from the main stem, so the tree or shrub has a broad-spreading outline. Two good examples are common flowering dogwood (*Cornus florida*) and doublefile viburnum (*Viburnum plicatum* var. *tomentosum*).

Keep 'Em Separate

Combining trees with different shapes is a great way to jazz up your winter garden—with one exception: *Never* crowd weeping trees in with other companions. To look their best, the graceful, arching branches need plenty of room to spread out and do their thing. It's fine to fill in the space below them with low-growing bulbs or groundcovers, but otherwise, give these beauties a bed they can call their own.

Grandma Putt's **GREEN THUMB TIPS**

Each time she made a new garden, Grandma Putt made it a point to combine plants with different flower forms: some daisies, some spikes, some buttons, some trumpets, and so on. She did the same with the forms of the plants themselves, contrasting low-growing carpeters with spiky clumps and rounded mounds with grasses or upright plants. This simple, but time-tested trick always made Grandma's gardens look great—and it'll work for you, too!

Jerry's Best Bets for...
Shapely Silhouettes

Looking for more examples of tree and shrub shapes? Take along this list while you're plant shopping. Including one or more examples of each shape will give your yard a big blast of winter excitement!

Weeping Trees and Shrubs

Golden weeping willow (*Salix alba* 'Tristis')

'Silver Frost' weeping pear (*Pyrus salicifolia* 'Silver Frost')

Weeping Canada hemlock (*Tsuga canadensis* 'Pendula')

Weeping Colorado spruce (*Picea pungens* 'Pendula')

Weeping Douglas fir (*Pseudotsuga menziesii* 'Pendula')

Weeping European birch (*Betula pendula* 'Tristis')

Weeping European hornbeam (*Carpinus betulus* 'Pendula')

Weeping green beech (*Fagus sylvatica* 'Pendula')

Weeping Higan cherry (*Prunus subhirtella* var. *pendula*)

Weeping white pine (*Pinus strobus* 'Pendula')

Weeping willow (*Salix babylonica*)

Pyramidal Trees and Shrubs

American holly (*Ilex opaca*)

'Aristocrat' callery pear (*Pyrus calleryana* 'Aristocrat')

Bald cypress (*Taxodium distichum*)

Birches (*Betula*)

Canadian hemlock (*Tsuga* canadensis)

Dawn redwood (*Metasequoia glyptostroboides*)

Eastern red cedar (*Juniperus virginiana*)

English holly (*Ilex aquifolium*)

Pin oak (*Quercus palustris*)

Sourwood (*Oxydendrum arboreum*)

Southern magnolia (*Magnolia grandiflora*)

Spruces (*Picea*)

Sweet gum (*Liquidambar styraciflua*)

Vase-Shaped Trees and Shrubs

Chinese dogwood (*Cornus kousa* 'Chinensis')

Crape myrtles (*Lagerstroemia*)

Hybrid elms (*Ulmus*)

Japanese zelkova (*Zelkova serrata*)

'Kwanzan' cherry (*Prunus serrulata* 'Kwanzan')

Paperbark maple (*Acer griseum*)

'Sea Green' juniper (*Juniperus chinensis* 'Sea Green')

Columnar and Fastigiate Trees and Shrubs

'Armstrong' red maple (*Acer rubrum* 'Armstrong')

'Arrowhead' sugar maple (*Acer saccharum* 'Arrowhead')

Fastigiate beech (*Fagus sylvatica* 'Fastigiata')

Fastigiate white pine (*Pinus strobus* 'Fastigiata')

'Graham Blandy' boxwood (*Buxus sempervirens* 'Graham Blandy')

'Helmond Pillar' barberry (*Berberis thunbergii* 'Helmond Pillar')

'Princeton Sentry' ginkgo (*Ginkgo biloba* 'Princeton Sentry')

CHAPTER 2

The Layered Look

The very best year-round gardens are like Grandma's Saturday-night soup—they contain a little bit of everything but the kitchen sink! A well-chosen mix of plants provides sure-fire, four-season excitement, and cuts down on your maintenance chores, too. In this chapter, you'll learn how to make the most of trees, shrubs, flowers, groundcovers, and vines.

PLANNING

You have to look at your yard all year long, so why not fill it with a wide variety of plants to guarantee you'll always have something of interest to look at? Let's take a peek at some of your options:

• Single trees and shrubs make eye-catching accents

• Groupings of trees and shrubs block an ugly view or provide shade

• Deciduous trees and shrubs change with the seasons, giving you something new to see throughout the year

• Evergreens are invaluable for year-round interest

• Look for long-blooming perennials to get the biggest bang for your gardening buck

• Experiment with pruning tricks to change the heights and bloom times of your perennials

• Bulbs aren't just for spring—they'll bloom in summer, fall, and even winter, too!

• Well-chosen ground-covers offer seasonal interest *and* cut down on mowing and trimming

Start with Trees, Please!

When you're looking for hard-working plants, you simply can't beat trees. Besides providing shelter for birds and wildlife, cooling shade in summer, and wind screening in winter, these long-lived lovelies are invaluable for adding four-season interest to any landscape. What more can you ask for?

Trees to the Rescue

Besides all of the other important jobs trees do, they give your yard what garden designers call "structure." In plain English, that means you can use 'em in all kinds of ways to make your yard into anything you want it to be. Plus, they're perfect problem-solvers, too! Here are a few ways I like to use trees in my landscape:

Create an oasis. A big yard filled with nothing but grass is about as inviting as the Sahara desert. But add a few trees, and bingo—you've got a place that says, "Come on out and sit a spell."

Divide and conquer. Trees make some of the niftiest "walls" you'll ever hope to find. Use them to create outdoor "rooms" in your yard—to divide your flower garden from the kids' play area, for example.

Block that view. Tired of looking at your neighbor's camper, or the busy street in front of your house? Just plant a few fast-growing trees, and presto—you've turned that old eyesore into a sight for sore eyes!

Try Trees in Threes

Don't make all of your trees fly solo! Instead of planting one here and one there, try growing them in groups of three instead. Plant a weed-smothering groundcover underneath to link them together, and you've got yourself a gorgeous grove effect. And you can go even one better by using four-season trees like river birch (*Betula nigra*) or dogwoods (*Cornus*). That simple grouping suddenly becomes an awesome year-round accent—with no extra work on your part!

Be a Super Shopper

Trees aren't just plain-Jane and practical—they're downright beautiful, too! When you're shopping for a new tree, take this handy checklist along to make sure your choice has what it takes to pull its own weight:

- ✔ Fabulous flowers in spring, summer, fall, or winter

- ✔ Bright berries in fall or winter

- ✔ Pretty leaves in spring and summer

- ✔ Showy color change in fall

- ✔ Evergreen foliage

- ✔ Bark with interesting patterns, shapes, or colors for fall and winter

No one tree has *all* of these traits, but many top-notch choices offer three, four, or even five of these multi-season features. The more your chosen tree can contribute, the merrier you'll be—I *guarantee* it!

NO-JIVE CHIVE SPRAY

MIX & FIX

Scale insects form tiny bumps on twigs as they suck the plant's sap, causing weak or stunted growth. If you spot these pests on your young trees and shrubs, scrape off as many as you can with your fingernail or a plastic spoon, then drench the affected parts with this simple spray.

¼ cup of dried chives
Water
Liquid soap

Pour 2 cups of boiling water over the chives and let them sit for one hour. Strain out the leaves, then mix 1 part of the liquid with 2 parts water. Add a few drops of liquid soap. Pour into a hand-held sprayer, shake, and apply to the point of run-off.

Gimme a Break!

If your yard gets too much wind to suit you, give it some shelter with a row or two of evergreen trees. Better yet, double up by planting a second row of flowering shrubs or small flowering trees along the inside edge of your windbreak. This easy-care pairing is guaranteed to fill your yard with color season after season. Plus, any plant with white or light-colored blooms will look like a million bucks when it's backed by an evergreen screen!

Evergreens Do Everything

When it comes to blocking ugly views or framing pretty ones, you simply can't find a better friend than an evergreen tree—or a whole bunch of them! For a dense, formal screen, plant your evergreens in a solid, straight row of all one kind of evergreen; try Leyland cypress (*Chamaecyparis leylandii*) in the South or arborvitaes (*Thuja*) in the North. For a less formal effect, combine two or three different evergreens with varying forms and textures: a long-needled pine (*Pinus*) with a dense, short-needled spruce (*Picea*), for instance.

> **Grandma Putt's GREEN THUMB TIPS**
>
> One of Grandma's least favorite garden chores was trimming straggly grass around tree trunks. If you feel the same, do what she did: Build beds around the base of each tree and fill them with multi-season perennials or groundcovers. Besides adding year-round interest, these mini-gardens will cut your trimming chores down to practically nothing!

The Rub on Shrubs

Like Rodney Dangerfield, these poor plants get no respect! In most yards, shrubs are simply a few overgrown odds and ends planted by clueless former owners, or else bargain-basement leftovers set out by penny-pinching developers to fill the bare soil around newly built homes. That's a downright shame, since these versatile, easy-care plants are some of the best sources of year-round interest you've ever seen!

Back to the Basics

So, just what *are* shrubs? Technically, they are woody-stemmed plants that have numerous spreading branches. Most people think that shrubs have to be a certain size—usually somewhere between 4 and 8 feet tall—but that definition just doesn't fly; they can be less than a foot tall all the way up to 15 feet or more in height. That means you're sure to find a shrub to fit every part of your yard. Best of all, well-chosen shrubs provide more ornamental value, season after season, than any other type of plant—*and* with a lot less work!

FLOWERING SHRUB ELIXIR

Don't waste your hard-earned dough on fancy, pre-packaged shrub fertilizers from your local garden center! Instead, just whip up a batch of this terrific tonic, and you'll have the best-looking flowering shrubs on the block.

½ can of beer
½ cup of fish emulsion
½ cup of ammonia
¼ cup of baby shampoo
2 tbsp. of hydrogen peroxide

Mix all of the ingredients together, and pour into a 20 gallon hose-end sprayer. Then every three weeks during the spring and summer, spray your shrubs until the tonic starts dripping off their leaves. That'll get 'em growin' like gangbusters!

Shrubs for Every Season

If trees are the walls of your outdoor garden "rooms," then shrubs are the furniture—the sturdy, dependable features that give your yard its day-to-day interest. But shrubs are a lot tougher to move than furniture, so it makes sense to choose them carefully.

Spend the bulk of your shrub budget on plants that look great in two or more seasons—with pretty flowers, interesting stems, bright fall color, evergreen foliage, and/or bountiful berries. One of my all-time favorites is oak-leaved hydrangea (*Hydrangea quercifolia*), with pale green spring leaves that turn deep green in summer and rich maroon in fall, white summer flowers, and attractive peeling stems in winter. Talk about getting a bang for your buck!

Ask Jerry

Q: My wife wants me to plant a forsythia for spring flowers, but I want a shrub that'll look good for more than a few weeks each year. Can you help?

A: Never fear—ol' Jer is here! You can have your forsythia and enjoy it all through the growing season, too; simply choose cultivars that have colorful foliage, such as the aptly named 'Gold Leaf', or those with white- or yellow-striped leaves, like 'Fiesta', 'Ilgwang', and 'Kumsun'.

Tough Love for Shrubs

Some shrubs have such good-looking leaves, they don't even need flowers! To get the biggest and brightest foliage on these beautiful bushes, try this tough-love tip: Whack 'em down to a foot or so above the ground every spring. Sounds harsh, I know, but you won't believe how quickly they bounce back, and they'll look all the better for it! This trick works great with purple-leaved smoke bush (*Cotinus coggygria*), elderberries (*Sambucus*), and ninebarks (*Physocarpus*).

Shrubby Slope Covers

Of all the tough sites we gardeners have to cope with, slopes have to be one of the toughest. Over the years, I've tried lots of different plants, and I have to say that spreading shrubs are some of the best slope covers around. Above ground, their branches and leaves do a super job of slowing down pelting raindrops, preventing soil erosion; below ground, the dense root systems knit together quickly to hold the soil in place. Lots of shrubs will work well for slopes, but the cream of the crop includes abelias, cotoneasters, forsythias, low-growing junipers, and spireas.

Spread 'Em!

Why is it that when folks plant shrubs, they always want to crowd 'em up close to the house? Shrubs always look their best—and need a *lot* less pruning, too—when they've got some space to spread out. One caution, though: If you want to plant a shrub at the entrance to your driveway, or anywhere else near the street, choose one that will stay below about 30 inches tall. That way, you'll always be able to see over it!

Easy-Care Perennials

You've built a good background of trees and shrubs—now it's time to do some exterior decorating! Perennial flowers are perfect for adding easy-care color throughout your yard, throughout the year.

Keep the Color Comin'

It used to be that perennials provided only seasonal spots of color, but not anymore. Look beyond those one-shot, early-summer favorites—peonies, poppies, delphiniums, and so on—and you'll find old favorites and new releases that bloom for two, three, four, or even five months of the year! Pincushion flowers (*Scabiosa*), catmint (*Nepeta* x *faassenii*), and red valerian (*Centranthus ruber*) are just three perfect perennials that don't know when to call it quits. For more everbloomers, check out "Jerry Best Bets for Four-Season Color" on page 32.

check out "Jerry Best Bets for Four-Season Color" on page 32.

Spread the Wealth

Psst! How'd you like to double or even triple your flower display in the same amount of space? Here's the secret: Look for perennials that bloom at different times. Peonies, for instance, come in "early," "midseason," and "late" cultivars; when the early ones are finishing, the midseason ones are just getting started, and so on. Asters, astilbes, daylilies (*Hemerocallis*), and irises are just a few perennials that offer this super season-extending option.

The Cutting Edge

The best way I know to turn ordinary perennials into bloomin' fools is to give 'em a good, hard pinch! You see, when flowers start to fade, plants start directing their energy toward seed formation. But when you pinch or snip off those spent blooms—in-the-know gardeners call this "deadheading"—many plants keep making more and more flowers.On those plants with fairly large flowers, take off individ-

---

CREATIVE COLOR COMBOS

With as few as two or three perennials, you can brighten up any spot in your yard for weeks or months on end. Here are a few ideas to get you going:

✿ Light yellow 'Moonshine' yarrow (*Achillea* 'Moonshine') with 'Blue Wonder' catmint (*Nepeta* x *faassenii* 'Blue Wonder')

✿ Blue Carpathian harebell (*Campanula carpatica*) with pale yellow 'Moonbeam' coreopsis (*Coreopsis verticillata* 'Moonbeam')

✿ Golden orange coneflower (*Rudbeckia hirta*) with reddish pink 'Autumn Joy' sedum (*Sedum* 'Autumn Joy')

✿ Pink fringed bleeding heart (*Dicentra eximia*) with bright yellow corydalis (*Corydalis lutea*)

ual blooms just above a bud or leaf. If there are many small blooms, it's easier to wait 'til most of them are done, then cut them all off with hedge shears; they'll be back in bloom in no time at all!

Vacation Planning

Are you one of those folks who loves to spend the summer camping in piney woods, sunbathing at the beach, or riding roller coasters at your favorite amusement park? If you spend lots of time away from home in the summer, then focus your gardening efforts on the seasons when you *are* home. Pairing spring-blooming and fall-flowering perennials in the same bed gives you a great show at the beginning and the end of the growing season. As a plus, the tall stems of the late bloomers will provide welcome shade for the more delicate spring flowers.

Short and Sweet

If you garden in a hot summer climate, you've probably noticed that your perennials tend to grow taller than they do in cooler areas. While their stems may be taller, they're also less sturdy, and that means you can get stuck with a *lot* of staking. To make this boring chore a thing of the past, try this great tip: Keep an eye out for cultivars that are listed as being dwarf or compact. They'll stand up all on their own, so you can toss those old stakes in the trash!

Ask Jerry

Q: *I planted some new perennials this year and thought I followed all the rules. They look healthy, but they don't seem to be growing very much. Should I be worried?*

A: Don't worry—be patient! Here's a handy rule of thumb that you need to know about perennials: First year, they sleep; second year, they creep; and third year, they leap. In other words, the first year, they're busy putting down roots, so you won't see much in the way of top growth. The second year, they're a bit farther along, but it's not until the third year that your garden will start looking like the lush, flower-filled paradise you planned for.

Annual Accents

24

To my mind, a yard without a few annual flowers is like an ice cream sundae with no cherry on top! No matter how much planning you put into selecting trees, shrubs, and perennials with multi-season interest, don't forget to leave a little room for these short-lived, but color-packed beauties, too.

Landscape Lingo

Just what *is* an annual, anyway? Botanists describe annuals as plants that sprout, grow, flower, set seeds, and die in a single season. We gardeners have a slightly different defini-tion: any plant that you have to sow or set out anew each year. Annuals come in two general types—cool-weather and warm-weather. Here's a rundown:

Cool-weather annuals. You'll also hear these called hardy or half-hardy annu-als, depending on how much frost they'll take. All thrive in cool conditions and generally are planted out in early spring. Most stop bloom-

---

Grandma Putt's

GREEN THUMB TIPS

It's a cinch to find plenty of summer flowers, but true gardeners want a bounty of bloom in spring and fall, as well! I still use a great trick I learned from Grandma Putt— plant cool-season annuals to liven up your early- *and* late-season garden. These hardy souls adore the cool temperatures of spring, then take a break during the dog days of summer before bouncing back in fall. I always enjoy the bright orange daisies of calendulas (*Calendula officinalis*). Or try Grandma's favorite: sweet alyssum (*Lobularia maritima*). Besides produc-ing carpets of white blooms for months, it smells wonderful, too!

ing, or at least slow down, when the weather heats up. Examples include pansies and sweet alyssum (*Lobularia maritima*).

Warm-weather annuals. Also called tender annuals, these thrive in hot summer weather and bloom from early summer to frost. They hate the cold, so don't be in a hurry to set them out in spring; wait until after the last spring frost date. Examples include sunflowers (*Helianthus annuus*) and zinnias.

> ### SEEDLING STARTER TONIC
>
> Give annual seedlings a break on moving day by serving them a sip of this starter tonic. This helps them recover quickly from transplanting shock.
>
> **1 tbsp. of fish emulsion**
> **1 tbsp. of ammonia**
> **1 tbsp. of Murphy's Oil Soap®**
> **1 tsp. of instant tea granules**
> **1 qt. of warm water**
>
> Mix all of the ingredients in the warm water. Pour into a hand-held sprayer, and mist the young plants several times a day until they're back on their feet and growing again.

MIX & FIX

Get Potted

Tired of having your beautiful flower garden fizzle out in late summer? It'll never happen again if you try this terrific trick: Simply plug in a few annuals to spruce things up! Buy an extra six-pack or two of annual transplants in spring and pot them up, or sow seeds in pots in late spring. Plant 'em out wherever you need a bit of extra color in early August, and presto—you've got a bounty of blooms to enjoy until Jack Frost rears his ugly head!

Fill 'Er Up

There's no way around it: When you plant a new four-season garden, there are going to be some gaps for the first year or two. While you're waiting for the perennials and groundcovers to grow together, Mother Nature's going to send some weeds to fill in those empty spaces, unless *you* plant 'em up first. And that's where the amazing annuals come in! Two of my favorites for temporary space fillers are silver-leaved dusty miller (*Senecio cineraria*)—it looks great with anything—and love-in-a-mist (*Nigella damascena*); just scatter the seeds where you want them to grow!

Spring's the Thing

Sure, annuals are tailor-made for summer sizzle—but don't forget to make the most of 'em in spring, too! Sweet-smelling stock (*Matthiola incana*), bright blue forget-me-nots (*Myosotis*), and happy-faced pansies (*Viola* x *wittrockiana*) are just the thing for lifting your spirits after a dull, dreary winter, so be sure to plan for some spring blooms.

Grandma Putt's
GREEN THUMB TIPS

While Grandma enjoyed experimenting with new annuals each year, there were a few standbys she simply had to find room for every spring. She made it a rule, though, *never* to plant the same annual in the same bed two years running—and this should be your rule, too. When you grow the same plant in the same spot year after year, it's easy for pests and diseases to get a foothold. But when you rotate your beds with different annuals from one year to the next, you have a great no-spray way to keep bad bugs and funky fungi at bay!

Fall Into Annuals

While we're on the subject of seasons: Do yourself a favor and tuck in a few annuals in autumn, too! My all-time favorites for early fall planting are the ornamental cabbages and kales (*Brassica oleracea*). They'll look good well into the winter, and may even live long enough to send up their yellow flowers the following spring. That's three seasons of interest from just one annual—talk about getting your money's worth!

Bulbs for a four-season garden? You bet! Sure, it's spring bloomers—daffodils, tulips, and the like—that get all of the press, but they're not the only game in town. With a little planning, it's possible to enjoy a bounty of bulbs all year long.

Floral and Hardy

Unlike the usual spring-flowering bulbs, summer-blooming bulbs are kind of a mixed bag. Some of them, like lilies, are hardy in most climates (meaning that you can plant them in fall or spring, and leave 'em in the ground year-round). Others, like cannas and dahlias, are cold-tender. If you live north of Zone 8, you'll need to plant them each spring and dig them up again in fall for winter storage indoors. Both kinds of bulbs have a lot to offer any four-season garden, but if you're looking for the most *wow* for the least work, hardy bulbs are your best bet.

Don't Spread 'Em

The biggest mistake people make when planting bulbs? Trying to spread them out too much! Whether you have 20 bulbs or 200, you'll get the biggest bang for your gardening buck by planting them in groups of five or more, with the individual bulbs no more than 6 inches apart.

Ask Jerry

Q: *Hey, Jer—how come I have luck with some bulbs and not others in my Deep South garden?*

A: Some bulbs—notably tulips and hyacinths—need a period of chilling to grow and bloom properly, and they don't get that if your soil stays warm in winter. But don't waste your hard-earned money buying "precooled" bulbs—do the job yourself! When you get new bulbs in early fall, simply pop them in the vegetable drawer of your refrigerator, and leave 'em there for five to six weeks. Plant them in December, and they'll brighten your beds and borders on schedule in spring!

Bulbs, Bulbs Everywhere!

Need some exciting new ideas for using bulbs in your yard? Here are five fun ways to get the most from your bulb budget:

1. Plant small, hardy bulbs—like crocuses and snowdrops (*Galanthus*)—in an informal patch of lawn; they'll bloom and die back before the mowing season starts.

COMPOST TEA

Compost tea is the most healthful drink any bulb or flower could ask for. It delivers a balanced supply of important nutrients—major *and* minor—and fends off diseases at the same time.

**1¹/₂ gal. of fresh compost
4¹/₂ gal. of warm water**

Pour the water into a 5-gallon bucket. Scoop the compost into a cotton, burlap, or pantyhose sack, tie it closed, and put it into the water. Cover the bucket and let it steep for three to seven days. Pour the solution into a watering can or hand-held sprayer, and give your plants a good spritzing with it every two to three weeks throughout the growing season. Dump the solids back into your compost pile.

2. Naturalize early daffodils in a wooded area that gets winter sun and summer shade. The flowers will finish up about the time the trees leaf out in late spring.

3. In fertile, sunny beds, plant tulips and hyacinths among peonies, daylilies (*Hemerocallis*), and other bushy perennials that'll hide the fading bulb foliage in early summer.

4. Plan ahead for lilies to take center stage in your summer garden by giving them excellent drainage and full sun. If you are growing fragrant Oriental lilies, which simply *demand* frequent sniffing, place a stepping stone nearby.

5. Make special beds for bulbs that need to be dug up and stored for winter, such as dahlias, so you won't disturb nearby plants each fall.

Early Birds Get the Best Bulbs

The sooner you get daffodils, tulips, and hardy bulbs in the ground in fall, the more time they'll have to grow roots before winter weather arrives. And since longer roots make for stronger plants, it just makes sense to get those bulbs in the ground right away—especially in cold climates! Here's a simple schedule to help you plan your bulb-planting sessions:

Zones 2 to 4:
September

Zones 5 to 7:
October or November

Zones 8 and 9:
November or December

Ask Jerry

Q: When I'm planting bulbs, can I just drop them in the hole, or do I have to plant them in any special way?

A: With some bulbs, it's anyone's guess as to which is the top and which is the bottom. But for most, there's an obvious difference: The top of the bulb comes to a point, while at the base, there is usually some sign of roots or a basal plate from which roots will grow later. So remember—look for the nose, not the toes, and plant your bulbs "heads up"!

Timesaving Groundcovers

Ready to put the finishing touches on your four-season yard? Well, then, I've got an idea that'll really "floor" you: plant groundcovers! These low-growing, low-maintenance plants are perfect for carpeting the ground beneath trees, under shrubs, and along walkways—wherever a tidy, well-groomed look is important.

The Great Cover-Up

Once you give groundcovers a try, you won't believe all of the ways that these hard-working plants can liven up your landscape! Here are a few ideas to get you started:

→ Use evergreen groundcovers to keep weeds at bay in high-visibility foundation plantings.

→ Cloak a slope with a carpet of flowering groundcovers—they'll help hold the soil, eliminate mowing chores, and look great, too!

→ Replace straggly patches of grass under trees and shrubs with shade-loving groundcovers, such as bugleweeds (*Ajuga*) and periwinkles (*Vinca*).

→ Convert unused lawn areas into masses of flowering or evergreen groundcovers, and you'll get a lot more seasonal interest for a lot less work!

MIX
&
FIX

GROUNDCOVER CHOW

Give your groundcovers a taste of this mix in spring, then stand back, and watch 'em grow!

3 parts bonemeal
3 parts greensand or wood ashes
1 part bloodmeal

Mix the ingredients together. Scatter 2 tablespoons around each clump of plants, and scratch into the soil surface.

Groundwork for Groundcovers

So, what makes a plant a great groundcover? First, it should grow in a variety of conditions, and second, it should grow vigorously with little or no care from you. Most important, it should spread quickly to create a dense, weed-smothering carpet. But you know what? Those are the same traits that make some plants truly troublesome weeds!

To keep your groundcovers from becoming ugly thugs, you need to choose them very carefully. When you're pairing them with other plants, like perennials and shrubs, use less vigorous groundcovers such as barrenworts

(*Epimedium*), so they won't crowd out their companions. But when you're growing groundcovers in masses, Japanese pachysandra (*Pachysandra terminalis*) and other strong spreaders are a better choice, because they'll fill in quickly and keep weeds out. Either way, install some kind of barrier—a row of bricks, maybe, or a plastic edging strip—between any groundcover and your lawn, so the groundcover won't escape and take over your yard!

Spotlight on...

Ornamental Grasses

Everyone knows that grasses make great groundcovers—that's why most of us have some kind of lawn around our home. But besides the typical turf-formers, there's a whole other world for homeowners to explore: ornamental grasses! These easy-care plants are all the rage, and no wonder; they come in all shapes, sizes, and colors, and they'll grow in just about any conditions you can imagine—sun or shade, wet soil or dry. Here's a quick overview of the two main types of ornamental grasses, to get you on your way to success!

Cool-season grasses. These grasses do most of their growing when it's cool out—below 75°F—so they look their best in late summer to fall, and again in spring. Many have evergreen leaves, and they tend to be low-growing. Examples include blue fescue (*Festuca glauca*) and blue oat grass (*Helictotrichon sempervirens*).

Warm-season grasses. These grow when temperatures are warm, from mid- to late spring through summer. They bloom from midsummer to fall, and many hold on to their tan foliage through winter. Examples include miscanthus and pampas grasses (*Cortaderia*).

Jerry's Best Bets for...
Four-Season Color

Ready to get growing with your new year-round garden? Here's a sampling of some of my favorite multi-season trees, shrubs, and perennials to help get you started. All of these look good in at least two seasons.

Trees

Atlas cedar
 (*Cedrus atlantica*)
Callery pear
 (*Pyrus calleryana*)
Colorado blue spruce
 (*Picea pungens* f. *glauca*)
Crabapples (*Malus*)
Flowering dogwood
 (*Cornus florida*)
Fringe tree
 (*Chionanthus virginicus*)
Hemlocks (*Tsuga*)
Hollies (*Ilex*)
Japanese flowering cherry
 (*Prunus serrulata*)
Kousa dogwood
 (*Cornus kousa*)
Magnolias (*Magnolia*)
Mountain ashes (*Sorbus*)
Paperbark maple
 (*Acer griseum*)
Pines (*Pinus*)
Redbuds (*Cercis*)
River birch (*Betula nigra*)
Serviceberries (*Amelanchier*)

Smoke bush
 (*Cotinus coggygria*)
Southern magnolia
 (*Magnolia grandiflora*)
'Winter King' hawthorn
 (*Crataegus viridis*
 'Winter King')
Witch hazels (*Hamamelis*)

Shrubs

Boxwoods (*Buxus*)
Burning bush
 (*Euonymus alatus*)
Common camellia
 (*Camellia japonica*)
European cranberry bush
 (*Viburnum opulus*)
False cypress
 (*Chamaecyparis*)
Fothergillas (*Fothergilla*)
Glossy abelia (*Abelia* x
 grandiflora)
Heavenly bamboo
 (*Nandina domestica*)
Japanese aucuba
 (*Aucuba japonica*)
Japanese holly (*Ilex crenata*)
Japanese pieris
 (*Pieris japonica*)
Mountain laurel
 (*Kalmia latifolia*)
Oak-leaved hydrangea
 (*Hydrangea quercifolia*)
Oregon grape holly
 (*Mahonia aquifolium*)

Red-osier dogwood
 (*Cornus stolonifera*)
Scarlet firethorn
 (*Pyracantha coccinea*)
Virginia sweetspire
 (*Itea virginica*)

Perennials

Anise hyssop
 (*Agastache foeniculum*)
'Autumn Joy' sedum
 (*Sedum* 'Autumn Joy')
Balloon flower
 (*Platycodon
 grandiflorus*)
Bearsfoot hellebore
 (*Helleborus foetidus*)
Coreopsis (*Coreopsis*)
Fringed bleeding heart
 (*Dicentra eximia*)
Heucheras (*Heuchera*)
Lenten rose (*Helleborus* x
 hybridus)
Orange coneflower
 (*Rudbeckia fulgida*)
Perennial candytuft
 (*Iberis sempervirens*)
Pincushion flowers
 (*Scabiosa*)
Red valerian
 (*Centranthus ruber*)
Wormwoods (*Artemisia*)
Yellow corydalis
 (*Corydalis lutea*)

CHAPTER 3

Four-Season Problem Solving

L et's face it, folks—it's rare to find a site that's absolutely perfect for a garden. But no matter what you're starting with, there are ways to deal with even the toughest gardening conditions. Deep shade or broiling sun, waterlogged or dry as a bone, in the steamy South or on a steep slope; you name it, and I've got timely tips to help you have the best four-season yard on the block!

PLANNING

Instead of spending all your free time taking care of your plants, why not put your plants to work for *you*? Once you know the tricks for coping with challenging sites, you can create a four-season yard that's as easy to care for as it is easy on the eyes!

- Remember that light conditions change as trees and shrubs mature, so full-sun sites will get shadier over time

- Light-colored bloomers can turn a gloomy garden into a pretty place

- In dry, shady sites, good soil preparation is the key to success

- Soaker hoses make post-planting watering a snap in *any* type of terrain

- Why fight wet spots? Fill 'em with moisture-loving bloomers for a no-fail show all season long

- Expand your plant options in soggy sites by raising the soil level to improve drainage

- Mulch is an absolute must for helping plants cope with dry-soil sites

Add Sparkle to Shady Sites

To my mind, a garden just isn't complete without a few trees—and that goes double if you're looking for year-round interest in your yard. But there's one indisputable fact of life: Where there are trees, there is shade. Sure, most flowers prefer sun, but with some garden smarts on your part, even the shadiest spaces can burst into bloom with loads of color. So let's go ahead and shine some light on this shady subject.

Let There Be Light

What's the most important thing you can know about your chosen garden site? The amount of sunlight it gets during the day. To figure it out, check the site every hour or so over the course of a sunny day—ideally in early or midsummer, after all of the trees have leafed out—and note whether the site is in sun or shade. At sunset, simply total up the number of hours the site was in sun.

A **full sun** site gets at least six hours of sunlight a day, ideally, with at least four of those hours in the afternoon. A site in **partial shade** means it gets between three and six hours of sun a day. A **shady** site gets three hours or less of sun a day.

Shady Thoughts

I often hear folks complain that their yard is too shady to grow flowers, but that doesn't have to be the case! True, shaded sites can be a challenge, but they can also be beautiful—and nothing beats a stroll through a shady garden on a hot summer afternoon.

When you're choosing plants for a four-season shade garden, look for light-colored blooms—white, pale yellow, and pastel pinks—because rich blues, purples, and reds just don't show up

well in shade. Plants with variegated foliage (leaves that are striped or spotted with yellow or white) are also ideal for brightening up the gloom!

Dry Shade Strategies

Shady sites with moist soil are a favorite for many wonderful woodland plants. But if you're stuck with a garden that's shady and *dry*—well, you need all the help you can get! Here are three quick tips to get you growing successfully:

1. Work lots of compost into your soil *before* planting—a layer 2 or 3 inches thick is just about right.

2. *After* planting, snake soaker hoses all through the bed, so it'll be easy to water regularly for the first year or two.

3. Be generous with mulch—2 to 3 inches of chopped leaves, shredded bark, or other organic mulch will cover the soaker hoses and keep the moisture right where the roots need it.

Gorgeous Grasses for Shade

There's no doubt about it—most ornamental grasses are real sun-lovers. But shady-site gardeners don't have to feel left out of the fun, 'cause there are some super-looking grasses that are just made for the shade! Here are a few great grassy options for sites with bright, all-day shade, or a half-day of sun and a half-day of shade:

Northern sea oats (*Chasmanthium latifolium*): Showy seed-

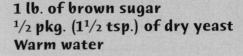

SLUGWEISER

Shady sites make ideal hangouts for slugs and snails, so be prepared to take control! To drown your slug sorrows, try this sure cure.

1 lb. of brown sugar
¹⁄₂ pkg. (1¹⁄₂ tsp.) of dry yeast
Warm water

Pour the sugar and yeast into a 1-gallon plastic jug, fill it with warm water, and let it sit for two days, uncovered. Then pour it into your slug traps, and let the good times roll!

MIX & FIX

heads and rich brown fall and winter color.

'Snowline' sedge (*Carex conica* 'Snowline'): White-edged leaves that are evergreen or semi-evergreen.

Striped sedge (*C. morrowii* 'Variegata'): Stiff, shiny, evergreen leaves edged in silvery white.

Variegated broad-leaved sedge (*C. siderosticha* 'Variegata'): Green-and-white-striped leaves.

Variegated hakone grass (*Hakonechloa macra* 'Aureola'): Gracefully arching, green-and-yellow-striped leaves.

Grandma Putt's

GREEN THUMB TIPS

When I was a young boy, I thought that Grandma Putt loved her shady garden just for its delicate-looking blooms and lush foliage. But it was years later before she admitted the *real* reason: It was the easiest-care planting she ever had! You see, shady gardens lose much less moisture to evaporation than sunny sites, so you don't need to water them nearly as often. The plants grow slower, too, so they need little or no extra fertilizer—just a compost mulch each spring. So if you want an attention-getting landscape, but don't have a lot of time to take care of it, a shady area can be your best friend!

Fun in the Sun

Sunny sites are tailor-made for spectacular four-season plantings. But sometimes, you can get a little too much of a good thing! No worries, though—I've got a slew of top-notch tips to help you make the most of any sun-baked site.

Color with a Kick

Bright, full-sun sites offer lots of exciting opportunities for fabulous flowers. You can use the richest colors—radiant reds, sunny yellows, awesome oranges, and passionate purples—that'll really knock your socks off! White flowers, too, can usually hold their own in strong sunlight, but stay away from pastels, because pale petals tend to look faded and tired in intense light.

Super Grasses for Screening

Need some privacy for your new deck or pool, but don't want to block the sun with trees and shrubs? Grow grasses instead! Here's a half-dozen sun-loving grasses that are just perfect for summer and fall screening:

Feather reed grass (*Calamagrostis* x *acutiflora* 'Stricta')

Flame grass (*Miscanthus sinensis* var. *purpurascens*)

Japanese silver grass (*Miscanthus sinensis*)

Pampas grass (*Cortaderia selloana*)

Purple moor grass (*Molinia caerulea*)

Switch grass (*Panicum virgatum*)

ALL-SEASON GREEN-UP TONIC

If any of your sun-lovers are looking a bit peaked, give them a taste of this sweet treat; they'll green up in a jiffy!

1 can of beer
1 cup of ammonia
$1/2$ cup of dishwashing liquid
$1/2$ cup of liquid lawn food
$1/2$ cup of molasses or clear corn syrup

Mix all of the ingredients together in a large bucket, then pour into a 20 gallon hose-end sprayer. Saturate your lawn, trees, shrubs, and flowers with this tonic every three weeks throughout the growing season.

MIX & FIX

Soak It to 'Em!

Many times, an ample supply of water can spell the difference between a spectacular sunny garden and a disappointing disaster.

To ensure your sun-lovers will get all the water they need, snake soaker hoses through the bed, so they run near each plant. Top them with a layer of mulch to cover them up and help the soil hold moisture at the same time. Because these hoses drip so slowly, the water has plenty of time to soak down to the roots—with no wasted run-off, either!

Don't Sweat the Sun

Too much sun? Enjoy it while you've got it! If you're building a four-season garden with trees and shrubs as well as lower-growing flowers, you'll have some shade before you know it. The change will happen gradually, so you may not notice right away, but your plants will. No need to spend a fortune to totally redo your yard, though: If your sun-lovers look spindly and bloom less, or they just don't look as vigorous as before, simply replace them as your budget permits with plants that prefer some shade.

Ask Jerry

Q: Is it possible for plants to get too much sun?

A: It sure is! Just like people, plants can get sunburn, especially when you move them suddenly from the shade to a sunny spot. Sunburn shows up as tan, bronzed, or scorched-looking patches on the leaves or flowers. To prevent it, expose indoor-grown plants to sunshine gradually—a few hours more each day over a week or so. If you see these symptoms on plants that are already in the garden, give them a long, cool drink right away, and move them to a shadier spot as soon as you can.

You *Can* Fool Mother Nature

It never fails: Gardeners who have shade wish they could grow sun-loving plants, and those with sun want to grow delicate shade-lovers. Those in the first group are pretty much out of luck, but with a little know-how, you sunny-site gardeners can enjoy the best of both worlds! Just try these three quick tricks:

➜ If it's woodland wildflowers you're after, simply plant them toward the back of your beds and borders. They'll bloom early, before the sun gets too hot, then die back to the ground just as the sturdier sun-lovers start leafing out.

➜ Plant shade-loving annuals and perennials on the north side of established shrubs, or on the shady side of tall perennial clumps.

➜ Mulch early, and water often! With a steady supply of moisture, many shade-loving plants can actually grow quite well in the sun, too.

Don't Get Bogged Down!

Tired of slogging around in that wet spot in your yard? You have two options: Either raise the root zone to improve the drainage, or turn that ugly mud puddle into a fantastic four-season garden—by filling it up with plants that actually *like* it wet and wild!

Soggy-Soil Strategies

Just as there are different kinds of shade, there are different kinds of wet sites, too. And in both cases, the secret to success is the same: Experiment with a variety of plants to determine which ones will thrive in your particular conditions.

But if you've tried a bunch of different plants and still can't get anything to grow, consider testing your soil's pH. If your soil turns out to be acidic (under 6.0 on the pH scale), add lime to bring the pH to a more normal level.

Raising the Roots

Too wet to dig down? Then it's time to grow up—with raised beds, that is! To try this approach, mix 1 part coarse builder's sand with 3 parts compost, rotted sawdust, and/or rotted manure. Dig it deeply into the soil, rake it smooth, and let the site settle for three or four weeks before planting. Another option is to build a low frame around the area with rocks or lumber, then fill it with a mix of top-soil and compost. With either method, you'll end up with a well-drained bed above a reservoir of damp soil—perfect for keeping deep-rooted plants happy during the dry days of summer.

Slippery When Wet

If you have clay soil, I can't give you better advice than this: Don't even *think* about digging or tilling when the ground is wet! Besides making your job 10 times harder, working soggy clay soil will leave you with a compacted mess—definitely not good

CREATIVE COLOR COMBOS

It's a snap to change a wet area from an eyesore to an eyeful—it's all a matter of pairing up the right plants. Here are a few of my favorite moist-soil combinations to get you growing:

✿ Red-osier dogwood (*Cornus stolonifera*) with red-fruited winter-berry (*Ilex verticillata*) and bright green cinnamon fern (*Osmunda cinnamomea*)

✿ Red 'Lord Baltimore' common rose mallow (*Hibiscus moscheutos 'Lord Baltimore'*) with white-flowered summersweet (*Clethra alnifolia*) and blue lobelia (*Lobelia siphilitica*)

✿ Pink Joe Pye weed (*Eupatorium purpureum*) with tan seedheads of feather reed grass (*Calamagrostis x acutiflora 'Stricta'*) and bright yellow sneezeweed (*Helenium autumnale*)

✿ Pink or white turtleheads (*Chelone*) with red cardinal flower (*Lobelia cardinalis*) and pink Chinese astilbe (*Astilbe chinensis*)

conditions for flowers to grow in. So before you dig in, pick up a handful of soil and squeeze it. It should be moist enough to stick together when you open your hand, but dry enough to break apart when you tap the clump lightly with your finger. If it sticks to your hand instead, wait a few days, and test again before digging.

Fall Into Planting

Trying to hack out planting holes in cold, soggy soil has to be one of the worst gardening jobs ever! So, if you're planning to start a year-round garden in a wet site, take my advice and wait until late summer or early fall to start digging. By that time, the ground should be dried out a bit, and the soil will be nice and warm—just right for getting new roots off to a strong start.

Go with the Flow

When is a wet area *not* a wet area? When it's dry! Sounds obvious, I know, but think

Grandma Putt's GREEN THUMB TIPS

Instead of dreading damp sites, Grandma always said that her best gardens grew there. The plants are large and lush, and you never need to worry about watering them. If you want to include some plants that need good drainage, such as pinks (*Dianthus*) or lavenders, try Grandma's trick: Make a 50-50 mix of sand and soil, and pile a few handfuls on top of the ground in your wet-site border. Set the plants on top of the mounds, and they'll grow like gangbusters!

about this: A site that's sort of soggy in spring, when rainfall is abundant, often becomes dry as a bone by the time summer rolls around. Should you forget about planting there? No way!

You see, many common perennials can actually grow fine in spring-wet, summer-dry conditions, so you could go ahead and grow a garden there as you normally would. Just avoid plants that demand well-drained soil, such as lavenders, artemisias, blanket flowers (*Gaillardia*), and pinks (*Dianthus*). Or, fill it with all kinds of moisture-loving flowers and foliage, then plan on watering often through the summer to keep 'em in top form.

Soggy Solution

If you've got a lawn area that holds water for days after a rain, don't abandon hope. You can spruce up the site by planting water-loving trees and shrubs. Dawn redwood (*Metasequoia glyptostroboides*), shrubby dogwoods (*Cornus*), and winterberry (*Ilex verticillata*)are good choices. These thirsty plants will suck up that extra water in no time!

Dazzling Drought-Busters

Unless you enjoy spending the summer with a hose permanently attached to your hand, it makes a lot of sense to plan ahead for those inevitable dry spells. So, don't let droughts get you down; try some of these top-notch tips to get rid of your watering worries for good!

Dry as a Bone? Try These Tricks

Dry-soil sites don't have to be as barren as a desert! With some good, old-fashioned garden smarts on your part, it's easy to turn parched patches into pretty, year-round plantings. Here are four quick tips that'll guarantee success:

1. Start with plants that naturally prefer their soil on the dry side—there are lots to choose from.

2. Pile on the organic matter! Spread a 2- to 3-inch layer of compost or chopped leaves over the site, then dig or till it into the soil to help hold moisture around the roots.

3. Wait until fall to plant new gardens. Rainfall is usually much more dependable (and plentiful) at this time of year.

4. After planting, lay a soaker hose between plants to allow hassle-free watering during dry spells. Make sure it comes within a few inches of each clump. If need be, hold it in place with wire pins made from old clothes hangers.

Pile It On

If dry soil is a common problem in your garden, I've got just the answer for you: mulch! A layer of shredded bark, chopped leaves, or other organic material works wonders to keep the soil moist and cool for great root growth. It stops soil from forming a water-repelling crust, and it adds organic matter, too—perfect for retaining moisture!

Be a Plant Psychic

It doesn't take special powers to tell if a particular plant will be drought-tolerant or not—you just have to know what to look for! Simply check its leaves for any of these clues: a covering of fuzz or dense hairs; a rubbery or waxy appearance; a silvery or blue color; or a slender, needle-like shape. Spot any one or more of these signs, and there's a good chance that the plant will do just fine where it's dry.

Easy Does It

Ready to transform that parched slope into a fabulous

FABULOUS FOLIAR FORMULA

For big, bright, shiny leaves in even the toughest soil, feed your foliage plants this fantastic formula every three weeks.

1 can of beer
1/2 cup of fish emulsion
1/2 cup of ammonia
1/4 cup of blackstrap molasses
1/4 cup of instant tea granules

Mix all of the ingredients together in a 20 gallon hose-end sprayer and apply thoroughly until it starts running off the leaves. This formula works best on plants that aren't blooming; if yours are in flower, aim the spray at the foliage, and try to avoid wetting the blooms.

MIX & FIX

44

four-season planting? Try this compost-as-you-go trick! In spring, mark off a strip across a slope that's about 3 feet wide by 4 or 5 feet long. Loosen the soil as best you can, then cover it with leaves, grass clippings, topsoil, and whatever else is handy. Add more kitchen scraps and garden trimmings all summer long, and mix the new stuff with the old using a rake or hoe.

The following spring, plant your perennials in the strip of compost, then start a new strip above or below it. In just a few seasons, you can transform a barren slope into a bounty of year-round bloomers, one strip at a time!

How Dry I Am

Clay soil holds on to water for a long time, but once it dries out, it's *really* dry! The surface cracks, and the soil breaks into cement-like chunks that just shed water. The best solution is to never let clay dry out completely. Before it becomes dust-dry, water it slowly and deeply—soaker hoses are perfect for this—and keep it topped with a layer of mulch.

Roll Out the Barrel

I wouldn't be without a rain barrel in my garden—and you shouldn't, either! You'll be amazed at how much water you can catch from even a small roof. Just make sure to keep a tight lid on the barrel (with a cutout for the downspout, of course), to stop mosquitoes from getting in and breeding in the standing water. Or add 1 tablespoon of olive oil to the water. That'll keep those pesky pests from making their home in your rain barrel!

MIX & FIX

NUTRIENT BOOST FOR NEGLECTED SOIL

If you have a site with poor, dry soil or seem to have lots of yellowed, sick-looking plants, try this surefire pick-me-up!

6 parts greensand or wood ashes
3 parts cottonseed meal
3 parts bonemeal

Mix the ingredients together. Add 2 cups of gypsum and 1 cup of limestone per gallon of blend. Apply 5 pounds per 100 sq. ft. a few weeks before planting, or work the mix around the bases of established plants.

Jerry's Best Bets for...
Tough Sites

What's the secret to creating a fantastic, year-round flower garden? It all boils down to one simple rule: Put the right plants in the right place! To get you started on your way to success, I've rounded up some of the most dependable multi-season candidates for any tough site.

Shady Characters

Bleeding hearts (*Dicentra*)
Creeping phlox (*Phlox stolonifera*)
Foamflowers (*Tiarella*)
Grape hollies (*Mahonia*)
Hardy begonia (*Begonia grandis* subsp. *evansiana*)
Hellebores (*Helleborus*)
Hostas (*Hosta*)
Lungworts (*Pulmonaria*)
Mountain laurel (*Kalmia latifolia*)
Oak-leaved hydrangea (*Hydrangea quercifolia*)
Pieris (*Pieris*)
Rhododendrons and azaleas (*Rhododendron*)
Spotted deadnettle (*Lamium maculatum*)
Woodland phlox (*Phlox divaricata*)

Sun-Lovers

Basket-of-gold (*Aurinia saxatilis*)
Blue false indigo (*Baptisia australis*)
Butterfly bushes (*Buddleia*)
Butterfly weed (*Asclepias tuberosa*)
Cherries (*Prunus*)
Chinese juniper (*Juniperus chinensis*)
Coral bells (*Heuchera sanguinea*)
Coreopsis (*Coreopsis*)
Crabapples (*Malus*)
Daylilies (*Hemerocallis*)
Magnolias (*Magnolia*)
Perennial candytuft (*Iberis sempervirens*)
Pines (*Pinus*)
Purple coneflowers (*Echinacea*)
Roses (*Rosa*)
Sages (*Salvia*)
Spruces (*Picea*)

Wonderful for Wet Areas

Astilbes (*Astilbe*)
Bee balm (*Monarda didyma*)
Japanese iris (*Iris ensata*)
Japanese primrose (*Primula japonica*)
Joe Pye weeds (*Eupatorium*)
Lobelias (*Lobelia*)
Red maple (*Acer rubrum*)
Rodgersias (*Rodgersia*)
Siberian iris (*Iris sibirica*)
Sour gum (*Nyssa sylvatica*)
Summersweet (*Clethra alnifolia*)
Swamp milkweed (*Asclepias incarnata*)
Virginia sweetspire (*Itea virginica*)
Willows (*Salix*)
Winterberry (*Ilex verticillata*)
Yellow flag (*Iris pseudacorus*)

Dry-Soil Delights

Basket-of-gold (*Aurinia saxatilis*)
Black-eyed Susans (*Rudbeckia*)
Blanket flower (*Gaillardia* x *grandiflora*)
Butterfly weed (*Asclepias tuberosa*)
Coreopsis (*Coreopsis*)
Hypericums (*Hypericum*)
Junipers (*Juniperus*)
Lavenders (*Lavandula*)
Moss phlox (*Phlox subulata*)
Perennial candytuft (*Iberis sempervirens*)
Redbuds (*Cercis*)
Russian sage (*Perovskia atriplicifolia*)
Scarlet firethorn (*Pyracantha coccinea*)
Wormwoods (*Artemisia*)
Yarrows (*Achillea*)
Yuccas (*Yucca*)

PART 2

GET READY FOR A SPRING FLING!

After a long, cold, and dreary winter, there's nothing like that first mild, sunny day to send folks scurrying to the great outdoors. But for most of them, March is still too early to see much in the way of flowers—except maybe for a few forsythias or a couple of crocuses. And the inevitable return of chilly weather sends these poor souls rushing back inside for another few weeks, until Jack Frost is gone for good and it's time to set out their annuals for summer color.

Well, that may be fine for most folks, but not for *you*. You want flowers *now*, and lots of 'em! When the gardener's form of March Madness strikes, I've got just the cure: a bounty of early-blooming trees, shrubs, perennials, annuals, bulbs, and groundcovers that'll welcome spring with a big bang. In the next three chapters, I'll share hundreds of handy hints for getting the growing season off to a rousing start in early spring—plus lots of super suggestions for keeping the color comin' as you gear up for summer, too!

CHAPTER 4

Early Spring Has Sprung

January may kick off the new year for most folks, but *March* is really where it's at if you're a die-hard gardener. From under your feet to high above your head, blooms are bursting out all over! To get you revved up and ready to go, I've packed this chapter with great tips on getting the most out of traditional spring favorites—plus some exciting new ideas and plants to make your yard look extra-special this year.

SPRING

It's time to get out there and get busy! Here's a bunch of things you can do to get your spring garden off to a great start:

- Gradually remove winter mulches

- Sow seeds of half-hardy annuals indoors

- Sow seeds of hardy annuals outdoors

- Start cannas and dahlias in pots indoors

- Plant shrubs and trees

- Pot up spring bulbs for indoor bloom

- Order summer bulbs

- Plant bare-root perennials and roses

- Divide fall-blooming perennials

- Stake floppy perennials before they sprawl

- Prune roses and late-flowering shrubs

- Prepare new beds for planting

- Fertilize emerging bulbs

With their bright blooms and no-fuss nature, it's easy to see why flowering bulbs get most of the attention at this time of year. But if you want a really *spectacular* show to kick off the growing season, don't forget to add early-flowering shrubs and trees to your yard as well!

Let's Get Catty

The furry, silver-gray "catkins" of pussy willow (*Salix discolor*) have long made this spring shrub a favorite with young folks—and the young at heart, too! It'll grow fine in full sun and average garden soil in Zones 4 to 8, but it really likes lots of moisture, so it's also a great choice for a soggy site.

Don't be shy about cutting budded branches to bring indoors in early spring—regular pruning is actually *good* for the plant! Left untrimmed, it'll get to be a big, scraggly shrub. But if you take out about a third of the branches each spring (cut 'em off a foot or so above the ground), your pussy willow will stay low and bushy. For something different, try redgold pussy willow (*S. gracilistyla* 'Melanostachys'), too: It has black catkins!

A Surprising Quince-idence!

For pure spring flower power, it's tough to beat hybrid flowering quince (*Chaenomeles* x *superba*)! These shrubs tend to be small in stature—usually 3 to 4 feet tall and wide—but their bright red, pink, white, or scarlet flowers make a big show in any garden. As a bonus, they produce greenish yellow fruits in fall, which you can harvest to make a tasty jelly! They'll grow fine in full sun and average soil in Zones 5 to 8.

Party Hardy

There's just nothin' like the glowing golden blooms of forsythia to send Ol' Man Winter on his way, double-quick! But not all forsythias are created equal—at least as far as hardiness goes. The plants themselves are hardy into Zone 4, but bitter winter cold can kill the flower buds—and there's not much point in having a forsythia that doesn't bloom! So if you live north of Zone 6, look for extra-hardy selections, such as 'Meadowlark' and 'Northern Sun'.

FANTASTIC FLOWERING SHRUB TONIC

A dose of this elixir in early spring will give your flowering shrubs the energy they need to produce a fantastic floral extravaganza!

1 tbsp. of baby shampoo
1 tsp. of hydrated lime
1 tsp. of iron sulfate
1 gal. of water

Mix all of these ingredients together. For an extra "kicker," add 1 tablespoon of my Liquid Iron to the mixture. Then spray the elixir on all of your flowering shrubs to the point of run-off.

Be a Smart Shrub Shopper

One of my favorite spring activities—and I bet one of yours, too—is visiting my local garden center to pick up some new plants. This is a great time to buy early-flowering shrubs, because you can see exactly what color their flowers are. Plus, if you get 'em in the ground now, they'll settle in without missing a beat. Here are some other, less obvious points to ponder as you shop:

→ Look for leaves that are healthy and free of dark spots or yellow patches.

→ Check that the potting soil is firm and free of weeds.

→ Avoid plants with visible pests, such as aphids or scale.

→ Make sure the pot has a readable plant tag, so you know exactly what you're buying!

Pruning Pointer

Whatever you do, don't be too quick to turn the pruning shears on your shrubs in spring. The general rule of thumb is to prune early-flowering shrubs *after* they're done blooming. Many of these plants need a whole year to develop new flower buds, so if you snip off the shoots *before* they bloom, you're also cutting yourself out of a spectacular flower display this year!

Spotlight on...

Fothergillas

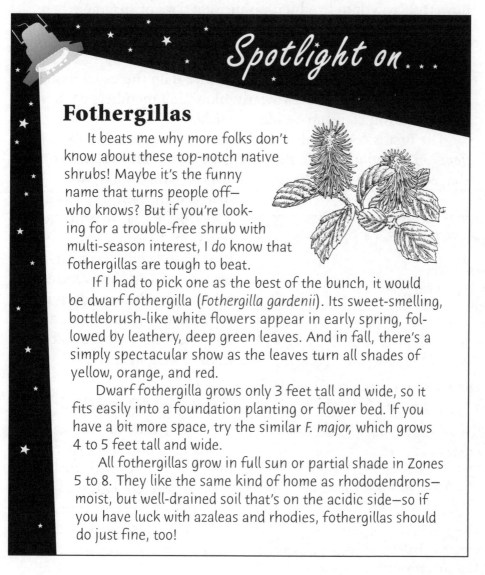

It beats me why more folks don't know about these top-notch native shrubs! Maybe it's the funny name that turns people off—who knows? But if you're looking for a trouble-free shrub with multi-season interest, I *do* know that fothergillas are tough to beat.

If I had to pick one as the best of the bunch, it would be dwarf fothergilla (*Fothergilla gardenii*). Its sweet-smelling, bottlebrush-like white flowers appear in early spring, followed by leathery, deep green leaves. And in fall, there's a simply spectacular show as the leaves turn all shades of yellow, orange, and red.

Dwarf fothergilla grows only 3 feet tall and wide, so it fits easily into a foundation planting or flower bed. If you have a bit more space, try the similar *F. major*, which grows 4 to 5 feet tall and wide.

All fothergillas grow in full sun or partial shade in Zones 5 to 8. They like the same kind of home as rhododendrons—moist, but well-drained soil that's on the acidic side—so if you have luck with azaleas and rhodies, fothergillas should do just fine, too!

Don't Be Shy!

One exception to the "no shrub pruning in spring" rule? Shrubs that flower on "new" wood (stems that are produced in the current growing season), such as butterfly bush (*Buddleia davidii*) and chastetrees (*Vitex*). Go ahead and give these summer-flowering shrubs a good hard trim—back to about a foot or so above the ground—and they'll spring back with a bunch of flowerful growth to brighten up the dog days of summer.

The Rhodies to Success

Looking for something a little zippier than the usual pastel-flowered spring shrubs? Two early-blooming members of the rhododendron clan can be just the ticket!

The first is commonly called Korean rhododendron (*Rhododendron mucronulatum*). Blooming on bare branches, its funnel-shaped, purplish pink flowers make a can't-miss show when paired with 'February Gold' daffodils. 'P.J.M.' hybrid rhododendrons bloom a few weeks later, with bright lavender-pink blooms against the evergreen foliage (which turns deep purple in winter). Give both a try, and you'll have all the color you need to ring in spring.

The Bare Facts

At this time of year, garden centers sell bare-root roses—dormant bushes with their roots protected with packing material and wrapped in plastic. Mail-order rose nurseries tend to ship bare-root plants around

MIX & FIX

ROSE REVIVAL TONICS

This dynamic duo will get your bare-root roses off and growing like champs. First, wash your newly purchased bare-root rosebushes, roots and all, in a bucket of warm water with the following added.

1 tbsp. of dishwashing liquid
¹⁄₄ tsp. of liquid bleach

Then, before planting, soak your bare-root rosebushes for about half an hour in a clean bucket filled with 1 gallon of warm water with the following added to it.

2 tbsp. of clear corn syrup
1 tsp. of dishwashing liquid
1 tsp. of ammonia

now, too. Granted, these plants don't *look* very lively, but good-quality bare-root roses are excellent buys. Treat 'em with my Rose Revival Tonics (at left), then give 'em deep, fertile soil in which to stretch out their roots, and they'll settle in quick as a wink!

Pass the Salt, Please

When you've almost finished planting a new rose-bush, just before you water it well and add mulch, sprinkle a tablespoon of Epsom salts over the soil's surface. Roses love the stuff, so I always give my established roses a spring feeding of Epsom salts, too. In spring, just after I remove the old winter mulch, I sprinkle a tablespoon over the soil around each bush. You won't believe the results—lots of vigorous new growth, and richer flower colors, too!

Rise 'n' Shine, Roses!

For folks in warmer climates—Zone 7 and south—it's time to start removing the winter protection from established roses. (Those of you in cooler areas should wait a few weeks; the end of March is usually fine.)

Once you remove the mulch, give your plants a week or two to soak up some sun, then check the canes carefully for signs of new buds. When those buds begin to swell, prune off the tips of any canes that appear to be dead and budless. Stop when you hit healthy green wood and an outward-facing bud.

ROBUST ROSE FOOD

Feed your established rosebushes first thing in the spring with this fabulous food. They'll love you for it!

5 lbs. of garden food
2 cups of bonemeal
1 cup of Epsom salts
1 cup of sugar
4 pulverized (dried) banana peels

Mix all of these ingredients together, and sprinkle a handful or two around the base of each plant.

MIX & FIX

54

The Berry Best

Ask gardeners "in the know" about their favorite four-season trees, and I guarantee that serviceberries (*Amelanchier*) will be right near the top of the list. Also called Juneberries and shadbush, these little-known natives have everything you could ask for—pretty white spring flowers, handsome summer foliage, fantastic fall color, and handsome gray bark for winter—all wrapped up in a good-looking, medium-sized tree that fits easily into just about any yard. They even have edible berries that rival the best blueberries for great flavor! Give 'em a site with partial shade or full sun and well-drained, acidic soil that does not dry out totally—then stand back and enjoy the show.

Ask Jerry

Q: *I'm looking for an easy-care, spring-flowering tree that'll really make a statement in my front yard. Any suggestions?*

A: You bet—try Eastern redbud (*Cercis canadensis*). In early spring, the bare stems are lined with the most vibrant pinkish purple flowers you'll ever see. They'll last for almost a month if the weather stays cool. For even more color, look for the cultivar 'Forest Pansy'; it has deep purple leaves that extend the show from spring to fall!

Searchin' Out the Sargent

Looking for something a little different than the run-of-the-mill flowering cherry for your four-season landscape? Well, then, my friends, I've got just the thing for you: Sargent cherry (*Prunus sargentii*). This 20- to 30-foot-tall beauty has pink flowers in early spring, followed by shiny leaves that start out reddish, turn deep green for summer, and then end the season a glowing red or bronze. And for the winter months, you'll enjoy the rich reddish brown bark that shines just like it's been freshly polished. Enjoy it planted alone as an accent or paired with other early bulbs and shrubs; either way, you'll know you've really got somethin' special!

The Hole Truth

When I was a boy, everyone said to dig a big, deep hole when you planted a tree. Well, things sure have changed over the years! Nowadays, the experts tell us to go ahead and dig a big hole, but don't make it *deep;* make it *wide.* It should be only as deep as

the root ball of the tree you're planting, but three times the width. Loosen the soil on the sides of the hole, too. Set the root ball in the middle of the hole, then refill the hole only with the soil you took out—don't add any compost or peat moss. Moist, loose soil is all those baby roots need to spread out and get your tree off to a sturdy start!

Don't Delay–Plant Today!

Back in the good old days, most trees were sold with bare roots, and early spring was the only good time to buy and plant them. Spring is still the best season for planting bare-root trees, or those that have been plucked from nursery fields and sold with their roots wrapped in burlap. Either condition is traumatic for the trees, so the sooner you get them planted, the better off you'll both be! The same goes for trees and shrubs you're transplanting in your own yard. And while you're at it, give 'em a taste of my Tree Transplanting Tonic, (at right)—it'll get 'em off on the right root, *guaranteed!*

TREE TRANSPLANTING TONIC

MIX & FIX

Energize your soil with this amazing mix to help it hold moisture and encourage good drainage.

⅓ cup of hydrogen peroxide
¼ cup of instant tea granules
¼ cup of whiskey
¼ cup of baby shampoo
2 tbsp. of fish emulsion
1 gal. of warm water

Mix all of these ingredients in a bucket, and pour it into the hole when you transplant a tree or shrub.

Great Starts Made Simple

While it doesn't pay to pamper trees and shrubs when you're makin' their beds, it's good green-thumb sense to give 'em some TLC *after* you get 'em in the ground. Just follow these steps:

Step 1: Use the leftover soil to form a raised ring around the edge of the planting hole. That'll direct water down to the roots, instead of letting it run off to who-knows-where.

Step 2: Using a gentle flow from a hose or watering can, fill the basin two or three times with water to give the roots a good, thorough soaking.

Step 3: Finish up by covering the soil with a 2-inch layer of mulch, such as shredded bark or chopped leaves, to keep the soil moist and wicked weeds at bay.

Dependable Perennials

Of course, trees and shrubs aren't the only garden residents making a comeback at this time of year—perennials, too, are ready for a return appearance! Here are some quick tips to help you choose the best of the bunch for your spring garden—and to get the others ready for their later display.

Primrose Primer

To my mind, spring just hasn't sprung until I've seen the first primroses (*Primula*) peeking up through the ground. These little cuties are so sturdy that they'll keep right on blooming even through a late snowfall! And they don't ask for much—just humus-rich soil that never totally dries out during the year. They'll grow fine in full sun in the North, but south of Zone 6, they'll appreciate a bit of afternoon shade.

Two of the earliest-appearing species are English primrose (*P. vulgaris*), with flat, pale yellow blooms, and cowslip primrose (*P. veris*), with nodding, fragrant, yellow flowers. And for a veritable rainbow of hues, be sure to grow lots of polyanthus primroses (*P.* x *polyantha*). All three have evergreen or semi-evergreen leaves and are hardy in Zones 4 to 8.

Watch Out for Weeds

When you're cleaning up your garden beds in spring, make double-sure you've removed all the weeds *before* adding a fresh layer of mulch. Don't expect the mulch to simply smother the weeds, because it won't!

Squeeze, Please!

There's nothing like a warm spring day to make you want to get busy in the garden. But don't even *think* about digging in right away—unless your soil passes the squeeze test, that is! Simply trowel up a handful of soil from the site, and give it a good squeeze. If it crumbles apart when you open your hand, it's too dry. (Water thoroughly, then let the area sit for two or three days, and test again.) If it clumps into a solid shape, it's too wet. But if it holds together without packing, it's just right—and you can get on with your digging!

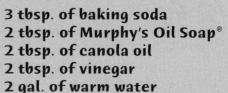

ALL-PURPOSE BUG/THUG SPRAY

MIX & FIX

To kill flower garden insects and diseases in one fell swoop, whip up a batch of my all-purpose spray. Apply in early spring, just as the bugs and thugs are waking up from their long winter's nap.

**3 tbsp. of baking soda
2 tbsp. of Murphy's Oil Soap®
2 tbsp. of canola oil
2 tbsp. of vinegar
2 gal. of warm water**

Mix all of the ingredients together, and mist-spray your perennials to the point of run-off.

No-Fail Mail Order

Have you ever bought perennials by mail? If so, then you were probably quite surprised when all you received was a tangled mass of roots topped with a tiny tuft of foliage. Well, these plants may not look very promising, but with a little care, they can repay you with loads of beautiful blooms for years to come! Here are a few tips to get them going:

➡ Prepare their bed *before* they arrive, so you can get 'em in the ground immediately.

➡ If you can't plant within three days of their arrival, plant them in pots until you have time to find them a permanent home.

➡ Before planting them anywhere, give all of your bare-root perennials a bath in my Root Revival Tonic (at right) to get 'em off to a great start!

Ask Jerry

Q: Hey, Jer—when's the best time to remove the mulch from my flower gardens?

A: Do it bit by bit, like I do, and you'll never be sorry! Early March is generally a good time to uncover early-flowering perennials and bulbs, but leave the mulch in the garden, so you can replace it quickly if Jack Frost makes a return appearance. About the time the forsythias are done blooming, start pulling the mulch away from the rest of your flowers. Once the new shoots have been uncovered for about a week, they're plenty tough, so you can rake the mulch off completely and use it to start a new compost pile.

Soak It to 'Em

Spring showers are great for spring flowers, but they won't do much good for your summer bloomers. But with a little work now and a handy item known as a soaker hose, you can save yourself a whole lot of hassle for the rest of the growing season!

Soaker hoses look like regular garden hoses, but they're usually black, with many tiny holes that gently ooze water when you turn on the spigot. It's easiest to lay a soaker hose in your beds in early spring,

before your plants are up and growing. Snake it back and forth among the clumps, or run it along the front edge of the bed, then give it a U-turn and run it back to the other end of the bed. Cover the hose with mulch, and you won't even see it—but it'll be ready for action if a summer drought hits!

Spring Into Wildflowers

Want to bring the beauty of nature to your backyard? Then check out the wonderful wildflowers known as spring ephemerals. These delicate beauties emerge in early spring, do their thing, and then retreat into the ground by midsummer. This makes them perfect for planting under deciduous trees that cast dense shade in the summer and fall! Some of the easiest-to-grow spring ephemerals include bloodroot (*Sanguinaria canadensis*), May apple (*Podophyllum peltatum*), and Virginia bluebells (*Mertensia virginica*).

Stake Early, Stake Often

Most folks don't think about supporting their perennials until the plants are falling over in summer—and that, my friends, is a mis-stake! The very best time to stake floppy perennials is in early spring, well *before* they start sprawling. Set out your stakes and sup-

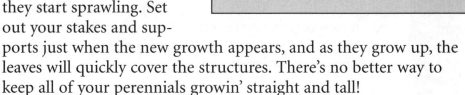

ROOT REVIVAL TONIC

Use this terrific tonic to give your bare-root perennials a bit of refreshment before they go into the garden.

¼ cup of brewed tea
1 tbsp. of dishwashing liquid
1 tbsp. of Epsom salts
1 gal. of water

Let the plants sit in this tonic for up to 24 hours. It'll rev up those tired roots and get 'em ready to grow—*guaranteed!*

MIX & FIX

ports just when the new growth appears, and as they grow up, the leaves will quickly cover the structures. There's no better way to keep all of your perennials growin' straight and tall!

Spotlight on...

Bleeding Hearts

They may look dainty, but bleeding hearts (*Dicentra*) are actually as tough as nails! Most folks are familiar with the old-fashioned common bleeding heart (*D. spectabilis*), with white-tipped, pink hearts that dangle gracefully from 3-foot-tall, arching stems in spring. For a real WOW, try the cultivar 'Gold Heart', which has bright yellow foliage that makes a striking contrast to the light pink blooms. On the down side, common bleeding hearts tend to die back by midsummer—especially if the soil they're growing in tends to dry out—so you're left with a big gap to fill in your flowerbed.

For true multi-season interest, I highly recommend its longer-flowering relative, fern-leaved bleeding heart (*D. eximia*). This beauty is more compact—usually about a foot tall. It doesn't start flowering until late spring or early summer, but its lacy, blue-green leaves make great partners for earlier flowering bulbs. And best of all, fern-leaved bleeding heart and its hybrids can keep blooming well into fall—that's almost 6 months of color! 'King of Hearts' is an especially good-looking selection, with ferny, powder blue foliage and large clusters of nodding, rosy pink hearts all season long.

All bleeding hearts thrive in moist, fertile, humus-rich soil in Zones 3 to 9. They can take full sun in cool climates, but in most parts of the country, a site with morning sun and afternoon shade is ideal for keeping these pretty perennials in peak form.

Give 'Em a Lift

In most parts of the country, early spring is the ideal time for dividing summer- and fall-flowering perennials to keep 'em strong and healthy. (It's also my favorite time to get out in the yard and work off that extra weight I picked up over the winter!) Here's my super-simple, three-step division process:

Step 1: Use a digging fork or shovel to loosen the soil around the outside of the clump, and then to lift the clump out of the ground.

Step 2: Drop the clump onto the ground so that it loosens up or even breaks apart. Then pull or cut away the healthiest-looking pieces, and toss the rest on your compost pile.

Step 3: Spade a 3-inch layer of compost into the soil, set the divisions in their new homes, and water them in with a good dose of my Perennial Pick-Me-Up (see page 62).

Let's Be Partners

Few of us have garden space to spare, so it just makes sense to use every square inch we've got. Well, here's a great way to get double the bloom without digging more beds— simply pair early spring bulbs with later-rising perennials! Daylilies (*Hemerocallis*) are one of my top picks for partnering bulbs in sunny spots, while hostas are super in sites that'll get

CREATIVE COLOR COMBOS

For a stunning early show that's sure to stop traffic, give some of these easy-care combinations a try!

✿ White star magnolia (*Magnolia stellata*) with 'Sissinghurst White' lungwort (*Pulmonaria* 'Sissinghurst White') and white 'Thalia' daffodils

✿ Bright yellow 'Tête-à-Tête' daffodils with pure blue Siberian squill (*Scilla siberica*) and green-flowered bearsfoot hellebore (*Helleborus foetidus*)

✿ Pinkish purple Eastern redbud (*Cercis canadensis*) with purplish pink spotted deadnettle (*Lamium maculatum*)

✿ Yellow border forsythia (*Forsythia* x *intermedia*) with rosy moss phlox (*Phlox subulata*)

summer shade. Besides providing summer and fall interest, the perennials will cover up the yellowing foliage from the ripening bulbs in late spring, which is a BIG plus!

MIX & FIX

PERENNIAL PICK-ME-UP

Give your just-divided perennials a taste of the following tonic to get 'em growin' like gangbusters!

**1 can of beer
1 cup of all-purpose plant food
$1/4$ cup of ammonia**

Mix the ingredients together, and pour them into a 20 gallon hose-end sprayer. Fill the balance of the sprayer jar with water, then saturate the ground around the perennials. Repeat one week later.

Lovely Leaves

When you're choosing pretty flowers for your spring gardens, don't forget to include some showy leaves, too! Some of the best perennials for fantastic spring foliage include golden creeping Jenny (*Lysimachia nummularia* 'Aurea'), dark-leaved heucheras (*Heuchera*), silvery lamb's ears (*Stachys byzantina*), and pink-stemmed, white-striped variegated Solomon's seal (*Polygonatum thunbergii* var. *odoratum* 'Variegatum'). All of these'll stay great-looking well into fall, too—what a bonus!

The Annual Parade

Most annuals don't strut their stuff until summertime, but there *are* a few that'll really brighten up even the earliest spring days. It's also the time to get the later bloomers off to a great start—so let's get growin'!

Season Pleasin' Pansies

There's no better way to welcome spring than with a passel of pansies (*Viola* x *wittrockiana*)! These perky little guys come in just about every color you can imagine, and they look as good in the garden as they do in pots on your porch or patio.

Pansies love cool weather, so don't hesitate to get 'em out early—*unless* they've just come from a warm greenhouse! To help 'em adjust from the warm and cozy indoors to the great out-doors, set the plants outside in a sheltered spot for an hour or two, then bring 'em back in at night. Each day after, leave them out for a few hours longer. By the end of a week or so, they'll be ready to live outside for good. The same advice goes for other indoor-grown early annuals, such as Johnny-jump-ups (*V. tricolor*) and common stock (*Matthiola incana*).

Bulb Buddies

Annuals and bulbs—talk about a perfect pair! Fast-growing, cold-loving annu-als make fantastic fillers around bulbs, adding loads of color while helping to hold the bulb flowers up and out of the mud. To get started, simply buy small annual trans-plants in cell packs, and tuck them in just as the bulbs poke their noses out of the ground. Some top-notch choices for annual bulb partners include forget-me-nots (*Myosotis sylvatica*), English daisies (*Bellis perennis*), and sweet alyssum (*Lobularia mar-itima*)—plus pansies, too!

MIX
&
FIX

SOIL ENERGIZER ELIXIR

Whatever kind of garden you're planning, you'll get great results if you perk up the soil before planting with this energizing elixir!

1 can of beer
1 cup of regular cola (not diet)
1 cup of dishwashing liquid
1 cup of antiseptic mouthwash
1/4 tsp. of instant tea granules

Mix these ingredients in a bucket or container, and fill a 20 gallon hose-end sprayer. Overspray the soil in your garden to the point of run-off (or until small puddles start to form), then let it sit at least two weeks. This recipe makes enough to cover 100 sq. ft. of garden area.

Fast-Track Fillers

To get even more mileage from annuals, use 'em to fill the spaces left *after* the bulbs themselves die back by early summer. Start the process *now* by scattering annual seeds around emerging bulb shoots and pressing them into the soil. By the time the bulbs are done, the annuals will be up and rarin' to grow! A few of my top favorites for this trick include California poppy (*Eschscholzia californica*), flowering tobacco (*Nicotiana alata*), and love-in-a-mist (*Nigella damascena*).

Grandma Putt's GREEN THUMB TIPS

Friends often asked Grandma Putt how she managed to grow such sturdy-looking seedlings, and her answer was always the same: "Keep 'em cool!" Sure, many seeds sprout best when they're warm (70° to 80°F). But once they're up, high temperatures make 'em grow too fast, so their stems get spindly and flop over. Grandma kept her new sprouts in a bright, but cool spot—50° to 60°F—and they were as bushy and healthy as you'd ever want to see!

A Bright Idea

Want to fill your yard with annuals this summer—*without* emptying your bank account? Well, then, start 'em yourself from seed; now's the perfect time! The seed packets will tell you all you need to know about the timing, sowing depth, and so on. But here's a little secret they *won't* tell you—the key to successful seed starting is *light*, and lots of it!

So before you start sowing, hit your local hardware store or home center and pick up one or two 4-foot, fluorescent shop lights. Hang them over a table or bench, no more than 2 inches above the pots. Gradually raise the lights as your seedlings grow, so the fluorescent bulbs stay 4 to 6 inches above their tops.

Seed Startin' Smarts

It's tough to stop funky fungi from attacking tender seedlings, so it makes darn good sense to keep 'em at bay in the first place! Here are some tips to help your seedlings stay free from dastardly diseases:

- → Use fresh, sterilized seed-starting mix and clean containers.

- → Cover seedlings after sowing with a sprinkling of milled sphagnum moss.

- → Keep the pots in an area with good air circulation.

- → Treat seedlings with my Damping-Off Prevention Tonic (at right).

DAMPING-OFF PREVENTION TONIC

You can foil the fungi that cause damping-off disease by dosing your seedlings with this terrific tonic.

4 tsp. of chamomile tea
1 tsp. of dishwashing liquid
1 qt. of boiling water

Mix these ingredients and let them steep for at least an hour (the stronger, the better). Strain, then cool. Mist-spray your seedlings with this tonic as soon as their little heads appear above the soil.

MIX & FIX

A Bounty of Bulbs

No doubt about it: Spring just wouldn't be spring without bulbs! These trouble-free treasures come in every color of the rainbow and—best of all—they'll spring back year after year with virtually no care from you. Early bulbs tend to be on the small side, so it's a snap to tuck them into just about any spot in your yard. They're definitely a great way to kick off your four-season landscape!

Container Color to Go

Do you have a few clumps of crocuses, irises, or other early bulbs to spare? Then try this tip: Dig 'em up as soon as their shoots appear, and pop them into pots. Leave 'em outdoors to spruce up a porch or patio, or to add a welcoming touch to your front steps. Or, bring the pots indoors and keep 'em in a cool, sunny spot to enjoy their beautiful blooms close up. When the flowers fade, plant the bulbs back in your yard, and they'll come back next year without missing a beat!

Keep 'Em High and Dry

There's only one thing that most bulbs can't stand, and that's soggy soil. A site that tends to be waterlogged—especially in winter and early spring—is prime territory for the funky fungi and bad bacteria that can rot bulbs quick as a wink.

What's the simplest way to get around this? Don't plant bulbs where water tends to puddle for hours after a rain. If your whole yard is on the damp side, then make sure you dig the soil extra-deep (at least a foot down, if you can) at planting time to promote better drainage. Setting the bulbs an inch or two closer to the soil surface can help, too!

Tiny Treasures

Sure, you know what a crocus is, and you know what a tulip is—but have you ever heard of a "crocus tulip"? These little guys are the early risers of the tulip clan, blooming at the same

Grandma Putt's GREEN THUMB TIPS

Grandma often sent me out to her garden on nice spring days to snip the seedpods off of her daffodils and tulips, so the bulbs would put their energy into next year's blooms, instead of into making seeds. We never bothered doing this on tiny bulbs like crocus, though. Grandma always said these little ones would come back fine without our help, and sure enough, she was right!

time as regular crocus and reaching only 4 to 6 inches tall in full flower.

Two of my favorite crocus tulips are *Tulipa humilis,* usually with red or magenta blooms, and *T. tarda,* with white-tipped, yellow petals. Unlike fancy hybrid tulips, which often fizzle out after a season or two, these sturdy species come back year after year, better than ever!

Brighten Bare Spots with Bulbs

Tired of looking at that scruffy soil underneath bushy old shrubs? Well then, plant a bunch of early spring bulbs there next fall! It'll be easy to tuck these little gems among the shrubs' roots, and the blooms will add a boatload of color before the shrubs leaf out again in the spring.

Look to the Leaves

Tulips of all kinds are super for spring color, but they can offer more than just rainbow-hued blooms—some have fantastic foliage, too. And since the leaves hang on a whole lot longer than the flowers do, choosing kinds with colorful foliage extends your tulip show from just a week or two to as much as three months!

'Toronto' and 'Red Riding Hood' are two of several tulips with deep maroon or purple spots or stripes on their leaves. For even more flash, try 'New Design' or 'Silverstream', with a white edge on each leaf, or yellow-edged 'Annelinde' or 'Garant'. You'll be glad you did!

BULB BOOSTER

Give your bulb beds a boost each year with a taste of this miracle mix!

**2 lbs. of bonemeal
2 lbs. of wood ashes
1 lb. of Epsom salts**

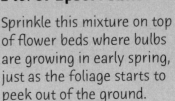

MIX & FIX

Sprinkle this mixture on top of flower beds where bulbs are growing in early spring, just as the foliage starts to peek out of the ground.

Let's Get Wired

Are your hyacinths too heavy to hold their heads up? Give 'em a little support, and they'll stand up straight and tall! All it takes is a piece of heavy wire about 10 inches long (the base of a wire coat hanger is perfect). Right before the flowers open, slip the wire into the top of the spike, down through the stem, and into the bulb—it's as easy as pie! Just remember to cut carefully when you snip off the spent flowers a few weeks later, so you don't ruin your shears on the wire.

Ask Jerry

Q: *I received a pretty pot full of flowering hyacinths for Easter. Is it worth trying to save them when they're done blooming?*

A: You bet it is! Here's how to do it: Snip off the flower stalks when the blooms fade, then keep the plants indoors for a few more weeks in a bright spot. Water them regularly, and fertilize once or twice. After the chance of frost has passed, plant the bulbs in your garden. It may take a year or two for them to flower again, but then they'll return each spring to liven up your yard. Talk about the gift that keeps on giving!

MIX & FIX

HOT BITE SPRAY

Want to keep pesky squirrels from nipping off the buds of your prized tulips? This spicy mixture'll make 'em think twice about taking a bite!

3 tbsp. of cayenne pepper
1 tbsp. of Tabasco® sauce
1 tbsp. of ammonia
1 tbsp. of baby shampoo
2 cups of hot water

Mix the cayenne pepper with the hot water in a bottle, and shake well. Let the mixture sit overnight, then pour off the liquid without disturbing the sediment. Mix the liquid with the other ingredients in a hand-held sprayer. Keep a batch on hand as long as new tulip buds are forming, and spritz the flower stems as often as you can to keep 'em hot, hot, hot! It's strong medicine, so make sure you wear rubber gloves while you're handling this brew.

Picture This!

What's the perfect tool for getting the best out of bulbs? Why, your camera, of course! Taking plenty of pictures of your yard in spring gives you an invaluable record of what you've already planted, and where everything is. It'll be easy to see where you need more bulbs, so you can order just what you need for next year without any guesswork. And come planting time, you can get 'em in the ground without planting new bulbs on top of existing ones!

Spotlight on...

Daffodils

They're a cinch to grow, and their bright blooms are a surefire sign of spring—so is it any wonder that gardeners go daffy over daffodils?

These foolproof flowers usually have yellow or white petals around a central yellow, white, pink, or red trumpet or cup. If you want something really different, look for double-flowered daffodils, which have extra petals in place of a cup or trumpet. They look more like roses or carnations than daffodils!

Most daffodils produce one bloom per stem, but for a real show, try multi-flowered (or cluster-flowered) types, such as 'Geranium' and 'Thalia'. They'll give you anywhere from 2 to 20 flowers on each and every stem!

Daffodils grow best in full sun, but they can take partial shade; in fact, sites under deciduous trees are ideal. It's fine if the soil is moist in spring and summer, but stay away from sites that tend to be soggy all winter—daffodils hate wet feet!

Bunny Barriers

Are rascally rabbits snacking on your bulb shoots as fast as they appear? Simply cut the bottoms out of those black plastic nursery pots you buy perennials in, and slip one bottomless pot over each group of shoots. Push the bottom inch or so of each pot into the soil to secure it. Leave the barriers in place for a few weeks, then slip them off again, and save 'em for next year.

You *Can* Fool Mother Nature

Want to see your spring bulbs a week or two earlier than everyone else's? Then plant 'em in an extra-warm, sunny spot, such as by a south-facing wall. House foundations also help provide heat—especially near a built-in chimney!

Get-Up-and-Grow Iris Tonic

For the most eye-catching bearded irises on the block, feed your plants a dose of this magical mix.

**6 parts hydrated lime
4 parts bonemeal**

Mix the ingredients together and sprinkle around established plants in early spring. Your irises will get off to a flying start!

Iris Rx

If you want to keep your bearded irises from getting "bored" later in the season, it's time to take steps against irises borers *now!* Early spring's the time for borers' cream-colored larvae to emerge from the eggs, which overwinter in garden debris and on the soil. But you can stop 'em before they start.

First, make sure you thoroughly clean up any iris leaves left from last year, then dust around the base of all the iris rhizomes with pyrethrin. Keep a close eye on the emerging leaves, too, and pick off any visible larvae by hand (wear gloves if you're squeamish). That should do the trick—and keep your irises in tip-top shape. And don't forget to feed your irises now with my Get-Up-and-Grow Iris Tonic (above), so they can thank you for your care with loads of beautiful blooms in early summer!

TENDER LOVING CARE

To get the longest show from tender bulbs, it's smart to give them a head start indoors in early spring, making sure they get lots of light. Wait until all danger of frost has passed before moving them outdoors. Here's how to get things growing:

Bulbs	Getting Started
Caladiums (*Caladium*)	Set the tubers 1 inch apart, with their knobby tops 1 to 2 inches deep, in trays of damp peat moss. They like to be very warm—75° to 80°F is ideal. Be sure to keep them moist. Once the leaves appear, move them into individual 4-inch pots.
Cannas (*Canna*)	Place the rhizomes in large individual pots, pressing them into the potting soil until they are just covered. Water lightly, and keep them at 70° to 75°F.
Dahlias (*Dahlia*)	In early to midspring, plant the tuberous roots in large, individual pots with their tops about 4 inches below the surface of the potting soil. Set them in a spot that stays about 75°F.
Elephant's ears (*Colocasia esculenta*)	Plant indoors 8 to 10 weeks before the last frost date in your area. Set the bulbs with their tops 2 inches below the surface of the potting soil, and keep them warm—about 75°F.
Tuberous begonias (*Begonia* Tuberhybrida Hybrids)	Set the tubers in trays or boxes of damp peat moss, and press them down (but don't cover them up). Place them in a warm spot—70° to 75°F is about right. Once the tubers sprout, transplant them to individual 6-inch pots.

Divine Vines and Groundcovers

Early spring's a fine time to get growing with vines and groundcovers. The earliest ankle-high ground-huggers will give you a bounty of blooms, and the weather's just right to get late bloomers started for summer and fall interest. It's also the season to look after later-flowering vines, so you're sure to have a great show come summer.

Timing Is Everything

Planning to add some vines to your yard this year? Then take my advice, friends: Now is the time to get their trellises in place, *before* you plant. The last thing you want to be doing is digging near delicate vine shoots and tramping on the soil later on in the season; you're likely to do a whole lot more harm than good!

MIX & FIX

CLEMATIS CHOW

If you want a really fine clematis vine, I've got just the ticket—a secret family recipe developed by my Grandma Putt.

5 gal. of well-cured horse or cow manure
½ cup of lime
½ cup of bonemeal

Mix the ingredients together in a wheelbarrow and spread over the root zone of your clematis, first thing in the spring. Your clematis will be as happy as a clam!

Clematis Made Simple

If you're looking to get the best show from your clematis vines, early spring's the ideal time to do some trimming—on most kinds, anyway. Just follow my handy guidelines to prune perfectly every time!

Whack these back! Clematis vines that start blooming after early summer make their flowers on this year's stems, so cut 'em

back hard in early spring to encourage lots of new growth. Prune down to 8 to 12 inches above the ground, just above a healthy pair of buds.

Once over lightly. Early, large-flowered clematis hybrids, like 'General Sikorski' and 'Niobe', bloom from late spring into early summer and may rebloom in late summer. Give 'em a light spring shape-up by cutting out any dead or damaged growth, then trim off the vine tips, just above any pair of plump, healthy buds.

Hold off on early bloomers. If you're growing alpine clematis (*C. alpina*) or anemone clematis (*C. montana*), *don't* prune them in early spring, or you'll cut off all of the buds! They really don't need pruning at all, but if the vines are getting messy-looking, trim them as soon as they're done flowering.

Thanks for Your Support

Tired of your beautiful bulb blooms falling facedown into the mud? Then try this nifty trick—pair 'em with a supporting cast of groundcovers! The leaves of low-growing groundcovers, like bugleweeds (*Ajuga*) and lesser periwinkle (*Vinca minor*), do a top-notch job holding tender bulb stems upright when spring winds blow. They'll also keep even the hardest spring showers from splashing mud around, so your bulb flowers stay neat and clean!

Groundcovers from the Ground Up

Established groundcovers are about as low-maintenance as you can get, so it's worth a little extra work to get 'em off to a great start. Dig out any grass and weeds that are already on the

74

site, then spread an inch of compost over the area and work it into the top 8 inches of soil. (Skip the compost for groundcovers that prefer lean soil, like junipers and sedums.) Add a generous dose of my Groundcover Starter Mix (below) at planting time, and your plants will fill in quick as a wink!

MIX & FIX

GROUNDCOVER STARTER MIX

Get new groundcovers growing like gangbusters with this power-packed punch.

3 parts bonemeal
1 part Epsom salts
1 part gypsum

Mix all of the ingredients together and scatter in the planting hole and on the soil surface, too.

Post-Planting Pointers

A little TLC goes a long way toward getting new groundcovers off to a great start. Here's a quick list of three things you can do to speed them along:

Step 1: Water thoroughly after planting, then spread a 1- to 2-inch-deep layer of mulch between the plants.

Step 2: Plan on a regular weeding session once a week for the first year.

Step 3: To fill in bare patches, loosen the soil, then move wandering stems into that area, and fasten them down with U-shaped pieces of wire.

Flocks of Phlox

For sunny yards, moss phlox (*Phlox subulata*) is a perfect choice. It forms 2- to 6-inch-tall carpets of evergreen, needle-like leaves that are smothered in pink, white, or purplish flowers in spring. It's hardy in Zones 2 to 9—in other words, just about everywhere.

In shadier sites, you have two terrific choices for early bloom: creeping phlox (*P. stolonifera*) and woodland phlox (*P. divaricata*). Creeping phlox offers pink, purple-blue, or white flowers atop 4- to 6-inch-tall stems. Woodland phlox is a bit taller, with lavender or white blooms on 8- to 12-inch-tall stems. It has a fabulous fragrance, too! Both of these will do great in Zones 3 to 8.

Chop 'Em Up

Besides a once-a-year grooming, the only care most ornamental grasses need is division. Cool-season grasses do best when you divide them every three years or so. Warm-season grasses, on the other hand, can live in one spot for many years without needing to be divided, so there are only three reasons to bother them:

1. If they outgrow their space,

2. If the center of the clump dies out, or

3. If the clumps start sprawling in midsummer.

Divide warm-season grasses in spring, just as new leaves are coming up; either spring or fall is fine for cool-season grasses. Follow the same steps you'd use to divide any other perennial: Dig up the clumps; cut 'em into sections; compost the old, woody portions; and replant the young, vigorous parts.

Problem Solved!

Here's a super-simple way to spruce up a large grass clump that has died out in the center: Cut the foliage back so you can see what you're doing, then use a post-hole digger to clean out the dead center of the clump. Fill the hole with fresh soil, and your grass will be back to growing on the right root in no time!

Grandma Putt's
GREEN THUMB TIPS

Dividing big grasses is a big job, so if you're planning to split up a really large grass plant, do what Grandma Putt always did—get someone to help you! Dig around the clump with a spade, and if it's small enough, haul it out of the hole to divide it. If it's too big to lift, chop it into pieces while it's still in the hole, then move the individual chunks.

Jerry's Best Bets for...
Early Color

Early spring's a super time to start off your four-season landscape, because you've got lots of fantastic flowers to choose from! Give any or all of these early risers a try:

Trees

Cornelian cherry
   (*Cornus mas*)
Japanese witch hazel
   (*Hamamelis japonica*)
Kobus magnolia
   (*Magnolia kobus*)
Purple-leaved plum
   (*Prunus cerasifera* var.
   atropurpurea)
Redbuds (*Cercis*)
Sargent cherry
   (*Prunus sargentii*)
Serviceberries
   (*Amelanchier*)
Star magnolia
   (*Magnolia stellata*)
Vernal witch hazel
   (*Hamamelis vernalis*)

Shrubs

Carolina rhododendron
   (*Rhododendron
   carolinianum*)
Flowering quinces
   (*Chaenomeles*)
Forsythias
   (*Forsythia*)

Fothergillas
   (*Fothergilla*)
Garland daphne
   (*Daphne cneorum*)
Japanese pieris
   (*Pieris japonica*)
Korean rhododendron
   (*Rhododendron
   mucronulatum*)
Oregon grape holly
   (*Mahonia aquifolium*)

'P.J.M.' rhododendrons
   (*Rhododendron* 'P.J.M.')
Royal azalea
   (*Rhododendron
   schlippenbachii*)
Spicebush
   (*Lindera benzoin*)
Winter jasmine
   (*Jasminum nudiflorum*)

Perennials

Barrenworts
   (*Epimedium*)
Basket-of-gold
   (*Aurinia saxatilis*)

Bearsfoot hellebore
   (*Helleborus foetidus*)
Bleeding hearts
   (*Dicentra*)
Bloodroot
   (*Sanguinaria canadensis*)
Corsican hellebore
   (*Helleborus argutifolius*)
Cowslip primrose
   (*Primula veris*)
Crested iris
   (*Iris cristata*)
Cushion spurge
   (*Euphorbia polychroma*)
Drumstick primrose
   (*Primula denticulata*)
Dutchman's breeches
   (*Dicentra cucullaria*)
English primrose
   (*Primula vulgaris*)
Foamflowers (*Tiarella*)
Lenten rose
   (*Helleborus* x *hybridus*)
Long-spurred columbine
   (*Aquilegia chrysantha*)
Lungworts
   (*Pulmonaria*)

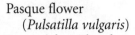

Pasque flower
(*Pulsatilla vulgaris*)
Perennial candytuft
(*Iberis sempervirens*)
Polyanthus primrose
(*Primula* x *polyantha*)
Rock cress
(*Aubrieta deltoidea*)
Siberian bugloss
(*Brunnera macrophylla*)
Snowdrop anemone
(*Anemone sylvestris*)
Violets (*Viola*)
Virginia bluebells
(*Mertensia virginica*)
Wall rock cress
(*Arabis caucasica*)
Wild columbine
(*Aquilegia canadensis*)
Woodland phlox
(*Phlox divaricata*)

Annuals and Biennials

Forget-me-nots
(*Myosotis*)
Johnny-jump-up
(*Viola tricolor*)
Pansy (*Viola* x *wittrockiana*)

Bulbs

Crocus tulips
(*Tulipa humilis* and
T. tarda)
Daffodils
(*Narcissus* Cyclamineus,
Short Cup, Triandrus,
and Trumpet types)
Danford iris
(*Iris danfordiae*)
Dutch crocus
(*Crocus vernus*)

Dutch hyacinth
(*Hyacinthus orientalis*)
Fosteriana tulips
(*Tulipa fosteriana* and
hybrids)
Glory-of-the-snow
(*Chionodoxa luciliae*)
Grape hyacinths
(*Muscari botryoides* and
M. latifolium)

Grecian windflower
(*Anemone blanda*)
Hybrid tulips
(*Tulipa* Single Early and
Double Early types)
Kaufmanniana tulips
(*Tulipa kaufmanniana*
and hybrids)
Reticulated iris
(*Iris reticulata*)
Siberian squill
(*Scilla siberica*)
Spring snowflake
(*Leucojum vernum*)
Striped squill
(*Puschkinia scilloides*)
Winter aconite
(*Eranthis hyemalis*)

Vines

Carolina jessamine
(*Gelsemium
sempervirens*)

Groundcovers

Allegheny pachysandra
(*Pachysandra
procumbens*)
Bergenias
(*Bergenia*)
Common periwinkle
(*Vinca minor*)
Creeping phlox
(*Phlox stolonifera*)
Giant periwinkle
(*Vinca major*)
Japanese pachysandra
(*Pachysandra terminalis*)
Moss phlox
(*Phlox subulata*)
Spotted deadnettle
(*Lamium maculatum*)

CHAPTER 5

Midspring Madness

The days are getting longer, the temperatures are getting milder, and you're just itchin' to get down and dirty. Midspring is a marvelous time of year to be a gardener, because a bounty of beautiful blooms are bustin' out all over. Read over this collection of super springtime tips and tricks, and you'll be rarin' to head outside and get busy on your best-looking landscape ever!

When your yard's overflowing with lush leaves and bright blooms, it can be tough to focus on the gardening jobs you need to get done during this season. Use this list to remind you of the tasks at hand—then be sure to take time to enjoy your handiwork!

- Remove winter mulch from flowers and roses
- Pull out any weeds as soon as you spot them
- Plant warm-season ornamental grasses and divide established clumps, if needed
- Plant container-grown perennials, vines, roses, shrubs, and trees (balled-and-burlapped shrubs and trees, too)
- Feed established flowers, groundcovers, vines, roses, shrubs, and trees
- Plant new groundcover patches and beds
- Prune spring-flowering trees and shrubs when they're done blooming
- Sow seeds of cold-hardy annuals outdoors
- Transplant annual seedlings into larger containers

There's no doubt about it: Midspring is prime time when it comes to flowering trees and shrubs. Best of all, these beauties ask for little of your time in return for their dependable spring display. So plant plenty of trees and shrubs in your yard for early color—but make sure they have other features that will add sparkle later on, too!

Jerry's Cherry Picks

When it comes to four-season trees, it's tough to beat my personal favorites: the flowering cherries (*Prunus*). These top-notch trees have it all: gorgeous spring blooms, handsome summer foliage, fantastic fall color, and beautiful bark to enjoy in winter. Talk about earning their keep!

One of the very best of the bunch is Japanese flowering cherry (*P. serrulata*), with pink or white midspring flowers, reddish fall color, and glossy, reddish brown bark. Paperbark cherry (*P. serrula*) also has exceptionally pretty, peeling bark. Or try autumn-flowering cherry (*P. subhirtella* 'Autumnalis'): Its pinkish white blooms open over a long period of time, often starting in late fall and continuing all through winter in mild climates!

TERRIFIC TREE CHOW

Give established trees a taste of this mix in spring, and they'll be rarin' to grow!

25 lbs. of garden food (5-10-5 is fine)
1 lb. of sugar
$\frac{1}{2}$ lb. of Epsom salts

Feed your trees by drilling holes in the ground out at the weep line (at the tip of the farthest branch), 8 to 10 inches deep and 18 to 24 inches apart. Fill the holes with 2 tablespoons of the above mixture, and sprinkle the remainder over the soil.

MIX & FIX

Don't Bleed 'Em Dry

Planning to do some pruning this spring? It's smart to trim spring-flowering trees and shrubs right after they're done blooming, because you know you won't be cutting off any of the flower buds. But whatever you do, *never* prune beeches (*Fagus*), birches (*Betula*), elms (*Ulmus*), or maples (*Acer*) in spring! These trees tend to "bleed" a whole lot of sap from pruning cuts at this time of year, so the wounds can take a long time to heal. And in the meantime, the poor trees are much easier targets for pests and diseases. Fortunately, it's a snap to prevent these problems—simply wait until early or midsummer to do any needed trimming on these bleedin' trees.

Let's Get Crabby

When you want a bounty of early blooms, crabapples (*Malus*) are a classic choice. But for a long time, these trees have gotten a bad rap, due to their messy fruits and devastating disease problems. Well, it's time to give these old dogs a new look!

Plant breeders have been busy over the past few years, and they've come up with some real winners. Fabulous spring flowers; disease-resistant summer foliage; red, orange, or yellow fall color; and eye-catching winter fruits—these hybrids have it all! Here are just a few of the very best: 'Adams', with reddish pink flowers and dark red fruits; 'David, with red buds, white flowers, and bright red fruits; 'Harvest Gold', with red buds, pale pinkish white flowers, and golden yellow fruits; and 'Jewelberry', with red buds, pinkish white flowers, and bright red fruits.

Saucy Saucer Magnolias

To gardeners in many parts of the country, nothing says spring like the beautiful blooms of the saucer magnolia (*Magnolia* x *soulangeana*). Unfortunately, frost can really do a number on this otherwise top-notch tree, turning those beautiful pink-and-white blooms into ugly brown mush overnight. But fortunately, planting later-blooming cultivars, such as 'Lennei' and 'Verbanica', can help prevent this problem.

For extra frost protection, plant the tree in the *coldest* spot in your yard, such as a north-facing site. Sounds crazy, maybe, but it really works! You see, cold temperatures slow the opening of the flower buds, so the petals will be more likely to escape the nip of late frosts.

Step-by-Step Tree Feeding

Want to keep early-blooming trees and shrubs happy and hearty? Feed 'em smart each spring. It's as easy as 1, 2, 3!

Step 1: Scatter organic or controlled-release fertilizer around the base of each plant.

Ask Jerry

Q: *I'd like to plant a bradford pear (Pyrus calleryana) in my yard, but I've been hearing that maybe they're not a good choice. What's up with these trees?*

A: It's true that bradford pears have a lot to offer—spring flowers, glossy summer leaves, great fall color, and interesting gray bark—but they do have some serious drawbacks, too. Their branches tend to grow upward close to the main trunk, creating weak "crotches" that snap easily when the tree is laden with ice or snow. If you really want to grow one, choose a cultivar selected for stronger branch angles, such as 'Chanticleer'.

Step 2: If your soil tends to be acidic (that's common in the eastern half of the country), add a dusting of lime to help keep the pH near neutral.

Step 3: Finish up with $\frac{1}{4}$ cup of Epsom salts for every 3 feet of plant height. Sprinkle it on the ground in a ring around the plant, out at the tips of the farthest branches.

These three simple steps will deepen flower and leaf colors, thicken flower petals, and improve your plants' root systems, too—and you'll have the best-looking landscape on the block!

Ring My Silverbell

For something really different to brighten your midspring garden, go for the silver—Carolina silverbell (*Halesia carolina*), that is! This pretty native tree thrives in acidic soil and enjoys the light shade cast by taller trees, so it's a first-class choice for woodland gardens. Just remember that the bell-shaped, white flowers dangle from the *undersides* of the branches, so plant it where you can look *up* at them. A slope rising away from your house, or a bed next to a ground-level deck or patio, is ideal.

Holly Cow!

When is a holly *not* a holly? When it's an Oregon grape holly (*Mahonia aquifolium*)! This out-of-the-ordinary shrub is a real winner when it comes to multi-season interest. Spikes of fragrant, yellow flowers in midspring are followed by grape-like clusters of purple-blue berries for summer and fall, and the holly-like, evergreen leaves look great all year long. In the North, give it a site sheltered from strong winds; in the South, keep it in some shade. And one more tip: Prune out one-third of the oldest stems each year to keep your plants bushy and beautiful!

SUPER SHRUB SOIL MIX

Get your new shrubs off to a spectacular start with a dose of this magical mix!

2 bushels of compost
½ cup of Epsom salts
½ cup of bonemeal
1 tbsp. of medicated baby powder

Mix all of these ingredients together in a container, and work about a cup into each hole when you plant your shrubs.

New Life for Old Shrubs

At one time or another, most of us have to deal with an old, overgrown shrub that's simply gotten too big for its own good. Instead of hiring someone to remove it, or using your own time and energy to dig it out, I've got another option: Try renewal pruning!

It's really easy to do: Every

year for three years running, cut out one-third of the branches close to the ground. By the second spring, you'll already see lots of new growth eager for the room you're about to create with your pruning saw. By the third (and final) rejuvenation pruning, you'll be taking out the last of the old wood—and your vigorous new shrub will have a whole new lease on life.

A Lovely Rose Look-Alike

If you love roses as much as I do, you can't wait until May or June for them to come into bloom. Well, you don't *have* to wait—kick off the season in midspring with a Japanese rose (*Kerria japonica*)!

Okay—it's not a true rose, but the flowers *do* look something like single or double golden roses. The long, arching stems are bright green, so they add lots of color to your yard all through winter, as well. This trouble-free shrub thrives in partial shade, or in a site with morning sun and afternoon shade, and it laughs at drought. Japanese rose spreads by suckers, so be sure to give it plenty of space; it's a super choice for covering slopes and other tough sites!

MIX & FIX

SPRING SHRUB RESTORER

This elixir is just the ticket for perking up tired old shrubs and getting them started on their way to a robust new life.

1 can of beer
1 cup of ammonia
1/2 cup of dishwashing liquid
1/2 cup of molasses or clear corn syrup

Mix all of these ingredients in a 20 gallon hose-end sprayer. Drench your shrubs thoroughly, including the undersides of the leaves. And if you have any left over, spray it on your trees, too!

A Java Jolt for Special Shrubs

Spring is a good time to fertilize most shrubs, but don't feed your azaleas and rhododendrons just yet—wait until *after* they bloom. Then give them a fertilizer that's specially formulated for plants that prefer acidic soil. Don't forget to toss your used coffee grounds around these shrubs, too—they'll love you for it!

Spotlight on...

Azaleas and Rhododendrons

Everyone thinks about azaleas and rhododendrons for midspring color—and little wonder! These beauties can really brighten up your yard early in the year. But did you know that with a little planning, you can actually enjoy their blooms for almost six months? It's true! Here are a few of the best bloomers, from earliest to latest:

Korean rhododendron (*Rhododendron mucronulatum*): Purple flowers in late winter or early spring; Zones 5 to 7.

'P.J.M.' rhododendron: Purplish pink flowers in early spring; Zones 5 to 9.

Hybrid azaleas: Red, pink, white, purple, or orange-red flowers in midspring; hardiness varies, but usually Zones 6 to 8.

Large-leaved rhododendrons: Large clusters of flowers in a wide range of colors in late spring; Zones 5 to 8 for most.

Royal azalea (*R. schlippenbachii*): Fragrant, pink flowers in late spring; Zones 5 to 8.

Flame azalea (*R. calendulaceum*): Red to orange-yellow blooms in early summer; Zones 5 to 9.

Sweet azalea (*R. arborescens*): Fragrant, white flowers in early to midsummer; Zones 5 to 9.

Swamp azalea (*R. viscosum*): Very fragrant, white to pinkish blooms in midsummer; Zones 4 to 8.

Plum-leaved azalea (*R. prunifolium*): Bright red or orange flowers in late summer; Zones 5 to 8.

All of these thrive in acidic, humus-rich soil. A spot with morning sun and afternoon shade, or light shade all day, encourages the best bloom display.

Smart Rose Shopping

If you're looking to add some new roses to your yard, mid-spring is a super time to shop for them. But don't be tempted to buy bagged or boxed roses now, because they simply won't have time to develop a good root system before summer heat arrives. Potted roses are a *much* better bet for midspring planting!

3-D Rose Pruning

Rose pruning can sound pretty complicated, but it doesn't have to be! Just remember my simple "3-D Rule": Trim out any dead, diseased, or damaged stems, cutting back to healthy, white-centered wood. Cut out any weak or crossing canes, too. A few basic cuts in early to midspring will go a long way toward getting any rose into prime form for bloom time.

ROSY FEEDING REGIME

Believe you me, roses are the hardest-working flowering plants in your garden. These beauties bloom only for the sake of showing off, as much as they can, for as long as they can. But all this hard work takes lots of energy—and that's where you come in! Follow this simple feeding routine, and your roses will have all the food they need to keep those blooms comin' along! Start with a dose of this elixir in mid- to late spring.

4 cups of bonemeal
1 cup of 5-10-5 garden fertilizer
1 cup of Epsom salts

Mix these ingredients together in a bucket, then give each bush 1 heaping tablespoon, or work in 4 pounds per 100 sq. ft. of rose bed. Then every three weeks after that, give 'em a drink of this terrific tonic.

1 cup of beer
2 tsp. of instant tea granules
1 tsp. of 5-10-5 fertilizer
1 tsp. of fish emulsion
1 tsp. of hydrogen peroxide
1 tsp. of dishwashing liquid
2 gal. of warm water

Mix the ingredients together, then water each plant with 1 pint of the solution in the morning. Stop feeding by July 15 in the North, and August 15 in the South.

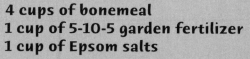

Dependable Perennials

Midspring is a terrific time in a year-round yard! Newly emerging perennials are full of lush leaves, and the blooms are coming along nicely, too. And because these surefire favorites come back year after year, they make ideal partners for spring-flowering trees and shrubs—the ultimate in easy-care companions!

Spread the Wealth

When the spring gardening bug bites, there's no cure like a shopping trip to your local garden center. But before you fill your cart with loads of already-in-bloom perennials, remember that you want a *four-season* garden—not just a *spring* garden! Sure, it's fine to buy a few new perennials now, but remember to leave room for later bloomers, too.

This Candytuft's Dandy

When it comes to picking perennials for a four-season yard, I'd never want to be without perennial candytuft (*Iberis sempervirens*). Unlike most perennials, which tend to die back to the ground in

MIX & FIX

FUNGUS FIGHTER

Get sweet on your peonies, and give 'em a dose of molasses to keep dastardly diseases away!

¹/₂ cup of molasses
¹/₂ cup of powdered milk
1 tsp. of baking soda
1 gal. of warm water

Mix the molasses, powdered milk, and baking soda into a paste. Place the mixture into the toe of an old nylon stocking, and let it steep in the warm water for several hours. Then strain, and use the remaining liquid as a fungus-fighting spray for peonies and other perennials every two weeks throughout the growing season. I guarantee you'll have no more fungus troubles!

winter, this little charmer forms tidy mounds of narrow, ever-green leaves that look great all year long. And as a bonus, perennial candytuft produces a bounty of snow-white blooms in midspring—a perfect contrast to the deep green leaves. The compact, shrubby plants take well to trimming—immediately after bloom is the best time—so they make super mini-hedges for edging sunny flower beds and borders.

Perennial Wise Buys

More and more folks are trying out mail-order plant sources, and it's easy to see why. Those glossy, photo-packed catalogs are enough to make even the most jaded gardener want to grab his or her checkbook! But before you spend your whole plant-buying budget shopping by mail order, keep these tips in mind:

Consider shipping costs. What looks like a good deal at first may not be, once you add the shipping and handling charges to your order!

Try a test order. If you're buying from a company for the first time, order just three or four plants. That should give you an idea of their quality (or lack thereof).

Check out quantity discounts. Many catalogs offer price breaks when you order three or more of each plant. Perennials look best in groups, so you're better off buying several each of a few plants, rather than singles of many different perennials.

Grandma Putt's
GREEN THUMB TIPS

When spring rains saturate the soil, earthworms move to the surface to escape drowning. But when they are exposed like that, they're easy prey for robins, toads, and other worm eaters. Grandma Putt knew that worms do important work in improving the soil, so there was no way she was going to let a single one of her helpers perish. If you want to protect these critters too, do what we did; after each rain, scoop up all the worms you can find, and give 'em a safe haven in your compost pile!

Keep the Compost Comin'

There's no doubt about it: Digging or tilling plenty of organic matter into your soil *before* planting perennials is the secret to a successful year-round yard. But don't think you're done there! Keep up the good work by adding more every chance you get. Each time you set out a new perennial, or lift a clump to divide it, toss a shovelful of compost into the hole before replanting. That'll really help keep your soil in tip-top shape.

Spotlight on...

Columbines

Unlike the big, bright, in-your-face blooms of high summer, spring bloomers tend to have more modest charms. But what they lack in bold color, they more than make up for with their delicate colors and simple elegance. Columbines (*Aquilegia*) are a perfect example: With their graceful, nodding blooms that are accented with long "spurs," it's easy to see why these old-fashioned favorites have stood the test of time. Ranging in height from 6 inches up to 3 feet, their mid- to late-spring flowers come in every color of the rainbow—white and black, too—and some even have multiple colors in a single bloom. And they're a real hit with hummingbirds!

Best of all, these easy keepers don't demand a lot of fussing from you. Hardy in Zones 3 to 9, they'll thrive in a site with average, well-drained soil. Full sun is fine in the North, but give them some shade in the South. Columbine plants usually die out after three or four years, so allow them to reseed, or grow new ones from seed if you want specific colors.

Pest Prevention—1, 2, 3!

One thing for certain is a great four-season landscape starts with top-quality plants. You don't want to bring weak, diseased, or pest-infested perennials home from the garden center, so it's smart to check them carefully *before* you buy. Follow the three steps below, and you'll be sure to get the very best for your gardening buck:

Step 1: Look at the leaves. The foliage should be an even green color (or whatever color they are supposed to be), with no signs of pests.

Step 2: Inspect the stems. They should be free of bumps and discolored patches.

Step 3: Take a peek at the roots. If possible, gently slide the plant out of its pot to check that it doesn't have discolored, dead, or tightly matted roots.

Forcing's the Issue

It's tempting to buy perennials in full bloom when you're on a spring shopping spree, but beware: Those plants may have been "forced" to bloom weeks earlier than they normally would. This is especially true of flowering perennials displayed in greenhouses in mid- to late spring, when the same perennials grown outdoors are barely emerging from the ground.

If you do fall for an indoor-grown perennial, treat it just as you would a tender annual seedling. First, set it outside in a shady spot for an hour or so, and then bring it back inside. Over a period of about a week, gradually give it more sun and a longer time outside, until it is adjusted to the great outdoors. Then plant it as usual. Keep in mind that it will flower at its normal time next year.

PERENNIAL DEPTH PERCEPTION

Planting your perennials properly is a key part of growing a great-looking four-season yard. To take the guesswork out of determining the correct depth, I've come up with this handy-dandy chart that'll make perfect planting a breeze!

Plant Type	Planting Tips
Most common perennials, including coreopsis (*Coreopsis*), hostas (*Hosta*), and phlox (*Phlox*)	Plant with the crown (the point where the roots and stems join) just at, or a smidge above, the soil surface.
Most perennials with taproots, including baby's breath (*Gypsophila paniculata*), blue false indigo (*Baptisia australis*), and hollyhock (*Alcea rosea*)	Plant with the crown just below ground level.
Bleeding hearts (*Dicentra*), peonies (*Paeonia*), and Oriental poppy (*Papaver orientale*)	Plant deep enough so that the tips of the eyes (new buds) are about 2 inches below ground level.

Let's Try Violets

There's something simply magical about a spring garden filled with the dainty blooms of violets (*Viola*). The classic sweet violet (*V. odorata*) is a true beauty, with sweetly scented flowers that appear all through spring. In ideal growing conditions (cool-climate gardens with rich, moist soil), sweet violet can be almost a pest, because it spreads by both runners and by reseeding. Purple is the most common color, but there are also white- and pink-flowered forms (such as 'White Czar' and 'Rosina').

Looking for more than a single season of interest? Then try purple-leaved violet (*V. riviniana* 'Purpurea'). It produces pretty purple flowers in spring and deep purple foliage thereafter.

91

Mix It Up

Ready to get *all* of your flowers growin' like gangbusters this spring? Give 'em a dose of this fortified drink and watch 'em soar to new heights! Take any combination of plant-based kitchen wastes—like table scraps (no meat or fats), potato peelings, and banana peels—and put them in your blender. Fill it with water, blend it all up, and pour it around the base of your perennials. They'll thank you for it with beautiful blooms!

Divide and Conquer

To keep your multi-season perennials in peak condition, plan on dividing most of 'em every three to five years. But don't divide all the perennials in one bed at one time; if you do, you'll have to wait a few years for them all to fill in and bloom well again. Instead, do a few each spring and fall. Besides saving you lots of work at one time, this trick'll keep your perennial plantings looking great year after year!

A Cagey Staking Solution

If you haven't yet staked your perennials, it's time to get busy! By late spring, it'll be too late to get those supports in without damaging stems and leaves in the process. To make your life easier, try this terrific

CREATIVE COLOR COMBOS

With so many top-notch perennials coming into play during midspring, it's easy to create all kinds of eye-catching combinations. Here are just a few ideas to get your creative juices going:

✿ White-flowered, variegated Japanese Solomon's seal (*Polygonatum odoratum* var. *thunbergii* 'Variegatum') underplanted with white- or pink-flowered spotted deadnettle (*Lamium maculatum*)

✿ Pale yellow 'Corbett' columbine (*Aquilegia canadensis* 'Corbett') with lilac-purple wild blue phlox (*Phlox divaricata*)

✿ Pink-flowered old-fashioned bleeding heart (*Dicentra spectabilis*) paired with the fuzzy white spikes of foamflower (*Tiarella cordifolia*)

✿ Bright golden yellow corydalis (*Corydalis lutea*) with purple-blue crested iris (*Iris cristata*)

tip: Pull those old metal tomato cages out of your garage, turn 'em upside down, and put 'em to work as supports for all kinds of bushy perennials. You can spray-paint them black or dark green, but I find that the rusty ones blend in just fine.

Grandma Putt's GREEN THUMB TIPS

When it comes time to dividing perennials, how do you know which ones to start with? I've used Grandma Putt's rule of thumb for years, and I know it'll work great for you, too! First, concentrate on the summer- and fall-flowering ones, so you can get them settled back in and growing strong as soon as possible. Leave the early bloomers—primroses, violets, and the like—until *after* they're done flowering. They'll have plenty of time to get ready for next year's show, and you won't lose any blooms this year, either!

Euphorbia Euphoria

What's a comfy bed without a few cushions—or a flower bed without a few cushion spurges (*Euphorbia polychroma*)? This problem-free cutie forms tidy mounds of pale green leaves that are topped with long-lasting, bright yellow, flower-like bracts all through spring. After the blooms fade, the dense clumps of foliage still look good through summer, then turn a rich red in fall. That's almost eight months of garden interest! All it asks for in return is full sun or light shade and average to poor, well-drained soil. Talk about a good deal!

Midspring, and the Trapping's Easy!

The mild, moist days of spring are prime time for slugs and snails in any yard. These slimy slitherers can chew huge, irregular holes in foliage or even eat entire leaves, taking a big bite out of your best four-season bloomers before you know it.

To trap them, set cabbage leaves or orange or grapefruit rinds around your plants to provide a daytime hiding place. Lift the traps each morning and scrape the collected pests into a container of soapy water. Within a few weeks, you'll notice a definite decrease in your slug and snail population!

GARDENERS' LEAST WANTED

Yesterday, your perennials were in tip-top shape; today, it looks like someone took a string trimmer to them. What happened? Chances are, animal pests are to blame. But who's doing the damage? Here are some of the most common signs.

What You See	Likely Culprit(s)
Chewed leaves, flowers, and shoots	Deer, groundhogs (woodchucks), rabbits
Shoots or flower buds nipped off and often left lying by the plants	Squirrels
Newly planted perennials and bulbs dug up and left on the soil surface	Cats, dogs, squirrels
Top growth is wilted; plant falls over; roots are gone; or fall-planted bulbs don't appear in spring	Pocket gophers, voles

Don't Wait for Weeds

Where weeds are concerned, it's *never* a good idea to put off until tomorrow what you should do today. Starting right now, make a habit of pulling any weed as soon as you see it. If you wait, it's just going to get bigger and harder to pull. And in the meantime, it's stealing water and nutrients from your flowers. Plus, pulling a few weeds every day or two is a whole lot easier on your back than hours-long weekend weeding sessions!

SUREFIRE SLUG SPRAY

This simple spray'll zap these slimy pests in a flash!

1¹/₂ cups of ammonia
1 tbsp. of Murphy's Oil Soap®
1¹/₂ cups of water

Mix these ingredients in a hand-held sprayer, and spray any areas where you see signs of slug activity.

MIX & FIX

By midspring, the days are getting milder, but Jack Frost can still make a surprise appearance. That means it's a little too soon to set out most common summer bedding plants—but there's still lots of other annual activity going on, both indoors and out!

Oh, Sow Easy!

Don't have the time, space, or inclination to start your own annual transplants? You can still enjoy the fun of growing them from seeds—just sow 'em in the great outdoors! Mid- to late spring is a terrific time to direct-sow a wide range of annual flowers.

You can get growing as soon as the soil is dry enough to crumble easily in your hand. Start with the hardiest annuals, like pot marigold (*Calendula officinalis*), then move on to more tender types, such as nasturtiums (*Tropaeolum majus*), as the weather warms up. For specifics on timing, spacing, and sowing depth, check the back of each seed packet—it'll tell you everything you need to know!

Grandma Putt's GREEN THUMB TIPS

Over the years, Grandma Putt noticed that some of her annual flowers were practically as dependable as perennials. She'd sow 'em just once (or set out transplants), and new seedlings would appear each spring after that from self-sown seeds. We used to call these "perennial annuals"—but by any name, they're fantastic fillers for your four-season yard! Here are some of the best to try: bells-of-Ireland (*Moluccella laevis*), cosmos (*Cosmos bipinnatus*), larkspur (*Consolida ajacis*), love-in-a-mist (*Nigella damascena*), spider flower (*Cleome hasslerana*), and sweet alyssum (*Lobularia maritima*).

Peat Pot Pointers

Here's a puzzle: You want to get a jump start by sowing seeds indoors, but the seed packet says your chosen annuals don't like to be transplanted. Well, here's an easy answer—sow 'em in peat pots!

Fill these handy-dandy containers with the same seed-starting mix you use for other indoor-sown seeds, then plant your seeds as usual. Come transplanting time, simply plop the whole thing—pot and all—in the planting hole. Your seedlings will never know they've been transplanted! Annual poppies (*Papaver*), morning glories (*Ipomoea*), nasturtiums (*Tropaeolum majus*), and sunflowers (*Helianthus annuus*) are just a few great candidates for this smart starting trick.

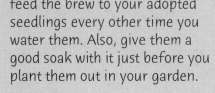

BEDDING PLANT BOOSTER

Don't let your bedding plants go hungry! While they are still in their six-packs, treat them to this nutritious mixture.

2 tsp. of fish emulsion
2 tsp. of dishwashing liquid
1 tsp. of whiskey
1 qt. of water

Mix all of these ingredients, and feed the brew to your adopted seedlings every other time you water them. Also, give them a good soak with it just before you plant them out in your garden.

MIX & FIX

Thinning Is In

With luck, so many seeds will sprout that you'll have to take some of them out to give the rest room to grow. Usually, the best time to thin is about three weeks after planting. *Never* pull out unwanted seedlings—that's likely to harm the roots of the seedlings you want to keep. Instead, snip off the extras with scissors, or else carefully dig them out with a trowel. Then either transplant them or pot them up.

A Bounty of Bulbs

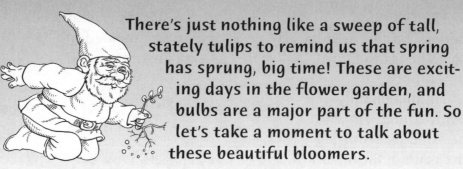

There's just nothing like a sweep of tall, stately tulips to remind us that spring has sprung, big time! These are exciting days in the flower garden, and bulbs are a major part of the fun. So let's take a moment to talk about these beautiful bloomers.

Planning Makes Perfect

When you see a traffic-stopping display of spring bulbs, you know that you're looking at the work of a *very* organized gardener! You see, growing great-looking bulbs doesn't take a lot of skill, but it does take advance planning.

Here's a fun and easy way to turn that task into a treat: Gather up all of those glossy bulb catalogs that arrive in midspring, and decide *now* what you'd like to grow for next year. You can easily see what you already have, so it's a snap to decide how many new bulbs you've got room for, and to figure out exactly which colors and heights would look best. As a bonus, bulb companies offer dandy discounts for early orders, so you'll save a bundle on next year's bulbs, too!

Grandma Putt's

GREEN THUMB TIPS

When April showers were lacking, Grandma Putt made it a point to keep her spring bulbs well watered—and you should do the same! Ample moisture will keep 'em going strong, so they can store plenty of food for next year's flowers. Grandma usually used a sprinkler, but nowadays, we're lucky enough to have soaker hoses; these handy items make it a cinch to soak the soil once or twice a week, as needed.

Hya, Cinth!

Who wouldn't love a midspring yard that's filled with fantastic fragrance? It's easier than you could ever imagine: Just plant a bunch of Dutch hyacinths (*H. orientalis*). The dense flower clusters come in just about every color of the rainbow, in both bright colors and pastels. They're a snap to grow in Zones 5 to 7; just give 'em full sun and average, well-drained soil.

Prefer your flowers a little more delicate-looking? Roman hyacinths (*H. orientalis* var. *albulus*) are an old-fashioned favorite, with multiple spikes of pink, blue, or white blooms that are much less formal-looking than their highly hybridized cousins. They're also a better choice for southern gardens, since they prefer the warmer temperatures of Zones 6 to 8.

Spotlight on . . .

Crown Imperials

Looking for something completely different to really wow your friends and family next spring? Plan on planting some crown imperials (*Fritillaria imperialis*) this fall. The bottom half of each 3- to 4-foot-tall stem bears whorls of slender, bright green leaves; the upper half is crowned with orange, yellow, or red bells topped with another tuft of leaves. This beauty thrives in full sun or partial shade and moist, but well-drained soil in Zones 5 to 8.

While I absolutely *love* crown imperials, I do have to warn you: They have a strong, musky odor that some people like, but others find appalling. Either way, it's probably best to avoid planting them close to your house; you want to *see* them, not *smell* them!

Think Snowflakes

By midspring, most of us are happy to see the last snowflakes melt away. But when you're growing a wide range of bulbs in your four-season landscape, you'll actually look forward to the return of your snowflakes (*Leucojum*) each spring!

Spring snowflakes (*L. vernum*) flower in early to midspring, with bell-shaped white blooms that are tipped with green atop 10-inch stems. Summer snowflakes (*L. aestivum*) are about twice as tall, with similar-looking flowers; they bloom in mid- to late spring (*not* in summer, as you might guess from the name). Both like sun or light shade and moist soil. Simply plant 'em once, and enjoy 'em year after year!

MIX & FIX

Bulb Soak

Get all your bulbs off to a great start by treating them to a sip of this super solution.

1 can of beer
2 tbsp. of dishwashing liquid
¼ tsp. of instant tea granules
2 gal. of water

Mix all of the ingredients together in a large bucket, and carefully dip the bulbs in the mix before planting.

Super Summer Jump Start

How'd you like to enjoy spectacular summer bulbs weeks earlier than your neighbors? You can, if you give your bulbs a head start by planting them indoors in early to midspring. Great candidates for this magnificent magic trick include caladiums, cannas, dahlias, and tuberous begonias, to name just a few.

Give 'em plenty of room—I like to use pots that are at least 6 inches wide and deep—and keep 'em warm (around 70°F). Water well at planting time, then wait until new growth starts before you water again. By the time all danger of frost has passed, they'll be growin' like gangbusters and ready for the garden. Your neighbors will be amazed—at least until you're nice enough to share your secret!

Grandma Putt's

GREEN THUMB TIPS

If you're as penny-wise as my Grandma Putt was, you'll love this little trick she used each year to double or even triple her dahlia display! Start the tubers in pots indoors in early spring, and keep them warm and moist to encourage new growth. When the shoots are about 6 inches tall, cut them off 1 inch above the soil line, then stick them halfway into a mixture of half sand and half compost. After watering lightly, cover the pot with a clear glass jar or a plastic bag, and set the pots in a place with bright, but indirect light. In four to six weeks, they'll be rooted and ready for the garden. The original plants? They'll be better off, too—much bushier than if they were left untrimmed!

Handy Planting

Midspring's a super time to get new lily bulbs in the ground—glads (*Gladiolus*), too! But after a day spent grubbing around in the garden planting bulbs, your fingernails can get mighty grimy. When I was a youngster, Grandma Putt used to get tired of nagging me to scrub my nails, so she had me try this trick: Before heading out to the garden, I lightly scratched my fingernails over a bar of soap. Come cleanup time, the dirt and soap would simply wash right out!

Tulip Tips

All leaves and no flowers make tulips mighty dull, indeed! So what happened? It's likely that the bulbs you bought weren't stored or handled properly. Tulips exposed to temperatures above 70°F in storage don't bloom well—if they bloom at all. There's not much you can do except be patient; you should have flowers the following year.

Divine Vines and Groundcovers

When you plant a bunch of vines, grasses, and groundcovers, you're doing more than some simple exterior decorating; you're adding an abundance of easy-care, multi-season color, too! Read on to find out how these versatile plants can turn a run-of-the-mill midspring yard into a real work of art.

Four Steps to Vonderful Vines

Midspring's the perfect time to add new vines to your four-season yard, so let's get growing! Here's how:

Step 1: Dig a hole 12 to 18 inches across, and about 1 foot deep.

Step 2: Set the plant in the hole so the crown (the point where the roots and stems meet) is about even with the soil surface—or 1 inch below ground level, for clematis.

Step 3: Fill in around the roots with soil, then water well.

Step 4: Spread a 2-inch-thick layer of organic mulch over the soil, keeping it an inch or two away from the stems.

Ask Jerry

Q: Hey, Jer—I planted a mountain clematis (Clematis montana) to get those beautiful white blooms that smell so nice. I give it a good trim each year in early spring, and it looks lush and healthy, but the darn thing just won't flower. What's up?

A: The answer's as simple as this: Keep your pruning shears in your pocket! You see, spring-flowering clematis bloom on stems that grew last summer. So when you prune your vine in March, you're cutting off all of this year's buds! If your vine really needs a trim, do it within two weeks *after* the flowers fade; then your vine will be fine the following spring.

Spring Training for Twiners

Even the most vigorous vines appreciate a little guidance from you in their early days. When the first shoots appear in spring, steer them in the direction you want them to grow. When they are tall enough, secure them to their support by fastening them loosely with coated-wire twist ties, pieces of old pantyhose, or strips of soft fabric.

ORNAMENTAL GRASS CHOW

Here's a fantastic formula for feeding your ornamental grasses that'll give 'em plenty of growing power.

**2 lbs. of dry oatmeal
2 lbs. of crushed dry dog food
1 handful of human hair**

Work a handful of this mixture into the soil, and then plant to your heart's content!

MIX & FIX

Classy Grasses for Midspring

Believe you me: There's nothin' like the moist weather and moderate temperatures of midspring to bring out the best in cool-season ornamental grasses! My favorites are the ones with colored or variegated foliage, because they make fantastic companions for all kinds of early-blooming bulbs, perennials, shrubs, and trees.

For a crisp contrast of bright green and white, you can't do better than variegated bulbous oat grass (*Arrhenatherum elatius* subsp. *bulbosum* 'Variegatum'). Its narrow, vertically striped leaves are absolutely elegant when paired with pure white blooms, such as tulips or pansies, and make a lively accent against rich red, bright pink, or deep blue flowers. Two other great spring grasses are golden wood millet (*Milium effusum* 'Aureum') and variegated foxtail grass (*Alopecurus pratensis* 'Aureovariegatus'). Both of these have bright yellow leaves that complement just about any companion you can think of!

The Kindest Cut

Most warm-season grasses look great standing in the garden all winter, but by springtime, they need a pretty harsh haircut to get ready for another season. Hand-held pruning shears are fine for smaller plants, but you'll need heavy artillery to tackle the big guys, like miscanthus: Use long-handled loppers or, better yet, a string trimmer with a saw blade attached.

Ask Jerry

Q: *I have an old patch of periwinkle that's looking a little tired. Any tips for freshening it up?*

A: Here's a great trick to keep *any* groundcover in top form: Set your lawn mower on its highest blade height, and run it over the whole patch in late winter, once every few years. The plants will come back stronger and bushier than ever!

Think Vinca

Pretty, persistent, and problem-free: That's what periwinkles (*Vinca*) are all about! These "bulletproof" groundcovers have glossy, evergreen leaves that look great all year long, plus purple-blue blooms all through spring—and sometimes later in the year, too. It doesn't take 'em long to fill in, either: Set the young plants about 1 foot apart, and by their second year, they'll send out running stems that root wherever they touch the ground. That'll create a solid, weed-free carpet in only two or three years.

Periwinkles are no prima donnas, either: They can grow just about anywhere—full sun to full shade in cooler areas, or partial to full shade in hot summer climates. They're so vigorous that they can easily overwhelm other perennials, but they're unmatched for filling in large areas under trees and shrubs!

Beautiful Barrenworts

Who says groundcovers have to be plain, green, and boring? Barrenworts (*Epimedium*) are beautiful enough to grow in beds and borders, with red, yellow, pink, lavender, or white flowers to light up your yard from mid- to late spring. After that comes the foliage: pale green or coppery brown in spring, deep green in summer, and rich red in fall.

But these magnificent multi-season plants aren't just pretty faces: They're tough enough to take on the dense shade and dry, root-filled soil under trees and shrubs, where few other plants can grow. They're hardy in Zones 5 to 9, so they can grow in many parts of the country. And best of all, barrenworts are practically problem-free; even bunnies and deer don't eat 'em!

Bulb Buddies for Bountiful Color

Looking to liven up an expanse of all-green English ivy (*Hedera helix*)? This fall, tuck in some small tulips, daffodils, or other early bulbs to enjoy beautiful blooms next spring.

Groundcover Ground Rules

When you follow the rule of using one groundcover plant per square foot of garden area, it's easy to see that filling a big space can be a pretty pricey proposition. So take my advice: If you have a small area—under a single shrub, for instance—feel free to experiment with some of the most unusual (and expensive) flowering groundcovers, such as foamflowers (*Tiarella*), lady's mantle (*Alchemilla mollis*), and lung-

worts (*Pulmonaria*). But when you've got a large space to fill, look to the classic leafy groundcovers like periwinkles (*Vinca*), ivies (*Hedera*), and lilyturfs (*Liriope*). These grow quickly and are easy to propagate, so a single tray of 50 or more plants will probably cost the same as just three or four of the "fancier" spreaders!

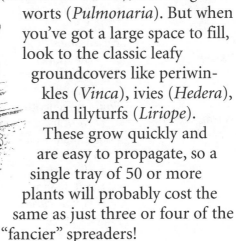

Jerry's Best Bets for...
Bright Blooms

The days are getting longer, the weather's getting milder, and the blooms are bustin' out all over! When you're planning your next year-round yard, use this handy list to make sure you've got a bounty of flowers on hand to celebrate the marvelous season of midspring.

Trees

Amur chokecherry
    (*Prunus maackii*)
Bradford pear
    (*Pyrus calleryana*)
Carolina silverbell
    (*Halesia carolina*)
Crabapples (*Malus*)
Flowering dogwood
    (*Cornus florida*)
Hawthorns (*Crataegus*)
Japanese flowering cherry
    (*Prunus serrulata*)
Mountain silverbell
    (*Halesia
    monticola*)
Paperbark cherry
    (*Prunus
    serrula*)
Redbuds
    (*Cercis*)
Sargent cherry
    (*Prunus sargentii*)
Saucer magnolia
    (*Magnolia* x
    soulangeana)
'Yoshino' flowering cherry
    (*Prunus yedoensis* x
    'Yoshino')

Shrubs

Barberries (*Berberis*)
Bridal wreath spireas
    (*Spiraea prunifolium* and
    S. vanhouttei)
Brooms (*Cytisus*)
Burkwood viburnum
    (*Viburnum* x *burkwoodii*)
Carolina rhododendron
    (*Rhododendron
    carolinianum*)
Evergreen azalea hybrids
    (*Rhododendron* x
    indicum)
False hollies
    (*Osmanthus*)
Flowering currants
    (*Ribes*)
Fountain leucothoe
    (*Leucothoe fontanesiana*)
Fragrant snowball
    (*Viburnum* x
    carlcephalum)
Garland daphne
    (*Daphne cneorum*)
Japanese rose
    (*Kerria japonica*)

Judd viburnum
    (*Viburnum* x *juddii*)
Kaempferi azalea
    (*Rhododendron* x
    kaempferi)
Korean azalea
    (*Rhododendron yedoense*
    var. *poukhanense*)
Koreanspice viburnum
    (*Viburnum carlesii*)
Oregon grape holly
    (*Mahonia aquifolium*)
Pink shell azalea
    (*Rhododendron vaseyi*)
Red-vein enkianthus
    (*Enkianthus
    campanulatus*)
Royal azalea (*Rhododendron
    schlippenbachii*)

Perennials

Bleeding hearts (*Dicentra*)
Bloody cranesbill
    (*Geranium sanguineum*)
Columbines (*Aquilegia*)
Crested iris (*Iris cristata*)
Fern-leaved peony
    (*Paeonia tenuifolia*)
Foamflower
    (*Tiarella cordifolia*)
Hellebores (*Helleborus*)
Maiden pinks
    (*Dianthus deltoides*)

Perennial candytuft
(*Iberis sempervirens*)
Primroses (*Primula*)
Rock cress
(*Aubrieta deltoidea*)
Sandworts (*Arenaria*)
Sea thrift
(*Armeria maritima*)
Siberian bugloss
(*Brunnera macrophylla*)
Solomon's seals
(*Polygonatum*)
Violets (*Viola*)

Virginia bluebells
(*Mertensia virginica*)
Wall rock cress
(*Arabis caucasica*)
Woodland phlox
(*Phlox divaricata*)
Yellow corydalis
(*Corydalis lutea*)

Annuals

Edging lobelia
(*Lobelia erinus*)
Forget-me-nots
(*Myosotis*)
Pansy (*Viola* x *wittrockiana*)
Stock (*Matthiola incana*)
Sweet alyssum
(*Lobularia maritima*)

Bulbs

Candy stripe tulip
(*Tulipa clusiana*)
Checkered lily
(*Fritillaria
meleagris*)
Cliff tulip
(*Tulipa saxatilis*)
Crown imperial
(*Fritillaria imperialis*)
Daffodils (*Narcissus*)
Golden garlic
(*Allium moly*)
Grape hyacinths
(*Muscari*)
Hyacinths
(*Hyacinthus*)
Hybrid tulips
(*Tulipa* Triumph and
Darwin types)
Spring snowflake
(*Leucojum vernum*)
Spring starflower
(*Ipheion uniflorum*)
Summer snowflake
(*Leucojum aestivum*)

Vines

Alpine clematis
(*Clematis alpina*)
Armand clematis
(*Clematis armandii*)
Carolina jessamine
(*Gelsemium
sempervirens*)
Five-leaved akebia
(*Akebia quinata*)
Japanese wisteria
(*Wisteria floribunda*)
Large-petaled clematis
(*Clematis macropetala*)
Mountain clematis
(*Clematis montana*)

Groundcovers

Barrenworts (*Epimedium*)
Bearberry
(*Arctostaphylos uva-ursi*)
Foamflowers (*Tiarella*)
Green-and-gold
(*Chrysogonum
virginianum*)
Moss phlox (*Phlox subulata*)
Skimmias (*Skimmia*)
Soapworts (*Saponaria*)
Spotted deadnettle
(*Lamium maculatum*)
Sweet woodruff
(*Galium odoratum*)

CHAPTER 6

Swing Into Late Spring

Say good-bye to ol' Jack Frost: Summertime is almost here! Every week brings more to enjoy—bright blooms, lush leaves, and fantastic fragrance—from the tallest trees right down to the lowest ground-huggers. Ready to learn my best tips and tricks for making the most of Mother Nature's late-spring bounty in your own backyard? Then let's go!

Late spring's a super time to be outdoors. So don't wait another minute: Take advantage of this great season to finish up your spring chores and get ready for summer!

- Prune spring-blooming shrubs as soon as the flowers are finished

- Refresh mulch around trees and shrubs

- Fertilize shrubs and roses

- Keep after those weeds

- Pinch back fall-flowering perennials

- Harden off indoor-grown seedlings

- Set out annual transplants

- Water new plantings

- Watch out for slugs, aphids, and fungal diseases

- Deadhead spring-blooming perennials and bulbs

- Divide crowded clumps of early bulbs

- Plant containers for loads of summer color

No doubt about it: Springtime is prime time for flowering trees and shrubs. By late spring, the show is slowing down a bit, because leaves are emerging and tend to cover up some of the blooms on taller trees. But closer to eye level, there are still some absolutely fabulous trees and shrubs that add loads of easy-care color to any four-season landscape.

This Hawthorn Has It All

You want beautiful blooms, fine fall color, bright berries, and great bark, too? Then you *need* 'Winter King' hawthorn (*Crataegus viridis* 'Winter King')! This top-notch selection has to be one of the hardest-working trees in any four-season landscape. Here's everything you get:

➡ Snowy white flowers that bloom from late spring to early summer

➡ Glossy green leaves that resist most common diseases

➡ Pretty golden yellow color, with some tinges of red and purple in fall

➡ Half-inch berries that turn bright red in mid- to late fall and last through much of the winter

➡ Light gray bark that peels off in patches, showing the rich cinnamon brown color underneath

Sounds great, huh? But wait—there's more! This wonderful tree grows only 20 to 30 feet tall and wide, so it fits perfectly in most home landscapes in Zones 5 to 9. Please, folks—do yourselves a favor and get one of these growing in your yard today. You'll thank me for it!

We All Fall for Ashes

Mountain ashes (*Sorbus*) sure don't get much attention from most gardeners—and that's a darn shame. These marvelous, multi-season trees have a lot to offer: clusters of white flowers in late spring, followed by long-lasting red-orange berries that stay from fall until at least midwinter.

Korean mountain ash (*S. alnifolia*) is a big 'un— 40 to 50 feet tall—so it's a fine choice if you have a large property. American mountain ash (*S. americana*) reaches only 30 feet, so it's a better option for most suburban yards. And you cold-climate gardeners take note: American mountain ash is hardy as far north as Zone 2, so it's a fantastic choice where other four-season trees simply can't survive!

MIX & FIX

TIMELY TREE TONIC

A couple of times during the growing season, treat your trees to a dose of this tonic to keep 'em in top shape.

1 cup of beer
4¹/₂ tbsp. of instant tea granules
1 tbsp. of baby shampoo
1 tbsp. of ammonia
1 tbsp. of whiskey
1 tbsp. of hydrogen peroxide
1 tbsp. of gelatin
2 gal. of warm water

Mix all of these ingredients in a bucket, and give each tree up to a quart of this tonic about once a month from late spring through summer.

A Shrub for All Seasons

Looking for year-round interest a bit closer to ground level? Well, then, I've got just the thing: rockspray cotoneaster (*Cotoneaster horizontalis*). The show starts in late spring with masses of tiny white flowers, which ripen into cranberry-like red fruits for fall and winter. A bonus is the small, rounded leaves, which start bright green, mature to deep green in summer, and take on red tones before dropping in fall. This super shrub grows only 2 to 3 feet tall, but can spread to 6 feet wide, so it's perfect as a four-season groundcover on sunny slopes, in foundation plantings, or around taller shrubs.

Put 'Em on Ice!

Oh, no! Just when you thought your yard was safe from frost, the weatherman warns that below-freezing temperatures are predicted overnight. Well, never fear—Jerry's here with a great tip: Spray your late-flowering trees and shrubs lightly with water, so that the buds will be protected by a thin layer of ice. No, I'm not crazy—think back to junior-high science class, when you learned that water gives off heat as it freezes. You may still lose some blossoms, but the little extra warmth should be just enough to protect later buds, so they can emerge in all of their splendor.

Fountain of Fun

Hey, shade gardeners—I've got a wonderful winner for you! Fountain leucothoe (*Leucothoe fontanesiana*)—pronounced lew-CO-thwee—gets its name from its arching branches as well as its drooping clusters of white flowers in late spring. The "evergreen" foliage is actually "ever-changing": rich red when new, deep green during the growing season, and reddish purple through the colder months. This trouble-free shrub grows only 2 feet tall and wide, so it's a great multi-season space-filler around azaleas, rhododendrons, silverbells (*Halesia*), and other acid-loving plants.

Don't Get Bamboozled

Say "bamboo" to most folks, and they'll say "No way!" You see, true bamboos have a bad reputation for quickly taking over whole yards. But here's a "bamboo" that even the most cautious gardener can enjoy: heavenly bamboo (*Nandina domestica*). Unlike true bamboos, this Southern

SHRUB STIMULATOR TONIC

Nothing can get your shrubs off to a super start like this powerful potion!

4 tbsp. of instant tea granules
4 tbsp. of bourbon, or ¹/₂ can of beer
2 tbsp. of dishwashing liquid
2 gal. of warm water

Mix all of these ingredients together, and sprinkle the mixture around all of your shrubs in late spring.

MIX & FIX

belle bears white flowers in late spring to early summer, followed by large clusters of bright red berries that last well into winter. The leaves are beautiful in their own right: red or bronze when new, deep green through summer, and red-tinged in fall and winter. Sun or shade, moist or dry, rich soil or poor—if you live in Zones 7 through 9, this heaven-sent shrub *definitely* belongs on your list of best year-round bloomers!

Spotlight on...

Lilacs

I'll be the first to admit that most lilacs (*Syringa*) are single-season plants: They look and smell great for a few weeks each year, then are nondescript for the other 11-plus months. But if you *do* have the space to tuck in at least one lilac, you won't be sorry—their incredible flowers and rich, old-fashioned fragrance make it worth your while!

If your space is limited, you can't do better than 'Miss Kim' lilac (*S. pubescens* subsp. *patula* 'Miss Kim'). This compact cutie grows only 5 to 6 feet tall, with fragrant, lavender-purple flowers in late spring. Its reddish purple fall color is an added bonus.

Have room for a small tree? Then try Japanese tree lilac (*S. reticulata*). It blooms slightly later than other lilacs, with strongly scented white flowers. In fall, the green leaves turn yellow, then they drop to reveal glossy, reddish brown stems that provide lots of winter interest.

Most common lilacs are prone to powdery mildew, a fungal disease that causes white patches on leaves—but *not* 'Miss Kim' or Japanese tree lilac. Both are hardy in Zones 3 to 7 and grow best in full sun and average to dry soil.

Viburnums? Vy Not!

If I could grow only one kind of multi-season shrub in my yard, there's no doubt that it would be viburnums. They've got it all—showy blooms, attractive foliage, great fall color, *and* beautiful berries, too! There are dozens of easy-care viburnums to choose from, and there's not a bad one in the bunch. Here are just a few of my favorite late-spring bloomers to get you started. Give 'em partial shade and well-drained soil, and they'll soon become your favorites, too!

➜ **Blue muffin viburnum** (*Viburnum dentatum* 'Christom'): White flowers; yellow and red fall color; blue berries into winter; Zones 3 to 9.

➜ **Doublefile viburnum** (*V. plicatum* var. *tomentosum*): White flowers on horizontally branched plants; red berries in summer; red fall color; Zones 5 to 8.

➜ **'Erie' linden viburnum** (*V. dilatatum* 'Erie'): Large clusters of white flowers; yellow, orange, and red fall color; red fruits in winter; Zones 5 to 8.

➜ **'Onondaga' Sargent viburnum** (*V. sargentii* 'Onondaga'): Pink-tinged, white flowers; red-tinged leaves that turn all red in fall; glossy red berries that last through winter; Zones 4 to 7.

ROSE AMBROSIA TONIC

If your roses could talk, they would have great things to say about this grand elixir, which gives them just what they need to grow strong and bloom like gangbusters.

1 cup of beer
2 tsp. of instant tea granules
1 tsp. of flower food
   (5-10-5 or 5-10-10)
1 tsp. of fish emulsion
1 tsp. of hydrogen peroxide
1 tsp. of dishwashing liquid

Mix all of these ingredients in 2 gallons of warm water, and give each of your roses 1 pint every three weeks throughout the growing season. Dribble it into the soil after you've watered, so it will penetrate deep into the root zone.

MIX & FIX

Rosy Thoughts

Beach rose, hedgehog rose, or sea tomato—by any name, rugosa rose (*Rosa rugosa*) smells just as sweet—and blooms just as abundantly! Even if you think you can't grow great roses, you can have success with this trouble-free shrub; in fact, it *hates* being sprayed. Give it full sun and well-drained soil, then stand back—it'll thank you with a bounty of fragrant, white, clear pink, or purplish pink flowers from late spring into fall, followed by large, plump, tomato-red "hips." Add in glossy, disease-resistant foliage that's green in summer and yellow in fall, and you've got the perfect rose for any year-round yard!

Dependable Perennials

Irises, peonies, and poppies—oh my! Late spring is a glorious time for folks to make the most of perennials in their year-round landscapes. With so many fabulous flowers to choose from, the hardest part of having a great-looking yard in late spring is deciding just which ones you want to grow. Well, I've got a boatload of top-notch tips to help you find the perfect perennials for your property—and to help you make them look their best, too!

Get the Blues

Want a perennial you can simply plant and forget? Then give blue false indigo (*Baptisia australis*) a try! With its masses of beautiful blue blooms arranged in showy, 4-foot-tall spikes, this multi-season plant is a perennial classic for late-spring beds and borders. Even after the blooms fade, the plants still look great, forming shrub-like clumps of blue-green leaves. They're marvelous at the back of a sunny border, or planted in masses around shrubs. What about maintenance? Well, don't even *think* about dividing blue false indigo, because it *hates* to be disturbed. Just cut the whole plant to the ground in late fall or early spring each year—that's it!

Pinch an Inch— or More!

Would you believe that the solution to most flower garden problems is as close as your fingertips? It's true! You see, crowded perennial clumps don't get much sun or air circulation around their stems, and these moist, dark areas are perfect places for bad bugs and funky fungi to hide. But if you pinch (or cut) out about a third of the stems each spring, right at ground level, the remaining stems will have plenty of room to grow strong and stay healthy. This trick is especially handy on "mildew magnets" like asters, bee balm (*Monarda didyma*), and garden phlox (*Phlox paniculata*).

Ask Jerry

Q: *I love the spiky blue flowers of delphiniums, but they sure don't like me! I'm lucky to get my plants to bloom once; after that, they seem to just disappear during our hot summers. Any hints?*

A: Don't take it personally! It's not *you* that delphiniums don't like—it's your climate. These late-spring bloomers thrive in areas with cool temperatures and simply melt away in summer heat. But don't give up; give larkspur (*Consolida ajacis*) a try. This easy annual looks a whole lot like delphiniums, with tall spikes of blue, pink, or white flowers. Scatter the seeds where you want them to grow any time from late fall to early spring; after that, they'll self-sow and come back every spring without any extra work.

Popular Poppies

Oriental poppies (*Papaver orientale*) definitely *aren't* multi-season perennials; in fact, they probably have the shortest season of any bloomer that you can name. But, oh—those huge flowers

114

are so spectacular that I can't imagine a late-spring garden without 'em!

Bright orange is the most common color, but there are other colors, too, including salmon-pink 'Helen Elizabeth', white 'Royal Wedding', and purplish pink 'Patty's Plum'. Or, for a real color punch, try fire-engine red 'Turkenlouis', with pretty fringed petals. Oriental poppy plants die back to the ground soon after bloom, leaving a big gap in your garden. Don't despair, though—just plant some annuals around the declining foliage, and they'll fill the space all summer, no problem!

PERENNIAL PLANTING POTION

To make sure your flowers get growing on the right root, feed them this magical mixture.

¹/₂ can of beer
¹/₂ cup of ammonia
2 tbsp. of hydrogen peroxide
1 tbsp. of dishwashing liquid
2 gal. of warm water

Mix all of the ingredients together, and soak the soil around each transplant. You can also sprinkle it over your blooming beauties throughout the summer.

Bet on Blooms

Have you ever bought a perennial just because of the beautiful picture in a glossy catalog? If you have, then chances are you've been disappointed when the actual blooms weren't anywhere as stunning as the picture suggested! I was a sucker for pretty pictures, too, until I learned this tip: Try to buy perennials in bloom. Seeing them in person is the only way to be sure you're getting the exact color you're looking for.

Let's Get Catty

I can't think of a prettier sight than a flower-filled border edged with the hazy blue blooms of catmints (*Nepeta*). No, I'm not taking about catNIP (*N. cataria*)—the weedy spreader that sends kitties off to never-never land. CatMINTS are the better-behaved and much showier cousins, forming mounds of small, aromatic, gray-green leaves that are practically smothered in slender spikes of purple-blue blooms in late spring. Rabbits and deer pass them by, and they're rarely bothered by bad bugs or dastardly diseases. Just give 'em well-drained soil and full sun or light shade, and they'll be as happy as clams.

And here's a bonus catmint tip: Whack your plants back by about half in midsummer, and they'll rebloom all the way into fall. Talk about getting your money's worth!

Spotlight on...

Bellflowers

What better way could there be to ring out spring than with the bell-shaped blooms of bellflowers (*Campanula*)? These pretty perennials have a limited color range—usually either purple-blue or white—but they come in an amazing array of sizes, from low-growing ground-huggers to dramatic spike-formers that easily reach eye level. Bellflowers strut their stuff mostly in late spring and early summer, so they're perfect partners for peonies, irises, and many other flowers of the season.

Looking for blooms over a longer period? You can't do better than Carpathian harebell (*C. carpatica*)! Give the 6- to 12-inch-tall plants a light trim in midsummer, and they'll flower all the way into fall. They're a snap to grow from seed and often flower the very first year, so you could even use 'em as annuals, although they're perfectly hardy in Zones 3 to 8. Just give 'em full sun (some afternoon shade is appreciated in hot summer areas), and soil that's evenly moist, but not soggy.

May Flowers Need Spring Showers

No doubt about it: Watering spring-planted perennials is the most important thing you can do to get them off to a great start. If you don't get any rain, you may need to water every day for the first week. After that, cut down to every three or four days for several weeks, then water once a week for the rest of the growing season.

Water-Wise Mulching

Late spring's an ideal time for mulching flower beds and borders to help 'em get through the summer heat ahead. Here's a top-notch tip for getting even more out of your mulch: *Never* apply it when the soil is dry. If you do, the mulch will absorb any rainwater that comes along, and allow most of it to evaporate before it can soak into the soil. So wait until after a heavy rain—or water thoroughly if no rain's on the way—then get that mulch on the ground, *pronto!*

Shhh! Late Sleepers!

By late spring, most perennials are up and growing like gangbusters. Sometimes, though, you may notice a space that's ominously empty, with no shoots that are visible at all. What's up—or rather, not up? Don't worry—some perennials just like to sleep in a bit in spring. Balloon flower

---

SIMPLE SOAP-AND-OIL SPRAY

Are pesky pests taking a bite out of your pretty perennials? Then send them packing with this surefire spray!

1 cup of vegetable oil
1 tbsp. of dishwashing liquid
1 cup of water

Mix the vegetable oil and dishwashing liquid. Add 1 or 2 teaspoons of the soap-and-oil mixture to the water in a hand-held sprayer. Shake to mix, then spray on plants to control aphids, whiteflies, and spider mites.

MIX & FIX

(*Platycodon grandiflorus*), butterfly weeds (*Asclepias*), and rose mallows (*Hibiscus*) are all notorious for scaring gardeners by their late appearance. But they usually sprout up quickly once the weather warms in early summer, and they'll make up for lost time in *no* time!

Scents-ible Planting

Taking time to smell the roses is super, but if you *really* want to get the most out of your four-season yard, remember to include plants with fragrant *foliage,* too! Aromatic herbs like lavenders, lemon balm (*Melissa officinalis*), and thymes make your yard smell great, and they can help deter pesky pests as well. They're perfect for planting along pathways and next to benches, where you can easily brush against them or rub their leaves to release the scents.

HERB SOIL BOOSTER TONIC

Want to liven up your year-round landscape with fragrant herbs? Then get 'em off on the right root with this super soil mix!

5 lbs. of lime
5 lbs. of gypsum
1 lb. of 5-10-5 garden food
1/2 cup of Epsom salts

Work this mix into each 50 sq. ft. of herb garden area to a depth of 12 to 18 inches, and then let it sit for 7 to 10 days before planting.

MIX & FIX

Late spring is a terrific time to plant herbs, so what are you waiting for? Pick out a few of your fragrant favorites, then make sure you add some of my Herb Soil Booster Tonic to the planting hole to give 'em a rip-roarin' start!

A Star for Your Yard

Here's a nifty perennial that has to be one of the best-kept secrets in the perennial world! Arkansas bluestar (*Amsonia hubrectii*) has everything you could ask for in a perennial: pretty, pale blue flowers in late spring; slender, bright green leaves; *and* bright yellow to orange fall color. Hardy in Zones 5 to 9, it grows in dense, tidy clumps that are 2 to 3 feet tall and wide—perfect for just about any site. And did I mention that this no-fuss plant has a cast-iron constitution? Give it full sun or light shade and well-drained soil, and this trouper will come back better and better every year. Dividing? Don't bother! Spraying for pests? Forget about it! So take the time to search out this fantastic multi-season bluestar—I know you'll love it as much as I do.

Spotlight on . . .

Peonies

To my mind, a late-spring garden simply isn't complete without at least one peony! These old-fashioned flowers are still favorites with gardeners of all ages, and little wonder— what can take the place of those huge, ruffled, sweet-smelling blossoms? To enjoy them as long as possible, plant a variety of early-, midseason-, and late-flowering cultivars. That will extend the bloom time from just a week or two to well over a month!

Peonies thrive in a sunny, well-drained site. They prefer cooler climates, so they grow best in Zones 3 to 7. But don't despair if you live farther south; even Zone 8 gardeners can succeed with peonies if they choose heat-tolerant (also called "low-chill") cultivars, such as 'Festiva Maxima'. Set the dormant roots so the buds are no deeper than 2 inches below the soil surface; otherwise, they may not bloom. Also, keep in mind that the heavy blooms of double-flowered peonies will need staking to stay upright. If you absolutely hate staking, stick with single-flowered cultivars, such as clear pink 'Bowl of Beauty' or red 'Scarlett O'Hara'.

Making More Wildflowers in Three Easy Steps

If you've ever tried to grow spring wildflowers, such as blood-root (*Sanguinaria canadensis*), from store-bought seed, you've probably not had much luck. You see, the seeds of these early risers hate to get dried out, so when they're packed in envelopes and stored for months, they're pretty much dead-on-arrival.

But don't think you have to pay a fortune to *buy* new wildflower plants; you just need to know the secret to success with their seeds. Find a friend who's already growing the plants you want, then follow these three easy steps:

Step 1: Starting in late spring, check the seedpods every few days. Gather the seeds as soon as they're ripe (usually just as they start to turn brown).

Step 2: Sow the seeds immediately—either in pots or in a "nursery bed" in a corner of your vegetable garden.

Step 3: Keep the soil moist through summer and fall, and you'll find a whole crop of seedlings next spring!

Livin' on the Edge

Need to get your yard looking great, but only have an hour or so to do it? Don't worry about weeding, and forget about mulching—just grab your lawn edger or flat-bladed spade. Cutting a sharp new edge around flower beds and shrub borders is the quickest *and* easiest way I know to give your whole property a perfectly manicured look!

FLOWER FEEDER

Use this all-purpose food to keep your flowers flourishing.

1 can of beer
2 tbsp. of fish emulsion
2 tbsp. of dishwashing liquid
2 tbsp. of ammonia
2 tbsp. of hydrogen peroxide
2 tbsp. of whiskey
1 tbsp. of clear corn syrup
1 tbsp. of unflavored gelatin
4 tsp. of instant tea granules
2 gal. of warm water

Mix all of the ingredients together, and water all your flowering plants every two weeks in the morning.

MIX & FIX

The Annual Parade

Things are really heating up with annual flowers right about now! The early bloomers you planted a month or two ago are in full flower, and the summer-lovers are rarin' to get in the ground and get growin'. So c'mon, and let's get busy—there's lots to do!

Tough Love for Transplants

If you started seeds of cold-tender annuals indoors in March or April, it's high time to introduce them to the great outdoors. Don't give 'em the shock treatment, though—ease 'em into the transition, and they'll come through with flying colors!

Start hardening-off annual seedlings at least a week before you plan to plant them outdoors. The first day, set them in a sheltered, shady spot (under a porch, perhaps, or next to a shrub) for an hour or two, then bring them inside again. The next day, leave them out for three or four hours. After that, gradually increase both the time they spend outside and the amount of sunshine they get. By the end of the week, they should be ready to stay outside full-time.

Grandma Putt's
GREEN THUMB TIPS

Just before you set out your indoor-grown annual transplants, do what Grandma Putt did: Water 'em with a solution of 1/4 cup of baking soda per gallon of water. This will temporarily stop growth and increase their strength, so they will shrug off the tougher conditions they'll initially face while growing outdoors.

Seedlings on Wheels

Tired of carrying all your annual transplants in and out every day while you're hardening them off? Here's a great trick: Set 'em in a wheelbarrow or toy wagon so you can easily wheel them wherever they need to go!

Plan Ahead for Late Arrivals

Whether you buy them already started or you grow your own, it's easy to get carried away when setting out bedding plants for summer color. But before you start filling every nook and cranny, remember to leave some room for other annuals!

You won't be planting seeds of tender annuals— like sunflowers (*Helianthus annuus*)—for another week or two, at least, so you'll need to leave some open ground for them. You'll also need space for dahlias, cannas, and any other summer bulbs you started indoors earlier in the spring, as well as for any begonias, coleus, and other tender perennials you need to keep inside until nighttime temperatures are at least 50°F. Sounds like common sense, but trust me—it's easy to forget to leave room for these gems, and you don't want to have to dig new beds in a hurry later on to make space for them!

> ### FLOWER-POWER PREP MIX
>
> Here's a flower-power mixture that'll really energize your beds and produce a bounty of bright, beautiful blooms.
>
> **4 cups of bonemeal**
> **2 cups of gypsum**
> **2 cups of Epsom salts**
> **1 cup of wood ashes**
> **1 cup of lime**
> **4 tbsp. of medicated baby powder**
> **1 tbsp. of baking powder**
>
> Combine all of these ingredients in a bucket, and work the mixture into the soil before you plant to get all your flowers off to a rip-roarin' start!

MIX & FIX

Three Steps to Perfect Planting

Ready to get growing? Wait for an overcast or drizzly day for transplanting, if you can, then follow these three easy steps:

Step 1: Dig a small hole for each transplant. (I suggest digging

122

all the holes first, by the way, so you can make sure you have the right number of plants to fill the space.)

Step 2: One at a time, set a plant into a hole so it's at the same depth it was growing before. Gently firm the soil around the roots.

Step 3: Water thoroughly, then give each plant a dose of my Transplant Tonic (below) to get it growin' on the right root.

Here's a Sweet Deal!

If you need a cheap, nearly instant groundcover to fill in around tulips, ornamental onions (*Allium*), and other late-spring bulbs, think sweet alyssum (*Lobularia maritima*)! Start with plants from the garden center, and pop 'em in anywhere. They'll fill the space in a flash and crowd out weeds in the process. This pretty—*and* pleasingly perfumed—annual is also a perfect partner for pansies (*Viola* x *wittrockiana*), primroses (*Primula*), and newly planted perennials!

Made Easy

You're going to mulch your annual flowers for summer anyway, so why not do it now? Believe you me—it's a heck of a lot easier to do it while they're still small! To make the job go even faster, set an upside-down flowerpot over each plant, then use a shovel or pitchfork to toss the mulch evenly over the whole bed. Remove all of the pots, and *presto*—you've got a perfectly mulched garden!

Transplant Tonic

This terrific tonic is perfect for getting all sorts of transplants off to a super-fast start!

1/2 **can of beer**
1 **tbsp. of ammonia**
1 **tbsp. of instant tea**
1 **tbsp. of baby shampoo**
1 **gal. of water**

Mix all of the ingredients together. Use 1 cup of the tonic to water each transplant.

Plan Ahead for the Dog Days

It's almost inevitable: No matter how perfectly you plan your four-season plantings, gaps are going to appear in mid- to late summer, as early bloomers finish and fall-flowering plants are weeks away from doing their thing. To keep your yard looking like a million bucks all summer long, try this trick the pros use: Pot up a few extra annuals in late spring, and keep them well-watered and fertilized for the next few weeks. Then, when you see empty spaces in your beds and borders, simply pop the full-sized annuals out of their pots and into the ground. *Voilà*—no more holes!

Spotlight on...

Chocolate

If you love chocolate as much as I do, then why not grow a *chocolate* garden? No, I'm not talking about cocoa plants— I'm talking about flowers that *smell* or *look* just like chocolate! Some of my favorite choco-scented bloomers include chocolate cosmos (*Cosmos atrosanguineus*), sweet sultan (*Amberboa moschata*), and chocolate daisy (*Berlandiera lyrata*). Then toss in some plants with chocolate-brown foliage, such as 'Chocolate Ruffles' heuchera, 'Chocolate Chip' bugleweed (*Ajuga* 'Chocolate Chip'), 'Chocolate' eupatorium (*Eupatorium rugosum* 'Chocolate'), and 'Chocolate Mint' geranium (*Pelargonium* 'Chocolate Mint').

You can even find brown flowers, too, like chocolate foxglove (*Digitalis parviflora*), 'Chocolate' morning glory (*Ipomoea imperialis* 'Chocolate'), chocolate soldiers (*Aquilegia viridiflora*), and 'Chocolate Royale' painted tongue (*Salpiglossis sinuata* 'Chocolate Royale'). The perfect finishing touch? Why— cocoa-shell mulch, of course!

A Bounty of Bulbs

Sure, there are lots of beautiful bloomers to choose from for your late-spring landscape, but don't forget about bulbs! Tulips, ornamental onions (*Allium*), bearded irises, and more—these Dutch dandies are still going strong. So get ready—I've got a bunch of bright ideas to help you make the most of bulbs in your own yard.

Off With Their Heads!

A five-minute stroll through your yard every day or two is the best thing you can do to keep your bulbs in top form. Take along a pair of garden shears and a bucket, and snip off the tops of spent daffodils, hyacinths, and tulips so they don't form seedheads. That way, your bulbs won't waste their strength making seeds; instead, they'll use all their energy to store food for next spring's show!

Ask Jerry

Q: *Hey, Jer—any tips for handling the yellowing foliage of spring bulbs, like daffodils and tulips? It sure looks awful! Can't I just cut it down?*

A: I know *exactly* what you mean, but believe me: Cutting down the leaves before they turn brown is one of the *worst* things you can do to your bulbs. They need all the time they can get to gather energy for the following year's flowers. Instead of cutting them down early, grow your bulbs among perennials, whose emerging foliage will quickly disguise the ripening bulb leaves. Groundcovers make great bulb buddies, too, for the same reason!

Wet Soil? Go Wild!

Spring bulbs are a snap for most folks to grow, since these forgiving flowers can adapt to almost any soil conditions. The exception? Soggy soil is a death sentence for most bulbs. But don't despair if your yard tends to be on the damp side—I've got a beautiful bulb tailor-made just for you! Quamash (*Camassia quamash*) is a lovely lily relative that's perfectly at home along streams, near ponds, or in other sites that stay moist all summer. In late spring to early summer, this North American native sends up 1- to 2-foot-tall spikes of starry blue, purple, or white flowers—definitely different from most other spring bloomers!

Hardy in Zones 5 to 8, quamash thrives in full sun, but likes afternoon shade in hot summer areas. Simply plant the bulbs 5 inches deep in fall, then forget 'em—they rarely need dividing.

Spotlight on...

Tulips

Let's face it: Spring just wouldn't be the same without the big, bold blooms of hybrid tulips. But did you know that the classic, large-flowered types are just the tip of the iceberg in the tulip world? Here are two other top tulips to try:

Spots and speckles. Since tulip foliage is around for several weeks longer than the flowers, choosing tulips with good-looking leaves gives you extra excitement with no extra effort. My personal favorites are the Greigii Hybrids, such as 'Red Riding Hood', which have maroon striping and/or speckling on the foliage.

Boom the bloom. Would you believe that you can get two or three times the color from the same space? It's true! Unlike common tulips, which produce one stem and one bloom, cluster-flowered (also called bouquet) tulips can have anywhere from two to five blooms per bulb. Two of the best are yellow 'Antoinette' and coral-pink 'Toronto'.

No matter which tulips you choose, give 'em full sun and well-drained soil for best growth. And if spring rains are lacking, plan on watering regularly; tulips need about an inch of water a week through spring to stay in tip-top shape.

126

TLC for Tender Bulbs

Once all danger of frost is past, it's high time to get tender summer bulbs in the ground. If you gave yours a jump start by potting them up indoors earlier in the spring, then harden them off and plant 'em just like potted perennials. Otherwise, plant them like you would hardy bulbs. Set tuberous begonias about 1 inch deep, caladiums and elephant's ears (*Colocasia esculenta*) about 2 inches deep, and dahlias about 4 inches deep. Give 'em a good drink to settle the soil, and they'll be up and growin' strong before you know it!

MIX & FIX

ELEPHANT'S EARS ELIXIR

To grow the biggest elephant's ears on the block, give 'em a regular taste of this power-packed tonic!

1 can of beer
1 cup of all-purpose plant food
¼ cup of ammonia

Mix the ingredients together, and pour them into a 20 gallon hose-end sprayer. Fill the balance of the sprayer with water. Every three weeks, spray the plants until the liquid runs off the leaves.

Don't Be Sad— Get Glads!

If you enjoy the big, beautiful blooms of gladiolus as much as I do, you'll *love* this great tip I learned from Grandma Putt: Instead of setting out the corms all at once, plant just a few of them every two weeks from mid- or late spring through midsummer. This handy hint will give you waves of beautiful blooms all summer long!

For even better results, give your gladiolus corms a good bath before planting. Mix 2½ tablespoons of Lysol® into 1 gallon of warm water, soak the corms in this mixture, and then plant them right away. This quick trick will stop pesky thrips in their tracks—so no more ugly streaks in the petals at bloom time!

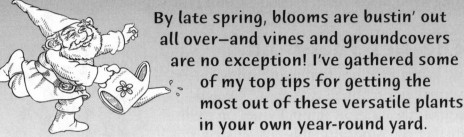

By late spring, blooms are bustin' out all over—and vines and groundcovers are no exception! I've gathered some of my top tips for getting the most out of these versatile plants in your own year-round yard. Planting, staking, training, and spraying—all the answers you need are right here!

Vines, Vines, See How They Climb

All true vines, whether they're annual or perennial, grow in one of three ways. So if you want to nip vine problems in the bud (so to speak), you need to give each kind a slightly different support system. Here's what you need to know:

Twining vines twist themselves around their support. They grow happily on any arbor, trellis, or openwork fence. Examples include morning glories (*Ipomoea*) and wisteria.

Clinging vines, like ivies (*Hedera*), send out rootlets that cling tightly to any surface they encounter.

Tendril vines, such as grapes and sweet peas (*Lathyrus odoratus*), pull themselves up with the help of little shoots that

---

SCAT CAT TONIC

Cats can be great pets, but they can also be real pests if they dig around or roll on tender vine shoots. Try this spicy solution to keep them away from your prized plantings.

5 tbsp. of flour
4 tbsp. of powdered mustard
3 tbsp. of cayenne pepper
2 tbsp. of chili powder
2 qts. of warm water

Mix all of the ingredients together. Sprinkle the solution around the areas you want to protect by keeping kitty away.

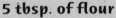

MIX & FIX

grow out from their stems or leaf tips. Clematis are similar, but they wrap their whole leafstalk around the support.

The Ties That Bind

When it comes to making supports for annual vines, not all twines are created equal! Always grow annual vines on trellises made from biodegradable cotton string or uncoated jute. At the end of the season, you can cut down the entire mass of withered stems and string, and chuck the whole thing onto your compost pile—easy as pie!

Grandma Putt's
GREEN THUMB TIPS

When you're choosing a site for a new vine, remember Grandma's words of wisdom: "Keep their roots in the shade and their heads in the sun." Look for spots where shrubs or walls will shelter the root zone, but where the shoots can rise up into the light with ease. The exception is shade-loving vines, like ivies and climbing hydrangea (*Hydrangea petiolaris*); let these scramble up a shady tree trunk or a cool north wall.

Do the Bugleweed Boogie

For a veritable carpet of ground-level color in shady spaces, you simply can't do better than bugleweeds (*Ajuga*). These superior spreaders produce tidy rosettes of bright green, bronze-brown, or multi-colored leaves that look great from early spring through late fall, plus 6-inch-tall spikes of blue, pink, or white blooms in late spring. For the quickest cover, choose fast-creeping common bugleweed (*A. reptans*); it'll fill large spaces in a flash! Upright bugleweed (*A. pyramidalis*) spreads much more slowly, so it's better as a filler around hostas, ferns, and other perennials.

Get Spacey

Here's my number one rule for planting ornamental grasses: Give 'em *plenty* of space at planting time. Warm-season grasses, especially—like Japanese silver grass (*Miscanthus sinensis*)—don't look like much in spring, but they can get mighty big by the end of the summer! So here's a handy rule of thumb: Plant them as far apart as they'll get tall. (It's okay to set them a little closer together if you're growing 'em on a slope, to get quicker cover.)

Spoil the Fun for Fungi

Ornamental grasses are pretty much problem-free, but every now and then, dastardly diseases can rear their ugly heads. Slow growth is the first sign that funky fungi may be around; you'll know for sure if you see dark streaks in the leaves. You probably don't want to hear this, but you really should remove infected plants from your yard; otherwise, the fungi can easily spread to your other grasses. For extra protection, treat your remaining grasses with my All-Around Disease Defense (below) right away; dividing overcrowded clumps can help, too.

ALL-AROUND DISEASE DEFENSE

Wet, rainy weather can foster funky fungi in your yard, especially in spring. But don't let the dreary days get you down—keep all of your plants happy and healthy with this elixir.

1 cup of chamomile tea
1 tsp. of dishwashing liquid
¹/₂ tsp. of vegetable oil
¹/₂ tsp. of peppermint oil
1 gal. of warm water

Mix all of the ingredients together in a bucket. Mist-spray your plants every week or so before the really hot weather (75°F or higher) sets in. This elixir is strong stuff, so test it on a few leaves and wait two or three days to make sure there's no damage before spraying any plant.

MIX & FIX

Glorious Container Gardens

When you're arranging your yard for four-season color, don't forget about the great planting options that container gardens can provide! These versatile features can look fabulous in any season, but late spring is prime time for getting them geared up for the big summer show. Here are some of my very best tips to help you on your way.

Big Is Beautiful

Where container plantings are concerned, bigger is *always* better. Small flowerpots leave little room for root growth and dry out in a snap, so plants are likely to grow poorly and look pathetic. Large containers, like wooden half-barrels, can hold a lot more soil, so there's plenty of root room. They hold more moisture, too, so you can take a break from watering once in a while without your plants getting parched. Best of all, large containers give you room for *lots* more bloomers—and that's what gardening is all about!

Keep 'Em in Check

Potted gardens aren't just pretty—they can be practical, too! They're a perfect place to grow good-looking, but fast-

Ask Jerry

Q: *I love decorating my deck with pots of pretty flowers, but I don't love spending every evening watering them all! Do you have any tips for making container gardening more fun and less work?*

A: I can give you the solution in one word: Mulch! The same secret that minimizes garden watering works perfectly for pots, too. After planting, top all of your containers with 1 to 2 inches of shredded bark, chopped leaves, or another good-looking organic mulch to keep soil cool and moist—just the way roots like it!

spreading perennials that you don't want to let loose in your beds and borders: thugs like obedient plant (*Physostegia virginiana*), chameleon plant (*Houttuynia cordata* 'Chameleon'), and ribbon grass (*Phalaris arundinacea* var. *picta*).

If your soil tends to be on the soggy side, containers are ideal for you, too! Fill 'em with plants that prefer well-drained soil, like lavenders, artemisias, and blanket flowers (*Gaillardia*).

Look-Alikes Make the Grade

I'm all for making the most of old-time garden smarts, but sometimes, there's a lot to be said for doing things the new way! In my Grandma Putt's day, clay pots were pretty much the only game in town. They looked

CREATIVE COLOR COMBOS

When it comes to creative container combinations that'll look good all summer long, the possibilities are endless! Here are just a few of my all-time favorites:

✿ Fragrant, fuzzy-leaved peppermint geranium (*Pelargonium tomentosum*) with white-variegated pineapple mint (*Mentha suaveolens* 'Variegata') and baby-powder-scented white heliotrope (*Heliotropium arborescens* 'Alba')

✿ Bright 'Profusion Orange' zinnia with purple-leaved 'Blackie' sweet potato vine (*Ipomoea batatas* 'Blackie') and the orange flowers and yellow-striped leaves of 'Pretoria' canna

✿ Silvery, lacy-leaved dusty miller (*Senecio cineraria*) and trailing, gray-leaved licorice plant (*Helichrysum petiolare*) with bright blue mealycup sage (*Salvia farinacea*) and sapphire blue edging lobelia (*Lobelia erinus*)

✿ Blue-green 'Blue Wedgwood' hosta with variegated Japanese Solomon's seal (*Polygonatum thunbergii* var. *odoratum* 'Variegatum') and silver-leaved 'White Nancy' spotted deadnettle (*Lamium maculatum* 'White Nancy')

nice, but they dried out in a flash, and they'd crack or crumble if touched by frost.

Well, all that's changed now, with the arrival of plastic, resin, and fiberglass planters that are dead ringers for true terra-cotta. Besides being a whole lot sturdier, these containers weigh practically nothing, and they need watering much less often. Best of all—at least as far as year-round bloomers are concerned—you can leave these look-alikes outside all year long with no chipping or cracking!

Do the Combo Mambo

Planning a great container garden doesn't take a design degree; in fact, it's as easy as 1, 2, 3! Just pick one plant from each category below, and you're *guaranteed* to have an eye-popping potted garden that anyone would envy!

Group 1: Upright or spiky plants are ideal for adding vertical interest in the center of the pot. Try dracaena spikes (*Dracaena marginata*), ornamental grasses, or cannas (to name just a few).

Group 2: Bushy flowering or foliage plants fill the main part of the container. Think of petunias, marigolds, and impatiens, for starters; there are lots of others!

Group 3: Vining or trailing plants spill out of the pot and down toward the ground, softening the edge of the containers. Examples include vinca vine (*Vinca major* 'Variegata'), English ivy (*Hedera helix*), and ivy geraniums (*Pelargonium peltatum*).

Share the Wealth

Here's a quick trick to make your property look like a million bucks: When you set out annual transplants in your beds and borders, save one or two plants out of each six-pack, and use those extras in your containers. That way, your potted plantings will tie right into the rest of your yard—and your neighbors will think you hired a pro to plan the elegant effect!

Use the News

Before adding potting soil to any container, line the base of the pot with a few sheets of newspaper to cover up the drainage holes. Excess water will still drain away, but the soil won't wash out along with it.

Uncontained Container Gardens

When you think of great container plants, what comes to mind? Annual flowers, right? But once you get into year-round bloomers, you'll be a lot more adventurous with your potted plantings! Just about anything you can grow in your yard, you can grow in a large planter: perennials, bulbs, vines, groundcovers, shrubs, and even small trees!

Of all the possible options, I'd have to say that shrubs are my favorites, since they look great every month of the year—especially the evergreen types. Plant 'em in the middle of the container, then fill in around their feet with bushy and trailing flowers for spring and summer color. After you pull out the frost-nipped flowers in fall, the shrub'll stay there to look wonderful all winter long!

MIX & FIX

ULTRA-LIGHT POTTING SOIL

To keep your really big pots and planters from being back-breakers, use this lightweight potting mix.

4 parts perlite, moistened
4 parts compost
1 part potting soil
¹/₂ part cow manure

Mix all of these ingredients together, then fill your containers. This mix dries out very quickly, particularly in the hot summer sun, so be sure to keep an eye on your flowers, and water them as needed.

Jerry's Best Bets for...
First-Rate Flowers

It's late spring, and blooms are bustin' out all over! Here's a rundown of some of the best bloomers for this season, so you can be sure to have your share of the fun in all parts of your yard.

Trees

European mountain ash
   (*Sorbus aucuparia*)
Golden-chain tree
   (*Laburnum* x *watereri*)
Hardy orange
   (*Poncirus trifoliata*)
Hawthorns (*Crataegus*)
Korean mountain ash
   (*Sorbus alnifolia*)
Kousa dogwood
   (*Cornus kousa*)
Pagoda dogwood
   (*Cornus alternifolia*)
Red horse chestnut
   (*Aesculus* x *carnea*)
Southern magnolia
   (*Magnolia grandiflora*)
Stellar dogwood
   (*Cornus* x *rutgersensis*)
Weeping willow-leaved pear
   (*Pyrus salicifolia*
   'Pendula')

Shrubs

American cranberry bush
   (*Viburnum trilobum*)
Burkwood daphne
   (*Daphne* x *burkwoodii*)
Catawba rhododendron
   (*Rhododendron
   catawbiense*)
Common lilac
   (*Syringa vulgaris*)
Cotoneasters (*Cotoneaster*)

Cranberry bush
   (*Viburnum opulus*)
Doublefile viburnum
   (*Viburnum plicatum* var.
   tomentosum)
Fountain leucothoe
   (*Leucothoe fontanesiana*)
Fraser photinia
   (*Photinia* x *fraseri*)
Heavenly bamboo
   (*Nandina domestica*)
Large-leaved rhododendron
   hybrids (*Rhododendron*)
Linden viburnum
   (*Viburnum dilatatum*)
Manchurian lilac (*Syringa
   pubescens* subsp. *patula*)
Meyer lilac (*Syringa meyeri*)
Pinxterbloom azalea
   (*Rhododendron
   periclymenoides*)
Red-leaved rose
   (*Rosa glauca*)
Roseshell azalea
   (*Rhododendron
   prinophyllum*)

Rugosa rose (*Rosa rugosa*)
Tea viburnum
   (*Viburnum setigerum*)
Yaku rhododendron
   (*Rhododendron
   yakushimanum*)

Perennials

Arkansas bluestar
   (*Amsonia hubrectii*)
Astilbes (*Astilbe*)
Bleeding hearts (*Dicentra*)
Blue false indigo
   (*Baptisia australis*)
Catmint
   (*Nepeta* x *faassenii*)
Clustered bellflower
   (*Campanula glomerata*)
Columbines (*Aquilegia*)
Dalmatian bellflower
   (*Campanula
   portenschlagiana*)
Hardy geraniums
   (*Geranium*)
Italian arum
   (*Arum italicum*)
Lupines (*Lupinus*)

Mountain bluet
  (*Centaurea montana*)
Oriental poppy
  (*Papaver orientale*)
Peonies (*Paeonia*)
Perennial flax
  (*Linum perenne*)
Roof iris (*Iris tectorum*)
Serbian bellflower
  (*Campanula
  poscharskyana*)
Siberian iris (*Iris sibirica*)

Annuals

Calendula
  (*Calendula officinalis*)
Coleus (*Solenostemon
  scutellarioides*)
Edging lobelia
  (*Lobelia erinus*)
Heliotrope
  (*Heliotropium
  arborescens*)
Marigolds (*Tagetes*)
Monkey flower
  (*Mimulus x hybridus*)
Pansies
  (*Viola* x *wittrockiana*)
Rocket candytuft
  (*Iberis amara*)
Snapdragon
  (*Antirrhinum majus*)

Stocks (*Matthiola*)
Sweet alyssum
  (*Lobularia maritima*)

Verbenas (*Verbena*)
Wax begonia
  (*Begonia hybrids*)

Bulbs

Baker tulip (*Tulipa bakeri*)
Bearded iris
  (*Iris* Bearded Hybrids)
Giant onion
  (*Allium giganteum*)
Hybrid tulips
  (*Tulipa* Cottage,
  Lily-Flowered, Double
  Late, and Parrot types)
Lily leek (*Allium moly*)
Persian onion
  (*Allium aflatunense*)
Quamash
  (*Camassia quamash*)

Spanish bluebells
  (*Hyacinthoides hispanica*)
Star-of-Bethlehem
  (*Ornithogalum
  umbellatum*)
Turkestan onion
  (*Allium karataviense*)
Wood hyacinths
  (*Hyacinthoides*)

Vines

Alpine clematis
  (*Clematis alpina*)
Anemone clematis
  (*Clematis montana*)
Armand clematis
  (*Clematis armandii*)

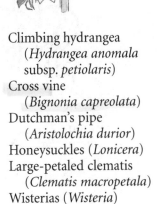

Climbing hydrangea
  (*Hydrangea anomala
  subsp. petiolaris*)
Cross vine
  (*Bignonia capreolata*)
Dutchman's pipe
  (*Aristolochia durior*)
Honeysuckles (*Lonicera*)
Large-petaled clematis
  (*Clematis macropetala*)
Wisterias (*Wisteria*)

Groundcovers

Barren strawberry
  (*Waldsteinia fragarioides*)
Bugleweeds (*Ajuga*)
Goldmoss stonecrop
  (*Sedum acre*)
Lily-of-the-valley
  (*Convallaria majalis*)
Mazus (*Mazus reptans*)
Rockspray cotoneaster
  (*Cotoneaster horizontalis*)
Snow-in-summer
  (*Cerastium tomentosum*)
Spotted deadnettle
  (*Lamium maculatum*)
Sweet woodruff
  (*Galium odoratum*)

PART 3

FUN IN THE SUMMER SUN!

Roses and lilacs and peonies—oh my! With so many beautiful bloomers to choose from, planning a garden that looks great in early summer is practically a no-brainer. And midsummer isn't too tough either, since that's when annual flowers really come into their glory. It's the weeks after that—those heat-drenched days from mid-July until early September—that are the true test of a gardener's skill. When you can honestly say that your yard looks as good in August as it did in April, you know you've really got something going on!

To make all of your dog-day dreams into reality, I've rounded up the very best of my summertime secrets to share with you. I've also dug through my notebooks for those pearls of hot-weather gardening wisdom that Grandma Putt shared with me so many years ago. With this treasure trove of time-tested gardening hints at your fingertips, you're *guaranteed* to have a traffic-stopping landscape that sails right through summer—and beyond!

CHAPTER 7

Early Summer Means Glorious Gardens

Ahhh, summertime! There's nothing like warm days, mild nights, and ample moisture to send plants blasting into bloom. From the trees overhead to the groundcovers at your feet—and in your beds and borders—fabulous flowers and lush leaves are looking better every day. Dive into this collection of tips and tricks for making the most of everything early summer has to offer.

Here's a quick rundown of some of the season's main chores to help you stay on top of things:

- Add mulch around recently planted annuals, perennials, and groundcovers
- Refresh mulches around existing plantings
- Snip or pinch off spent flowers to prevent seed formation
- Water new plantings thoroughly if rain is lacking
- Divide overcrowded spring bulbs as they go dormant
- Keep up the never-ending fight against weeds
- Pinch perennials (especially mums) to encourage dense, bushy growth
- Keep an eye out for pests and diseases
- Take cuttings of trees, shrubs, vines, groundcovers, and perennials
- Set out remaining cold-tender annuals and bulbs
- Sow biennial and perennial seeds now for blooms next year
- Keep sowing annual seeds outdoors for late summer and fall flowers

Small trees and shrubs are the stars of this season, and there's not a bad one in the bunch. Sun or shade, moist soil or dry—you name the site, and I've got a bunch of wonderful woody plants that'll make your yard the envy of all your neighbors!

Livin' on the Fringe

White fringe tree, grancy graybeard, or old-man's beard—whatever you call it, this super small tree (*Chionanthus virginicus*) definitely deserves a place in your year-round landscape. It's a real beauty in early summer, with clouds of cascading, fringe-like white flowers that smell honey-sweet. The deep green summer leaves turn bright yellow in fall, and if your tree is a female (it's pretty hard to tell), it may produce sprays of blue berries then, too.

This native tree grows about 20 feet tall and wide—a perfect size for just about any yard—and is hardy in Zones 5 to 9. It grows well in full sun, but it can also take partial shade—a plus if you already have a few large trees. Acidic soil is a must, so if you have luck with azaleas and rhododendrons, give this great little tree a try; you'll be glad you did!

MULCH MOISTURIZER TONIC

When you give your trees and shrubs a fresh layer of organic mulch in early summer, overspray it with this super tonic to give it a little extra kick.

1 can of regular cola (not diet)
1/2 cup of ammonia
1/2 cup of antiseptic mouthwash
1/2 cup of baby shampoo

Mix all of these ingredients in a 20 gallon hose-end sprayer, and give the mulch a long, cool drink.

MIX & FIX

140

Cutting Remarks

Did you know that early summer's a perfect time to take cuttings of your favorite woody plants? It's true that tree cuttings can be a little tricky, but many shrubs are as easy to propagate this way as perennials, so it's worth trying; you've got nothing to lose! Follow these four simple steps:

Step 1: On a cool or cloudy day, snip off 4- to 6-inch-long stem tips from the tree or shrub you want to propagate.

Step 2: Use a sharp knife to cut each stem about $1/4$ inch below a node (the spot where a leaf or leaf pair joins the stem), and pinch off the lowest set of leaves.

Step 3: Dip the base of each cutting in a rooting hormone (available at your local garden center), then insert the bottom third of the stem into damp sand or potting soil.

Step 4: Water lightly, then set the planted cuttings in bright, but indirect light. Once new growth appears, it's time to celebrate: You just made a new shrub or tree for free!

A Fishy Trick

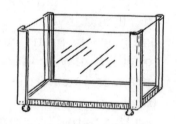

For extra-quick rooting, treat your tree and shrub cuttings to a little R and R in their own private sauna room. You see, leafy cuttings love high humidity, so it's just plain smart to keep them in some kind of enclosure until they have formed new roots. A tank-type terrarium or aquarium makes a perfect humidity chamber, and you can often pick one up for a song at a garage sale. Or try a clear plastic sweater box—that'll work just as well!

Layering's a Piece of Cake

Looking for a super-easy way to share a favorite shrub with a friend? Then try layering. It's sort of like taking cuttings, but you leave the shoots attached to the parent plant until they make roots, so you don't have to worry about them wilting.

All you do is choose a flexible stem near the base of the shrub, then bend it down to the ground. Loosen the soil a little bit where the stem touches it, scratch or nick the stem slightly, nestle it into the soil, and then set a rock over it to hold it down. (Leave a few inches of the stem tip exposed, please.) Keep the area moist, and in a few months, you'll have a rooted stem that's ready for a new home!

A Tree for All Seasons

Imagine, if you will, foot-long clusters of pure white blooms practically dripping with sweet perfume in early summer. Now, imagine pretty leaves that are almost yellow when new, then bright green, and then rich yellow again at summer's end. And don't forget about smooth, silvery gray bark that practically gleams on even the dullest winter day. Sounds too good to be true? Not if you plant an American yellowwood (*Cladrastis kentukea*)!

Grandma Putt's

GREEN THUMB TIPS

Early summer's prime time for mulching flower beds and borders—and don't forget to freshen up the mulch around your trees and shrubs while you're at it! No need to rake off the old mulch—just do what my Grandma Putt did, and cover it with an inch or two of fresh material. Douse with a drink of Grandma's magical Mulch Moisturizer Tonic (see page 139), and your trees and shrubs'll be all set for the summer.

This little-known native tree deserves a *lot* more attention from four-season gardeners, since it looks great every single month of the year. Yellowwood grows pretty slowly, eventually reaching 30 to 40 feet tall, and thrives in full sun and average soil in Zones 4 to 8. It takes a few years to reach flowering size, so don't delay; get one of these terrific trees growing in your yard today!

141

A Snip in Time

By now, your spring-flowering shrubs and trees are past their prime, so it's the perfect time to pull out your pruning shears for a little cleanup work. Believe you me: Pruning in early summer is a lot more pleasant than in winter's finger-numbing cold. But more important—at least as far as your plants are concerned—trimming early-blooming trees and shrubs now will give their new growth plenty of time to form flower buds for next year's show. Flowering quinces (*Chaenomeles*), Japanese rose (*Kerria japonica*), early spireas (*Spiraea*), weigelas (*Weigela*), and lilacs (*Syringa*) are a few good candidates for a trim this season.

Amazing Azaleas

Sure, everyone thinks of azaleas for stunning spring color—but that's not *all* these multi-season shrubs have to offer! A number of native azaleas are perfect for summer color in lightly shaded yards with moist, but well-drained, acidic soil. Among the best bets for early summer are coast azalea (*Rhododendron atlanticum*), pinxterbloom azalea (*R. periclymenoides*), swamp azalea (*R. viscosum*), and sweet azalea (*R. arborescens*). These four deciduous shrubs all have white or pale pink blooms that are incredibly fragrant—just perfect for perfuming your whole yard!

MIX & FIX

BEETLE JUICE

This stuff will stop any kind of pesky beetle right in its tracks!

¹/₂ cup of beetles (alive or dead)
2 cups of water

Collect the beetles and whirl 'em up with the water in an old blender (one you'll *never* again use for food preparation). Strain the liquid through cheesecloth. Pour about ¹/₄ cup into a 1 gallon hand-held sprayer, and fill the rest of the jar with water. Drench the soil around new plants to keep beetles from getting started. If they're already on the scene, spray your shrubs and roses from top to bottom, and make sure you coat both sides of the leaves. Always wear gloves when handling this mixture.

Six Steps for Ravishing Roses

143

Don't let the thought of growing roses intimidate you; it's a whole lot easier than you could ever imagine. Just follow these six simple steps to have the most beautiful roses on the block!

Step 1: Start with a site that gets full morning sun, and at least 6 hours of sun for the whole day.

Step 2: Check the soil pH often, and add lime or sulfur as needed to keep it between 5.5 and 6.5.

Step 3: Fertilize with an organic or timed-release rose fertilizer in early spring. After the first buds form, begin feeding them my Rose Ambrosia Tonic (see page 111) every three weeks. Stop feeding eight weeks before the first frost is expected.

Step 4: Keep the plants mulched with 2 inches of organic material, such as pine needles, chopped leaves, or compost.

Step 5: If rain is lacking, make sure your roses get the equivalent of 1 inch of water each week throughout the growing season.

Step 6: Snip off faded flowers often to encourage new buds on repeat-flowering roses, such as Hybrid Teas, Floribundas, and most shrub roses. They'll keep flowering well into fall!

Ask Jerry

Q: *I'd love to try my hand at growing roses, but I sure don't want to spend my summer weekends spraying, pinching, and pruning. Can you recommend a fuss-free rose for me?*

A: I sure can—give 'Knock Out' a try! This bullet-proof rose is a real beauty—bright reddish pink flowers from late spring through frost, and lightly fragrant, too. But best of all, it's practically immune to black spot and other funky fungi that can make rose growing a real hassle—and that means no spraying!

144

Perfect Plant Buddies

Want to get twice the flower power from your rosebush? Then try this trick I learned from Grandma Putt: Plant a clematis next to it! The clematis will climb up and over the rose, so it'll look like the bush has two different kinds of flowers. You can pair a clematis and rose that bloom at the same time for one spectacular show, or choose ones that flower at different times to extend the color. Sturdy shrub roses make the best supports, while smaller clematis (those that mature at 8 to 10 feet tall) are the best choice for partners.

ROSE APHID ANTIDOTE

Keep pesky pests off your prized roses with this simple citrus solution.

**1 lemon or orange peel,
    coarsely chopped
1 tbsp. of baby shampoo
2 cups of water**

Put these ingredients into a blender, and blend on high for 10 to 15 seconds. Use a coffee filter to strain out the pulp. Pour the liquid into a hand-held sprayer. Before applying this tonic, blast your roses with a strong spray of water from your garden hose to dislodge some of the aphids. About 10 minutes later, thoroughly spray buds and young stems with this mix. Repeat after four days, and your aphid problem should be history!

Banana Bonanza

Did you know that your breakfast leftovers can make a fantastic food for your roses? You'd better believe it! Simply work banana skins (or whole, overripe bananas) into the soil near the base of your bushes. The potassium in their skins gives roses a power-packed snack that'll help the plants fend off pests and diseases, plus deliver a bounty of beautiful blossoms!

Get to Know This Rose

If you're growing roses mainly for cut flowers, it makes sense to plant Hybrid Teas for their big, perfectly shaped, long-stemmed blooms. Unfortunately, the bushes themselves are often downright ugly!

When you're ready for a rose that's more than just a pretty

face, here's a winner that perfectly fills the bill: red-leaved rose (*Rosa glauca*). This 6- to 8-foot-tall shrub looks great all year long, with single, pink blooms in late spring to early summer; purple-tinged, gray-green leaves all summer; and reddish purple, bristly stems all winter. My favorite feature shows up in fall, when the clustered, oval fruits turn from green to orange to red, then stay on the plant well into winter. Best of all, this rose doesn't need fancy pruning, fertilizing, *or* spraying. Treat it more like a regular shrub than a rose, and it'll treat you to multi-season beauty year after year!

Got Milk?

If dusty gray patches are a familiar sight on the leaves and buds of your roses, you've got problems with powdery mildew. Fortunately, I've got the perfect chemical-free solution for you. Simply stir up a 50-50 mix of milk and water, then spray away; once a week is about right. Sounds too good to be true, I know, but it really works!

Dependable Perennials

Early summer is a glorious time in the flower garden, especially where perennials are concerned. So many classic perennials bloom during this season that creating color-packed beds and borders is practically a no-brainer! In this section, I've concentrated on tips to help you keep *all* your bloomers strong and healthy—plus pointers for making more plants to fill your yard with even more color next year.

Seeing Red (Valerian, That Is)

With so many fantastic perennials to choose from for early summer flowers, it's tough to pin down just a few to highlight for you. But here's one I just couldn't resist telling you about: red valerian (*Centranthus ruber*). Also known as Jupiter's beard, this old-fashioned flower was a favorite with my Grandma Putt, and I wouldn't ever be without it, either!

Starting in early summer, this sun-loving perennial produces showy clusters of rosy pink flowers—perfect partners for peonies, lupines, irises, and other seasonal bloomers. Even without your help, it will keep blooming into autumn; but the more you pinch off the old flowers, the more new ones you'll get. Red valerian is a snap to grow from seed and can bloom the very first year.

MIX & FIX

IRIS ENERGIZER TONIC

To get an eyeful of early-summer irises, treat your plants to this tasty tonic!

¹/₂ cup of beer
Vitamin B₁ plant starter
 (mixed at 25 percent of the
 recommended rate)
2 tbsp. of dishwashing liquid
1 gal. of warm water

Mix the ingredients together in a bucket and drench the soil around your irises to keep 'em growing right.

Livin' on the Shady Side

Strong summer sun can really be tough on pale-petaled perennials, so plan ahead to provide them with a little protection. Morning sun is usually fine, but light afternoon shade is a must to keep astilbes, bleeding hearts (*Dicentra*), foxgloves (*Digitalis*), and other delicate bloomers from frying. Fortunately, that also works out well for you, since light-colored flowers are ideal for brightening up shady sites!

Florist Flowers—for Free!

Sure, flowers look great in your yard, but they're also wonderful for bringing beauty *into* your home. With a little planning, your perennial beds and borders can provide you with a wealth of bright blooms and lush leaves all through the growing season. For even more flowers, set aside a sunny, out-of-the-way spot for a separate cutting garden; that way, you can harvest to your heart's content without spoiling the display in more visible areas.

Concentrate on perennials that flower in your favorite colors—especially those that match the interior decor of the rooms you plan to bedeck with blooms. And whatever you do, avoid perennials that are touted as low-growing or dwarf. Compact cultivars are super for reducing staking chores in a regular garden, but for cutting, you want the longest stems you can get!

Spotlight on...

Irises

Irises are one of those amazing plants that can be in bloom practically year-round. But when you think of the two best-known types—bearded irises and Siberian irises (*Iris sibirica*)—it's easy to see why early summer is prime time for these beautiful bloomers!

Bearded irises come in a veritable rainbow of colors and range in height from 8 inches to 3 feet tall or more, so you're sure to find one that's perfect for any sunny, well-drained part of your yard. Most bloom only in late spring or early summer, but if you grow reblooming cultivars—such as 'Immortality' and 'Baby Blessed'—you can get a bonus burst of bloom in late summer or fall!

Siberian irises are another classic addition to beds and borders in Zones 2 to 9. They prefer more moisture than beardeds and can even tolerate wet feet, so they are perfect for soggy sites. Blue, purple, white, or yellow blooms in early summer aren't the only thing they have to offer; their grass-like leaves are eye-catching all through the growing season, and the seedpods are good-looking well into fall, too. That's a whole lot of *wow* from one trouble-free flower!

Thrip Tips

Pretty peony blooms aren't prized only by year-round gardeners; they're popular with thrips, too! These tiny thugs are so small you can barely spot them, but you can sure see their damage: brownish streaks on the petals, and sometimes deformed buds, as well. To double-check, tap a damaged bloom over a piece of black paper; most flower thrips are light colored, so the dark paper makes them more visible. These pesky pests can be tough to control, but I've got just the thing for you: Simply whip up a batch of my great Garlic Tea Tonic, below.

Say Good-Bye, Buds!

Sometimes, you can actually get better blooms by pinching off some flower buds. Sounds crazy, I know, but it works—honest! You see, pinching out the smaller side buds from a cluster directs all that stem's energy into the main bud, so you get a bigger bloom. That's how florists get those huge "football" mums, and it works great on dahlias, peonies, and roses, too.

If you'd rather have *more*, although slightly smaller blooms, do just the opposite: Pinch out the main bud on the stem, and let the smaller side buds get all the energy.

Summer Sowing Secrets

Everyone thinks of spring as prime seed-sowing time, but guess what—early summer is actually the *perfect* time to start perennial seeds! Forget about

MIX & FIX

GARLIC TEA TONIC

When thrips zero in on your prize peonies, zap 'em with this elixir.

5 cloves of unpeeled garlic, coarsely chopped
2 cups of boiling water
1 tsp. of baby shampoo

Place the chopped garlic in a heat-proof bowl, and pour the boiling water over it. Steep overnight. Strain through a coffee filter, and pour the liquid into a hand-held sprayer along with the baby shampoo. Spray on affected plants, then store the rest at room temperature.

fussing with heat mats and plant lights; the air is already warm, so you can sow seeds right outside. Just keep them evenly moist, and they'll sprout up quick as a wink. Transplant them into individual pots in mid- or late summer, and by fall, they'll be the perfect size to move to your garden for next year's flowers. By the way, this same trick works beautifully with foxgloves (*Digitalis*), forget-me-nots (*Myosotis*), and other biennials, too!

Get Grounded

Sure, you can sow perennial seeds in pots, but I've got an even easier option for you: Plant 'em right in the ground! All you need is a good location—a sunny, sheltered site with loose, well-drained soil; a corner of your vegetable garden is a perfect place. Sow the seeds in shallow rows, or scatter them evenly over the soil surface, then sift a little vermiculite over the area to cover them. Water carefully to avoid washing out the seeds, then shelter the seedbed with burlap or a sheet of newspaper; remove it as soon as seedlings sprout up.

> ### SEED AND SOIL ENERGIZER TONIC
>
> This potion will get your seeds off to a rip-roaring start.
>
> **1 tsp. of dishwashing liquid**
> **1 tsp. of ammonia**
> **1 tsp. of whiskey**
> **1 qt. of weak tea**
>
> Mix all of these ingredients together, pour into a hand-held sprayer, and shake gently. Then once a day, mist the surface of your seedbeds.

A Lot Off the Top, Please

Are your early-flowering perennials looking a bit ragged about now? Here's a terrific trick that'll perk 'em up in no time: Just whack 'em back! If you have only a few plants, use hand-held pruning shears; for larger patches, hedge shears, a string trimmer, or even a lawn mower can make quick work of the job. Either way, trim the plants down to about 2 inches above the ground. They'll grow back in no time, with fresh new foliage that'll look great for the rest of the growing season.

Play a Supporting Role

By now, hopefully, all of your perennials are perfectly staked and growin' straight and tall. But what if you missed a clump or two in the spring rush? No need to deal with sprawling stems for the rest of the season—just try this handy hint! Take a long piece of yarn or soft twine, and gently wrap it a few times around the plant to gather up the stems. Carefully slip a cage or hoop over the plant, push the cage legs into the soil to secure them, then remove the tie to let the plant resume its full-bodied form inside the support.

Grandma Putt's GREEN THUMB TIPS

When my Grandma Putt had a new flower garden to fill, she'd never blow her whole budget buying already-started plants. Instead, she'd pick up a few packs of seeds and grow 'em herself for pennies a plant. You can do it, too—even if you've never tried starting seeds before! Here are five choices for early-summer sowing: black-eyed Susans (*Rudbeckia*), blanket flower (*Gaillardia* x *grandiflora*), lance-leaved coreopsis (*Coreopsis lanceolata*), shasta daisy (*Chrysanthemum* x *superbum*), and yarrows (*Achillea*).

Trimmin' Time!

Want to forget about staking your perennials altogether? Then it's time to take a little off the top! Cutting plants back by about half in early summer will have the most noticeable impact on reducing their size and increasing their bushiness.

Pinching off the top 2 inches or so of stem tips a few weeks from now, in midsummer, won't affect the final height much, but it *will* encourage branching in the upper part of the plants, so you'll end up with more blooms. Experiment with pruning and pinching at different times and heights to find the perfect combinations for your particular perennials.

Cut and Watch 'Em Come Again

If you're like me, you hate to let *anything* go to waste! So when you pinch or trim back perennials in early summer for size control, don't toss those clippings on your compost pile: Use 'em to make *new* plants to fill your yard or share with friends. Snip the leaves off the bottom half of each 4- to 6-inch-long cutting, then insert the bared stems into moist sand or a 50-50 mixture of peat moss and perlite. Set the potted cuttings in a site with bright, but indirect light, and keep the rooting material moist. In just a few weeks, you can have dozens or even hundreds of beautiful new perennials! Asters, bee balms (*Monarda*), catmints (*Nepeta*), mums (*Chrysanthemum*), phlox, and stonecrops (*Sedum*) are just a few top candidates for cutting.

To Feed, or Not to Feed?

It all boils down to where you live! In the Southeast, where heat and humidity are inseparable, it's important to fertilize your perennials several times during the summer. They're growing "fast and furious," so they need a steady supply of food to stay strong and healthy.

But in arid climates, where summers are hot and *dry*, it's best to hold off on the fertilizer. The last thing you want to do is encourage lush growth that'll wither away when dog-day dry spells arrive! Spreading an inch or two of compost around your plants in early spring, then topping it with another 2 inches of

BUG-BE-GONE SPRAY

Perennial pests can really get out of hand in areas with long, hot summers, so be prepared with this potent spray.

1 cup of Murphy's Oil Soap®
1 cup of antiseptic mouthwash
1 cup of tobacco tea*

Mix all of the ingredients together in a 20 gallon hose-end sprayer, and soak your plants to the point of run-off.

*Place half a handful of chewing tobacco in an old nylon stocking, and soak it in a gallon of hot water until the mixture is dark brown.

MIX & FIX

152

chopped leaves or shredded bark is the perfect recipe for keeping your plants in great shape all year round—and with no summer feeding needed.

Snip off Trouble

Ever notice weird-looking, silvery squiggles on the leaves of your columbines (*Aquilegia*) or chrysanthemums? Don't worry: They're not some mystical messages from aliens! Those winding tunnels within the leaves are caused by leaf miners, the larvae of tiny flies. It's practically impossible to control them with sprays, so I suggest simply snipping off affected leaves and tossing them in the trash.

CRAZY DAISY SPRAY

If you grow painted daisy (*Tanacetum coccineum*)—also called pyrethrum daisy—its early-summer blooms give you the makings for a great homemade pest spray.

$1/8$ cup of 70% isopropyl alcohol
1 cup of packed, fresh painted daisy flower heads

Pour the alcohol over the flower heads and let it sit overnight. Strain out the flowers, then store the extract in a labeled and sealed container. When you need it, mix the extract with three quarts of water and apply with a hand-held sprayer to control a wide range of garden pests.

Coreopsis: You Can't Beat 'Em

Color-packed and trouble-free, coreopsis plants bring a bit of sunshine everywhere they grow! For a long bloom season plus great cut flowers, large-flowered coreopsis (*Coreopsis grandiflora*) and lance-leaved coreopsis (*C. lanceolata*) are both winners. If you pick the golden yellow blooms regularly (or deadhead them), both kinds can flower from late spring through late summer. For a softer yellow, 'Moonbeam' thread-leaved coreopsis (*C. verticillata* 'Moonbeam') is a top-notch choice. It blooms from early summer right through fall—even if you don't bother taking off the spent flowers!

A Pinch in Time Means Better Blooms

Ever notice that the mums growing in your garden are never quite as full and bushy as they were when you bought 'em? Well, the secret is right at your fingertips! Simply pinch off the tips of the growing stems twice—once when the shoots are 6 to 8 inches tall, and again about four weeks later. This quick trick will keep your mums compact and cushion-like, plus encourage more blooms, to boot!

Spotlight on...

Hardy Geraniums

Sure, everyone knows about zonal geraniums (*Pelargonium*)—those bright red, pink, or white flowers that show up in summer gardens and window boxes all across the country. But it beats me why more folks don't grow *hardy geraniums* (*Geranium*)!

These no-fail perennials come in such a wide variety of colors and sizes that it's easy to find one (or more) that's just perfect for any garden. I love 'em all, but to my mind, the cream of this top-notch crop is bloody cranesbill (*G. sanguineum*). It grows in just about any climate (Zones 3 to 9), with dense, 1-foot-tall mounds of starry green leaves that turn fire-engine red in fall. And let's not forget about the magenta, pink, or white summer flowers! Bloody cranesbill and other compact geraniums look super near the front of beds and borders; taller kinds, such as mourning widow (*G. phaeum*), make great groundcovers around shrubs and roses.

Don't Let Diseases Get You Down

When it comes to keeping flower garden diseases at bay, an ounce of prevention is worth *way* more than a pound of fungicide! Put these three super secrets to work in your yard right away to keep perennials, bulbs, and other blooms in tip-top shape:

Don't crowd your plants. Leave plenty of "breathing room" around each clump for good air circulation.

Keep things tidy. Stake or trim taller plants to keep them from flopping over on their companions, and use mulch to prevent soil from splashing up on flowers and foliage.

Water wisely. Never let your plants go to bed wet! Instead, water them early in the day; that way, the leaves will dry off quickly and stop diseases from spreading.

MIX & FIX

FRAGRANT PEST FIGHTER

People love perfumed perennials, but pests sure don't! So the next time you're out in your flower garden, gather the ingredients for this aromatic pest-control spray.

¹/₂ cup of fresh tansy (*Tanacetum vulgare*) or mugwort (*Artemisia vulgaris*) leaves
¹/₂ cup of fresh lavender flowers and/or leaves
¹/₂ cup of fresh sage (*Salvia officinalis*) leaves
Boiling water
2 cups of room-temperature water
1 teaspoon of Murphy's Oil Soap®

Place the leaves and flowers in a 1-quart glass jar; fill with boiling water, cover, and let sit until cool. Add ¹/₈ cup of that liquid to the 2 cups of room-temperature water and the Murphy's Oil Soap®. Pour into a hand-held sprayer, and apply to all your flowers to keep pests at bay!

Strike up the band, 'cause this parade's on its way, big time! Annual flowers are really coming into their own about now, and there's still time to plant more. So don't delay—check out this collection of my top annual tips for early summer, then get out in your garden and put 'em to work!

A Super Seed-Sowing Secret

Some annuals simply *hate* being transplanted—so what's a gardener to do? Sow 'em right where you want to grow 'em! It's tempting to get them in the ground early, but you won't do these heat-lovers any favors sowing them in cold soil. But by early summer, the soil is getting warm to the touch, and seeds will sprout up in no time at all. Good candidates for direct sowing in early summer include four-o'clocks (*Mirabilis jalapa*), lavatera (*Lavatera trimestris*), morning glories (*Ipomoea*), and zinnias.

Tees, Please

By this time of year, some early-flowering perennials start to die back to the ground, where their roots stay dormant until next spring. You may think you'll remember where they are, but trust me: When you're trying to tuck in just a few more annual flowers,

Ask Jerry

Q: *It seems like every time I sow seeds outdoors, they keel over as soon as the sprouts appear. Any ideas to help keep this from happening again?*

A: You bet! To give your seedlings a disease-free start this year, I want you to sprinkle the soil around just-sown seeds with Jell-O® powder. The gelatin helps your baby plants hold water, and the sugar feeds the good microorganisms in the soil. Any flavor will do, but I like to use lemon the best, since it will repel some pests, too!

it's all too easy to plunge your trowel into that "empty" spot, damaging or even destroying the sleeping perennial! I did it myself way too many times, until I found this terrific trick: Take some old golf tees, and insert them into the soil around the base of the plants (or bulbs) you want to protect. They'll remind you where it's not safe to dig, so you can go ahead and plant your annuals without worry!

Grandma Putt's

GREEN THUMB TIPS

My Grandma Putt knew that thinning crowded seedlings was a must, but she hated the thought of killing all those healthy little sprouts. She came up with a great solution that I still use today—and I know you'll love it, too! Instead of pulling out or snipping off the extra baby plants, carefully lift them out with a spoon or tiny trowel, and pot them up or plant them in a corner of your vegetable garden. Then when you need color to fill a bare spot later on, simply pop the extras into your flower garden. Your beds and borders will look as lush and lovely in fall as they do in early summer!

Annuals to the Rescue

Once your summer bloomers are in full swing, it's the perfect time to start thinking about flowers for fall color. Whenever gaps appear in your garden, scatter seeds of fast-growing annuals there, and they'll fill that space in no time flat! Some of my favorite annual fillers for late flowers include calendula (*Calendula officinalis*), California poppy (*Eschscholzia californica*), bachelor's buttons (*Centaurea cyanus*), marigolds (*Tagetes*), snapdragon (*Antirrhinum majus*), sweet alyssum (*Lobularia maritima*), verbenas, and zinnias.

Get Wired!

You may see a neatly planted flower bed, but rabbits and other pesky critters see an "all-you-can-eat salad bar" sign! Annual transplants are most at risk from these hungry little fellas during their first week in the garden, so protect them from the get-go by covering them up with small cages made of poultry wire. Take off the cages once plants start growing, or leave them on and let the stems grow right up through them.

Some Sage Advice

Some snooty gardeners may look down on scarlet sage (*Salvia splendens*) as too common, but not me. When it comes to flowers, I say, the brighter, the better! But even if shocking scarlet just doesn't work for your color scheme, you can still enjoy the spiky blooms of this dependable annual. Thanks to busy plant breeders, scarlet sage now comes in a whole host of colors, including purple, pink, salmon, burgundy, lavender, and creamy white. The red-flowered ones'll take as much sun as you can give 'em; the other colors seem to do better with a bit of shade. Pinch off the spent flowers regularly, and these tried-and-true bloomers will flower from early summer up to frost.

Coleus for the New Millennium

If you haven't grown coleus (*Solenostemon scutellarioides*) for a few years, it's time to give them another look—they've come a long way! For starters, they're not just for shade anymore; in fact, some of the best cultivars pos-

ANNUAL ABUNDANCE ELIXIR

Ready for the best-looking flower beds on the block? Give your annuals a generous dose of this tonic every few weeks, then stand back!

1 cup of beer
2 tbsp. of fish emulsion
2 tbsp. of dishwashing liquid
2 tbsp. of ammonia
2 tbsp. of whiskey
1 tbsp. of corn syrup
1 tbsp. of instant tea granules

Mix all of these ingredients with 2 gallons of warm water in a watering can. Drench your annuals every three weeks during the growing season to keep them blooming all summer long.

MIX & FIX

itively thrive in full sun. And don't think you always have to buy a mix of seedlings in different colors; nowadays, nurseries reproduce the best coleus by cuttings, so you can choose the heights and colors that are best for your borders. Another big plus is that cutting-grown coleus are much less likely to flower than seed-grown plants—that means a *lot* less pinching to keep your coleus looking their best!

Avoid a Feeding Frenzy

Lots of foliage, but few flowers? Most annuals enjoy rich soil, but it's possible for them to get too much of a good thing! Hold off on high-nitrogen fertilizers, and avoid working fresh farm animal manures into the soil just before planting.

Keep Cutworms at Bay

Ever head out for a happy morning stroll through your flowers, only to find the tops of your carefully sown seedlings nipped off and lying on the soil? There's a good chance that cutworms were at work. These smooth, 1- to 2-inch-long, grayish or brown-

Ask Jerry

Q: *I love petunias, but they don't seem to like me much! They look great right after I plant them, but by the end of June, they hardly bloom at all. What am I doing wrong?*

A: Petunias generally aren't too picky, but there *are* a few tricks to keeping 'em in tip-top shape. Mulching them well right after planting will help a lot; so will pinching off the spent blooms (including the little green "cup" at the base of the bloom, because that's where the seeds form). After the first main flush of bloom, whack all your plants back by half, then water thoroughly and give 'em a dose of my Annual Abundance Elixir (see page 157). They'll be back in bloom in no time!

ish caterpillars curl up to sleep in the soil during the day, then creep out to attack seedlings and small plants at night.

The very best way to head these pests off at the pass is to put a collar around each seedling. I sink my mini corrals 2 inches into the ground, with about 3 inches showing above. Collars made from any of these materials will give first-rate protection:

- Aluminum foil
- Cardboard tubes from wrapping paper, toilet paper, or paper towels
- Mailing tubes
- Paper or plastic cups with the bottoms cut out
- Soup cans minus the ends

SLUG-IT-OUT TONIC

Slimy slugs can really do a number on tender annual seedlings, sometimes eating them whole! Send those slithering pests packing with a dose of this beery brew.

1 can of beer
1 tbsp. of sugar
1 tsp. of baker's yeast

Mix these ingredients in a bowl, and let 'em sit for 24 hours. Then pour the mixture into shallow aluminum pie pans, and set the pans so the rims are just at ground level in various areas of your garden. You'll catch lots and lots of slugs, and you'll know they died very happy!

MIX & FIX

A Bounty of Bulbs

Say good-bye to tulips, daffodils, and other early bloomers—it's time for summer bulbs to take center stage. I've got a bunch of top-notch bulb blurbs to share with you, so let's get busy!

Divide and Multiply

One of my favorite things about growing bulbs is their generous nature. You plant 'em once, and they just keep making more of themselves; pretty soon, you've got a bunch of new bulbs for free! Over time, clumps can get overcrowded, so if you notice them blooming less than before, that's your clue that it's time to dig, divide, and replant those bulbs.

Early summer is the ideal season for dividing spring bulbs, since they're heading into their resting period now. I strongly suggest using a wooden craft stick or some other label to mark the clumps you want to divide *before* their leaves die back totally, so

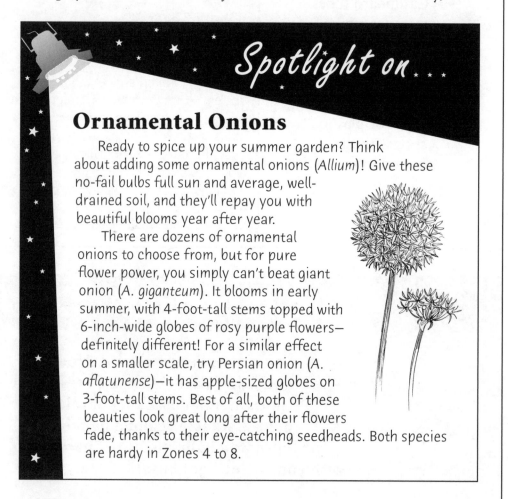

Spotlight on...

Ornamental Onions

Ready to spice up your summer garden? Think about adding some ornamental onions (*Allium*)! Give these no-fail bulbs full sun and average, well-drained soil, and they'll repay you with beautiful blooms year after year.

There are dozens of ornamental onions to choose from, but for pure flower power, you simply can't beat giant onion (*A. giganteum*). It blooms in early summer, with 4-foot-tall stems topped with 6-inch-wide globes of rosy purple flowers—definitely different! For a similar effect on a smaller scale, try Persian onion (*A. aflatunense*)—it has apple-sized globes on 3-foot-tall stems. Best of all, both of these beauties look great long after their flowers fade, thanks to their eye-catching seedheads. Both species are hardy in Zones 4 to 8.

you can find them later. When you're ready, dig up the clumps, separate them, and replant in more spacious quarters. That'll give 'em more room to bloom!

Glad to Know Ya!

To my mind, no bulb says summer like the elegant, spiky flowers of gladiolus. But if you hate the bother of planting new corms each year, you don't have to go without these beautiful bloomers—try hardy gladiolus (*Gladiolus communis* subsp. *byzantinus*) instead! Each small corm produces a graceful spike of 10 to 20 flowers, usually in magenta-pink, but sometimes in soft pink or white. Unlike eye-high common glads, hardy glads grow only 2 to 3 feet tall, so they *never* need staking! Plant these old-fashioned favorites in fall or early spring, in full sun and average soil. They can survive winters outdoors in Zones 5 to 10.

Begonias for Beginners

Once all danger of frost has passed, it's safe to set out tuberous begonias for a splash of summer color. These beauties like bright, but indirect light and moist, cool soil, so mulch 'em with lots of chopped leaves or compost after planting. Water often during dry spells, but be sure to let the soil surface dry out a bit between waterings, because begonias *hate* wet feet!

HOT BUG BREW

Want to get all of those bad bugs out of your flower beds—*pronto*? Give 'em a shot of this spicy solution!

3 hot green peppers (canned or fresh)
3 medium cloves of garlic
1 small onion
1 tbsp. of dishwashing liquid
3 cups of water

Purée the peppers, garlic, and onion in a blender. Pour the purée into a jar, and add the dishwashing liquid and water. Let stand for 24 hours, then strain out the pulp with cheesecloth or pantyhose. Use a hand-held sprayer to apply the remaining liquid to bug-infested bulbs and perennials.

MIX & FIX

Divine Vines and Groundcovers

The arrival of warm weather is what your vines have been waiting for to shoot up like skyrockets! Groundcovers, too, thrive at this time of year, making emerald carpets of lush leaves sprinkled with beautiful blooms. These easy-care plants don't need much fussing, but they do appreciate a little TLC right about now—so here's a bunch of super secrets to help keep 'em in fine form.

MIX & FIX

ALL-SEASON CLEAN-UP TONIC

To keep all of your plants in tip-top shape, apply this tonic in early evening every two weeks throughout the growing season.

1 cup of dishwashing liquid
1 cup of tobacco tea*
1 cup of antiseptic mouthwash
Warm water

Mix the dishwashing liquid, tobacco tea, and mouthwash in a 20 gallon hose-end sprayer, filling the balance of the jar with warm water. Liberally apply this mixture to groundcovers, vines, shrubs, trees, perennials, and other plants to discourage insects and prevent disease during the growing season.

*Place half a handful of chewing tobacco in an old nylon stocking, and soak it in a gallon of hot water until the mixture is dark brown.

A Fine Time for Trimmin' Vines

Most vines grow just fine without fancy pruning, but if you want them to look their very best, it's smart to give them a trim every few years. Dead, diseased, and damaged stems are fair game for pruning pretty much any season, and removing them is the first step in *any* vine-pruning project. But when it comes to trimming live, healthy stems, timing is everything!

First, figure out when the vine flowers, then prune *after* the flowers have faded. Early summer is prime pruning time for spring-flowering vines, such as early-blooming clematis. Hold off on pruning summer bloomers, such as passionflowers (*Passiflora*), until fall, and wait until winter or early spring to trim fall-flowering vines.

Demystifying Wisteria

If you've ever seen a wisteria vine in full glory, positively dripping with late-spring blooms, you'll know why so many folks want one for their own yards. But all that beauty comes at a price: painstaking pruning several times a year! If you're up for the chal-

Spotlight on . . .

Hybrid Clematis

Sure, there are lots of spectacular summer vines to choose from, but to my mind, clematis has to be the queen of them all! The large-flowered hybrids come in a wide range of colors—just about every one but pure yellow, plus many multi-colors— with flat, single, semidouble, or double blooms up to 8 inches across. Talk about flower power! When you're choosing a planting site, remember Grandma Putt's rule of thumb: "Clematis like to have their head in the sun and their feet in the shade." In other words, make sure your vines will get full sun, but set the plants so their roots will be shaded by a shrub, groundcover, or post. A generous layer of mulch can also serve the purpose of keeping the roots cool and moist. And don't stress over pruning; see "Clematis Made Simple" on page 72 for the full scoop.

lenge, here's a quick overview of the process of pruning an established vine:

Early summer. As soon as the flowers fade, trim back each side shoot to about 1 foot. If there are so many side shoots that you can hardly see what you're doing, don't hesitate to cut out some of them altogether, right back to the main stem. You can take out well over half of them and not hurt the plant!

Mid- to late summer. As the side shoots grow out again, they can get long and scraggly-looking. Trim 'em all again, a foot out from the early-summer cut.

Late winter or early spring. Prune the side shoots back to 1 foot (about where you made the early-summer cut the previous year).

Training Camp for Wayward Climbers

If you've planted a new vine this year, make it a point to check back every few days, to see if it needs any help. Twirling the stem tips around their support may be all they need to get them growing onward and upward. If a little extra assistance is in order, tie the stems to their trellis with soft yarn or strips of old pantyhose. Once they grab hold, an occasional pinch or snip will be enough to keep wayward stems goin' in the right direction!

Stop the Flop

Fed up with floppy ornamental grasses? Then try this trick: Whack 'em back by about half their height in early summer, and they'll hold their heads up straight and tall for the rest of the year!

Grandma Putt's
GREEN THUMB TIPS

Like most of us, Grandma Putt always had plenty of leftover coffee grounds. But she *never* threw hers in the trash; instead, she sprinkled this black gold on the soil around her vines and groundcovers (shrubs, too). Try it in your own yard, and see if you don't end up with the bloomingest plants on the block!

Spread 'Em

If you've got a steep slope that's a real hassle to mow, why not solve your problems once and for all—by getting rid of that grass and growing groundcovers there instead? Sloping sites tend to be as dry as a bone, so be sure to stick with groundcovers that are touted as drought-tolerant, like rock roses (*Helianthemum*) and two-row stonecrop (*Sedum spurium*). For extra-quick coverage, keep an eye out for plants that spread by underground roots, or that have stems that root wherever they touch the ground, like periwinkles (*Vinca*) for shade and showy evening primrose (*Oenothera speciosa*) for sun. They're sure to fill in fast.

You're Grounded, Vines!

Vines show off best when they can rise up high, but many can do double duty as groundcovers if you let 'em sprawl. They're especially nice cascading down slopes, and they'll smother weeds like nobody's business! Here's a rundown of my five favorite vines for growin' at ground level:

Ask Jerry

Q: *I want to mulch my newly planted groundcover slope, but no matter what I try, the mulch always ends up washing down to the bottom. Any suggestions?*

A: When it comes to covering slopes, all mulches are *not* created equal! Stay away from lightweight materials like bark nuggets and cocoa hulls, because they readily float and wash away. Shredded hardwood mulches are your best bet (with softwood types as a second choice), because they tend to knit together and stay in place.

1. Climbing hydrangea (*Hydrangea petiolaris*)

2. Five-leaved akebia (*Akebia quinata*)

3. Honeysuckles (*Lonicera*)

4. Mountain clematis (*Clematis montana*)

5. Sweet autumn clematis (*C. terniflora*)

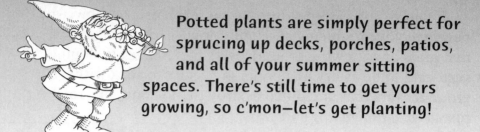

Potted plants are simply perfect for sprucing up decks, porches, patios, and all of your summer sitting spaces. There's still time to get yours growing, so c'mon—let's get planting!

Potted Plant Pick-Me-Up

Potted perennials and shrubs are a lot less work than annuals, because they can grow in the same container for several years without replanting. But after a year or two of vigorous growth, the soil can get mighty tired, and your plants just won't look as lush and healthy as before. I've found the perfect trick to pep up tired soil: Just add 1 can of beer or one shot of bourbon, scotch, vodka, or gin—plus 1 ounce of dishwashing liquid—to 1 gallon of water. Use this liquid to replace plain water when you mix up your favorite plant food, and I *guarantee* it'll liven things up like nobody's business!

MIX & FIX

YEAR-ROUND REFRESHER

Use this elixir every three weeks from spring through fall to keep your potted plants healthy and happy. (In warm climates, you can use it year-round.)

**1 cup of beer
1 cup of baby shampoo
1 cup of liquid lawn food
1/2 cup of molasses
2 tbsp. of fish emulsion
Ammonia**

Mix the beer, shampoo, lawn food, molasses, and fish emulsion in a 20 gallon hose-end sprayer. Fill the balance of the sprayer jar with ammonia, then spray away!

Corral Those Containers

It's easy to go crazy with container plantings, but when you have pots scattered all over your property, hauling water around can get to be a real drag. To make your life easier, group all of your containers in one or two highly visible spots—ideally, close to a water source. That'll make maintenance a snap, and your plants will stay healthier and happier, too!

Be Wise About Whiteflies

Container gardens are a perfect place to showcase extra-special plants you've picked up on shopping expeditions to your local greenhouse. But sometimes, when you bring those beauties home, you're bringing along some unwanted visitors: tiny white flies called (not surprisingly) whiteflies! These pesky little pests thrive in greenhouse conditions, but they can bother your outdoor plants, too, so it's smart to take precautions.

First, before you buy *any* greenhouse-grown plant, give it a good shake to make sure you don't see any whiteflies flitting around. If you spot the pests after you get the plants home, mix together 1 cup of sour milk, 2 tablespoons of flour, and 1 quart of warm water, then spray the mixture over the infested plants. Spray again a week later to catch any new flies that have hatched from hidden eggs—then say good-bye to whiteflies!

CONTAINER PLANT FOOD

To give your container gardens a real boost, make this marvelous master mix of fortified water.

1 tbsp. of 15-30-15 plant food
1/2 tsp. of gelatin
1/2 tsp. of dishwashing liquid
1/2 tsp. of corn syrup
1/2 tsp. of whiskey
1/4 tsp. of instant tea granules

Mix all of these ingredients in a 1-gallon milk jug, filling the balance of the jug with water. Then add 1/2 cup of this mixture to every gallon of water you use to water all of your container plants.

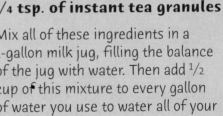

A Houseplant Holiday

Once you're sure Jack Frost is gone for good, why not bring your houseplants out to the garden for a summer vacation? There's nothing like a bit of fresh air and sunshine to really perk them up for another winter indoors! But remember that they're used to the still air and limited light of your home, so don't plunk 'em out on your deck and expect them to be happy about it.

Just like folks who spend most of their time indoors, plants can get sunburned if they suddenly sit outside with no protection. So set them in a sheltered, shady space at first, then gradually expose them to more sun over the period of a week or so. With this little bit of TLC at the beginning, your houseplants will be in for a long, relaxing vacation outdoors!

Ask Jerry

Q: *Hey, Jer—have any good tips for making less of a mess when watering hanging baskets? I'm tired of getting soaked every time I water!*

A: Try tossing your leftover ice cubes into the basket; they'll slowly melt and supply water without running out the bottom. Or, snap an old shower cap around the base of the basket before you water to catch any drips, then remove it when you're done.

Quick Wick Watering

Thinking of spending some of your own summer vacation away from home? Your potted plants don't have to do without water while you're gone—*if* you set up this super-simple automatic watering system! Here's all you need to do: Before you pot up each plant, run one end of a piece of cotton cord or rope through the drainage hole and into the pot, leaving a long piece outside. Then fill a milk jug with water and set the other end of the cord into it. Keep the jug filled with water, and the plants will draw up the water they need on their own!

Potted Herbs Make Perfect Scents

As much as I love choosing fabulous flowers for my potted gardens, I have to admit to having a real soft spot for herbs, as well. Granted—the plants themselves often aren't especially showy, but oh, those wonderful scents! Once you've experimented with growing herbs in containers, you'll be hooked, too. Here's why:

→ The plants themselves will thrive, because pots provide the excellent drainage that many herbs demand.

→ Containers are a safe haven for creeping herbs, like mints, which could otherwise quickly take over your beds and borders.

→ Herbs are a delight in pots on porches, decks, patios, and other sitting areas. Just reach out and touch 'em, and you'll be rewarded with their sensational scents!

The Pick of the Pots

While there are all sorts of pots you can buy, why not use your imagination and come up with your own? You can make a container out of just about anything: a leaky washtub, a cracked jug, or even an old boot! Look around your house for quirky containers. As long as they have some kind of drainage hole, they're fair game for flowers!

PERFECT POTTING SOIL

If you've got a lot of flowers to pot up, you'll need plenty of potting soil. So mix up a big batch of this simple blend, and keep it handy!

1 part topsoil
1 part peat moss
1 part vermiculite
1 part compost

Mix all of the ingredients together and use for potting up all kinds of annuals, perennials, and bulbs—shrubs, too!

The Real Dirt on Container Soil

Whatever you do, *don't* fill your pots and planters with soil straight from your garden. It'll pack down as hard as a rock in a few weeks, making it tough for roots to spread—and poor roots mean poor top growth, too. Plus, garden soil is simply loaded with weed seeds, and possibly insects and diseases, as well. But it's easy to nip all these problems in the bud: Just whip up some of my Perfect Potting Soil (above) and use that instead!

Jerry's Best Bets for...
A Summer Spectacle

Looking to liven up your yard in early summer? It's a piece of cake! Just pick a bunch of the plants below, and your flower-filled yard'll be the envy of all your neighbors.

Trees

American fringe tree
 (*Chionanthus virginicus*)
American yellowwood
 (*Cladrastis kentukea*)
Chinese fringe tree
 (*Chionanthus retusus*)
Japanese snowbell
 (*Styrax japonicus*)
Kousa dogwood
 (*Cornus kousa*)
Persian lilac
 (*Syringa* x *persica*)
Southern magnolia
 (*Magnolia grandiflora*)
Sweet bay
 (*Magnolia virginiana*)

Shrubs

Beautyberries (*Callicarpa*)
Chokeberries (*Aronia*)
Coast azalea
 (*Rhododendron atlanticum*)

Elderberries
 (*Sambucus*)
Flame azalea
 (*Rhododendron calendulaceum*)
Hills-of-snow
 (*Hydrangea arborescens*)
Mock oranges
 (*Philadelphus*)
Mountain laurel
 (*Kalmia latifolia*)
Red-twig dogwood
 (*Cornus alba*)
Roses (*Rosa*)
Scotch broom
 (*Cytisus scoparius*)
Spireas
 (*Spiraea*)
Viburnums
 (*Viburnum*)
Weigelas
 (*Weigela*)

Perennials

Avens (*Geum*)
Baby's breaths
 (*Gypsophila*)
Beardtongues
 (*Penstemon*)
Bee balms
 (*Monarda*)
Bellflowers
 (*Campanula*)
Campions
 (*Lychnis*)

Carolina lupine
 (*Thermopsis villosa*)
Catmint
 (*Nepeta* x *faassenii*)
Coral bells
 (*Heuchera*)
Coreopsis
 (*Coreopsis*)
Delphiniums
 (*Delphinium*)
Foxgloves
 (*Digitalis*)
Gas plant
 (*Dictamnus albus*)
Globe thistles
 (*Echinops*)

Hardy geraniums
 (*Geranium*)
Hollyhock
 (*Alcea rosea*)
Lemon lily
 (*Hemerocallis lilioasphodelus*)
Mountain bluet
 (*Centaurea montana*)

Oriental poppy
(*Papaver orientale*)
Painted daisy
(*Tanacetum coccineum*)
Peonies (*Paeonia*)
Pinks (*Dianthus*)
Siberian iris
(*Iris sibirica*)

Annuals

Bacopa
(*Sutera cordata*)
Bells-of-Ireland
(*Moluccella laevis*)
Calendula
(*Calendula officinalis*)
Cosmos (*Cosmos
sulphureus*)
Edging lobelia
(*Lobelia erinus*)
Floss flower
(*Ageratum
houstonianum*)
Geraniums
(*Pelargonium*)
Impatiens
(*Impatiens*)
Love-in-a-mist
(*Nigella*)
Marigolds
(*Tagetes*)
Mealycup sage
(*Salvia farinacea*)
Nasturtium
(*Tropaeolum majus*)
Petunias (*Petunia*)

Scarlet sage
(*Salvia splendens*)
Snapdragons
(*Antirrhinum*)
Sweet alyssum
(*Lobularia maritima*)
Wax begonia
(*Begonia semperflorens*)
Wishbone flowers
(*Torenia*)

Bulbs

Asiatic Hybrid lilies
(*Lilium*)
Bearded irises
(*Iris* Bearded Hybrids)
Hardy gladiolus
(*Gladiolus communis*
subsp. *byzantinus*)
Ornamental onions
(*Allium*)
Persian buttercup
(*Ranunculus asiaticus*)
Pineapple lilies
(*Eucomis*)
Tuberous begonias
(*Begonia*)

Vines

Black-eyed Susan vine
(*Thunbergia alata*)
Clematis
(*Clematis*)
Climbing hydrangea
(*Hydrangea anomala*
subsp. *petiolaris*)

Honeysuckles
(*Lonicera*)
Mandevilla
(*Mandevilla laxa*)
Wisterias (*Wisteria*)

Groundcovers

Bigroot geranium
(*Geranium
macrorrhizum*)
Hardy ice plant
(*Delosperma cooperi*)
Lowbush blueberry
(*Vaccinium
angustifolium*)
Partridgeberry
(*Mitchella repens*)
Periwinkles
(*Vinca*)
Sweet woodruff
(*Galium odoratum*)
Woolly yarrow
(*Achillea tomentosa*)

CHAPTER 8

Midsummer's a Dream

When it comes to pure flower power, your midsummer yard is where it's at! There's just nothing like warm weather to bring out the beauty of beds and borders packed with perennials, annuals, bulbs, shrubs, and more. I've rounded up a boatload of my very best tips for getting the most out of every part of your yard, so get ready to have the most gorgeous gardens on your block!

SUMMER

Here's a quick rundown of some yard and garden chores you'll need to keep up with during this busy season. Yep, there's lots to do—but be sure you take time to just *enjoy* your beautiful bloomers, too!

- Pinch spent blooms off of perennials, annuals, and bulbs as they fade
- Water all parts of your yard in dry weather
- Keep after those weeds
- Watch out for pest and disease problems
- Fertilize annuals, perennials, bulbs, and roses

- Cut back early-flowering annuals and perennials to get a new flush of foliage
- Check mulch thickness, and add more, if needed
- Direct-sow seeds of fast-growing annuals for fall color
- Check staked and trellised plants, and add additional ties or supports if needed
- Bring annual, perennial, and rose blooms indoors for beautiful bouquets
- Keep container gardens fed and watered

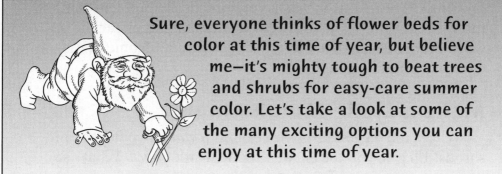

Sure, everyone thinks of flower beds for color at this time of year, but believe me—it's mighty tough to beat trees and shrubs for easy-care summer color. Let's take a look at some of the many exciting options you can enjoy at this time of year.

Treat Yourself to This Tree

I'll bet you didn't know that lily-of-the-valley grows on trees! Well, it's not the *usual* lily-of-the-valley (*Convallaria majalis*) I'm talking about; it's the lily-of-the-valley tree (*Oxydendrum arboreum*). This out-of-the-ordinary landscape gem would be a winner any time of year, but it's extra-special because it's one of the few trees that flowers in midsummer—with drooping sprays of fragrant, white flowers that look much like those of the spring-blooming groundcover. It produces another amazing show in autumn, when the leaves turn shades of rich red or purple. Lily-of-the-valley tree grows in Zones 5 to 9 and can take anything from full sun to full shade; plus, it grows only 20 to 25 feet tall—a perfect size for even a small backyard!

A Multi-Season Marvel

Stunning, white summer blooms, fabulous fall color, and beautiful bark for winter—stewartias have it all! These super, small- to medium-sized trees positively thrive in partial shade,

Ask Jerry

Q: *I know I'm supposed to water the trees I planted this spring, but it takes forever to water each one by hand. Any advice?*

A: You betcha! The answer's as close as your recycling bin. Dig out the plastic milk jugs, then use an ice pick or nail to poke a few small holes around the sides, about an inch above the base. Place the jugs around the root zone, fill 'em with water, walk away, and let your plants drink up!

174

so they're a perfect choice if you already have a few large trees growing in your yard. Stewartias are practically problem-free and rarely need pruning; just set 'em out in evenly moist, acidic soil when they're small, then stand back to enjoy a lifetime of easy-care, year-round beauty!

Make a Little Mulch Magic

What's the biggest favor you can do for *all* of your trees and shrubs? I'll give you the answer in one word: *mulch!* What's so special about this stuff? Let's take a look:

➜ Mulch helps keep the soil moist and at an even temperature—just right for healthy root growth.

➜ Organic mulches (shredded bark, chopped leaves, and the like) release nutrients and humus as they break down, providing a perfect food for your plants.

➜ A thick layer of mulch stops most weed seeds from sprouting, and the ones that *do* pop through are easy to pull out.

➜ Nothin' looks better than a neatly mulched yard!

Be a Mulch Manager

Now that I've sold you on the *whys* of mulching trees and shrubs, I've got a few *do's* and *don'ts* to get you on your way:

✔ *Do* plan to reapply organic mulches at least once a year—

MIX & FIX

CATERPILLAR KILLER TONIC

To keep caterpillars in check and away from your shrubs, brew up a batch of this aromatic elixir.

¹/₂ lb. of wormwood (*Artemisia*) leaves
2 tbsp. of Murphy's Oil Soap®
4 cups of warm water

Simmer the wormwood leaves in 2 cups of the warm water for 30 minutes or so. Strain out the leaves, then add the liquid and the Murphy's Oil Soap® to 2 more cups of warm water. Apply with a 6 gallon hose-end sprayer to the point of run-off. Repeat as necessary until the caterpillars are history! This tonic will protect flowers, too.

sometime from midspring to midsummer, and again in mid- to late summer, if needed. (You want to keep a 2- to 3-inch-thick layer on the soil at all times.)

✔ *Don't* think that if a little mulch is good, a lot is better. Piling mounds of mulch around the base of any tree can rot the bark and provide a perfect breeding ground for pest and disease problems.

✔ *Do* try to get your hands on shredded cedar or eucalyptus mulch—this stuff is *fantastic* for keeping bad bugs at bay. To make it go farther, spread an inch or so over the soil, then top it with another mulch material. This works great in flower gardens, too!

✔ *Don't* use rocks or gravel as mulch. Sure, these materials last a long time, but they don't do a darn bit of good for your soil!

REPOTTING BOOSTER TONIC

When your rooted cuttings are ready for transplanting, a dose of this terrific tonic will help 'em adjust to their new homes in a jiffy.

MIX & FIX

¹/₂ cup of weak tea water*
¹/₂ tsp. of all-purpose plant food
¹/₂ tsp. of vitamin B₁ plant starter
1 gal. of warm water

Mix all of the ingredients together, and gently pour the tonic through the soil of your repotted plants. Allow the pots to drain for 15 minutes or so, then pour off any excess in the tray, and treat your trees and shrubs to the leftovers!

*Soak a used tea bag and 1 teaspoon of dishwashing liquid in a gallon of warm water until the water is light brown.

Spotlight on...

Hydrangeas

When it comes to pure flower power, few summer-flowering shrubs can beat the huge blooms of hydrangeas.

The best known of the bunch, big-leaved hydrangea (*Hydrangea macrophylla*), bears blue flowers when grown in acidic soil and pink flowers in near-neutral or alkaline soil. Also known as florist's hydrangea, this shrub grows 3 to 6 feet tall and is hardy in Zones 6 to 8.

Peegee hydrangea (*H. paniculata* 'Grandiflora') was popular back in Grandma Putt's day, and it's still a winner. Depending on how you prune it, this white-flowered beauty can be a 4-foot-tall shrub or a 12-foot-tall tree. It's hardy in Zones 4 to 9.

Oak-leaved hydrangea (*H. quercifolia*) is the least well-known of these three, but it deserves a *lot* more attention from year-round gardeners! Hardy in Zones 5 through 8, this 6-foot-tall shrub has long-lasting clusters of white blooms, plus good-looking leaves, maroon fall color, and attractive, peeling bark.

All of these super shrubs appreciate humus-rich soil. Sunny sites bring out the best blooms, but then evenly moist soil is a must; plants in partial shade can tolerate slightly drier conditions. Prune big-leaved hydrangea immediately after bloom; late winter is a fine time for any needed trimming on the others.

Root Reconnaissance

If you took cuttings of your favorite trees and shrubs in early summer, now's the time to start checking for roots. If you don't see any roots peeking out of the bottom of the pots' drainage holes, gently tug on the cuttings. If you feel some resistance, there's a good chance roots are forming. When the cuttings are well rooted, move them into individual 2-inch pots. Once they've rooted into those pots, you can move them to larger pots for the winter, or plant them right in your yard.

BLACK SPOT REMOVER TONIC

Stop those pesky black spots from messing up your roses with this tomatoey tonic.

15 tomato leaves
2 small onions
¹/₄ cup of rubbing alcohol

Chop the tomato leaves and onions into tiny pieces, and steep them in the alcohol overnight. Use a small, sponge-type paintbrush to apply the brew to both the tops and the bottoms of any affected rose leaves.

MIX & FIX

Seeing Spots? Remove 'Em!

If you live where the weather's on the humid side, there's a good chance you're noticing some black spots on your rose foliage right about now. Fortunately, you can stop these spots in their tracks if you catch them early by painting every speckled leaf with my Black Spot Remover Tonic (above). And the next time you go rose shopping, look for roses that are touted as black spot-resistant, such as 'Carefree Sunshine' and 'Knock Out', to avoid the problem in the first place.

Small-Space Solutions

Think you don't have enough space for some new shrubs in your yard? Think again! If you have room for perennials, you have room for shrubs—*if* you choose the right ones. You see, some shrubs are so tough that you can whack 'em down to a foot or so above the ground each winter and have 'em spring right back! Best of all, these "cut-back" shrubs are more than just space-savers; the hard pruning they get every year encourages lush, vigorous growth that looks great all through the growing season. Some of my favorite candidates for this tough-love treatment include butterfly bush (*Buddleia davidii*), chastetrees (*Vitex*), elderberries (*Sambucus*), and smoke bushes (*Cotinus*). Give this trick a try—you'll be glad you did!

Dependable Perennials

Beds and borders positively packed with bright blooms and lush leaves—now *that's* what midsummer is all about! I've got a bunch of top-notch summer bloomers to share with you, as well as some super secrets for keeping all of your perennials in tip-top shape.

Ask Jerry

Q: *I'm really getting burned out with watering my flower gardens, Jerry! I do a little bit every day, but before I get them all done, the flowers in the first beds are already wilting. Any suggestions?*

A: Repeat after me: *Slow and steady is the key!* Frequent, shallow watering does more harm than good, because it encourages roots to form very close to the soil surface, where they're way more susceptible to drought. Instead, I want you to thoroughly soak the top 6 inches of soil, then hold off on watering again until the top 2 inches dry out. That'll get your perennials to send their roots down deep, and you won't have to spend all summer with a garden hose in your hand!

Spotlight on...

Hostas

Hostas are probably the hottest thing going for shade gardens nowadays, and no wonder—they'll adapt to just about any climate (Zones 3 to 9) and grow just fine in average garden soil. Forget about staking (they *never* need it), and don't worry about feeding them much either; they'll thrive with virtually no fussing from you.

Hostas are best known for their fabulous foliage, and what lovely leaves they are, too! Long and narrow or as broad as a paddle; smooth or puckered; and in all shades of green, plus blue, gold, and an amazing variety of variegations—the possible combinations are endless! Considering that hostas come in such a wide range of sizes, from just a few inches across (like 'Pandora's Box') to 5 feet wide or more ('Sum and Substance' is one), you can find a hosta that's just perfect for any part of your yard.

Whichever one you choose, make sure you find out how big it is supposed to get *before* you choose a site for it. Nursery-grown plants tend to all be pretty much the same size when you buy them, but once they mature (in three to six years), the big ones can take up a whole lot of space!

Dig This!

Watering wisely is one of the most important things any gardener needs to learn—and fortunately, it's also one of the easiest. The trick is knowing *when* you need to water, and the answer's right under your feet! Before you turn on the hose or grab your sprinkling can, pull back the mulch in a small area of your flower garden, then dig down a few inches with your trowel. If the top 2 inches are dry, it's time to water; if not, then wait a day or two and test again.

Don't Get Spaced Out

No matter how carefully you plan, it's inevitable that gaps will appear in your perennial garden right about now. But don't think you have to put up with this problem, 'cause that just isn't so! If you followed my advice about potting up extra annuals in spring, now's the time to put those babies to work filling empty spaces in your garden. Or, check out the sales racks at your local garden center; you may be able to find some leftover annuals that'll do the job. If all else fails, fill the space with a piece of garden art, such as a small statue, or even a picturesque old watering can. Your neighbors will wonder why your gardens always look great, even when theirs are in a midsummer slump!

Beware of Gift Plants

Gardeners are generous folks, and most are more than happy to share pieces of their favorite plants

MIX & FIX

Quassia Slug Spray

There's no getting around it: Slugs love perennials, and hostas in particular. But don't despair—here's a magical mixer that'll really knock those slimy slitherers for a loop.

4 oz. of quassia chips (available at health food stores)
1 gal. of water

Crush, grind, or chop the chips, add them to the water in a bucket, and let steep for 12 to 24 hours. Strain through cheesecloth, then spray the liquid on hostas and other slug-prone plants.

with appreciative friends. But before you let a new addition loose in your yard, keep this in mind: If the giver has enough to share, that likely means that the original plant has produced plenty of seedlings or offsets. And that can translate into a garden thug—a perennial that might end up taking over your yard if you don't keep digging it out and finding new homes for the offspring. Talk about a gift that keeps on giving!

My advice? Set aside a spot in your yard where you can grow these gift plants for a few years. After that, you'll know whether you can safely move them to your garden or else discreetly dispose of them.

Grandma Putt's
GREEN THUMB TIPS

To help your beautiful bouquets last as long as possible, do what my Grandma Putt always did: Toss a copper penny and a cube of sugar into the vase to keep the flowers fresher. Or, mix 2 tablespoons of clear corn syrup into a quart of very warm water, then use that to fill the vase. Either way, you'll be *amazed* at the results!

Cut Flowers for Free

All work and no play makes gardening no fun at all! Well, it's easy to put the bloom back into your life—just gather some of your flowers to enjoy inside your home. Here's how:

Step 1: Take a bucket of water with you when you head out to cut your flowers, and plunge the stems into the water as soon as you pick them. (Early morning's the best time, by the way, since the petals are full of water.)

Step 2: Gather a variety of different flower forms—some spikes, some rounded blooms, and so on. And don't forget to pick a few leaves as well to provide a backdrop for the bright blooms.

Step 3: Set the bucket in a cool, humid place for a few hours to give the blooms and leaves a chance to perk up again, then arrange 'em to your heart's content!

Yahoo for Yarrow

Now here's a perennial that does double duty: a beautiful border bloomer and a perfect fresh-cut or dried flower, too! I'm taking about yarrow (*Achillea*)—a summer favorite with long-lasting, flat-topped heads of tiny flowers in shades of yellow, pink, salmon, red, and white. 'Moonshine', with pale yellow blooms, is one of my all-time favorites, but each year, breeders bring out more amazing colors, such as cherry-red 'Summer Wine'. Give 'em full sun and well-drained soil, and divide 'em every two to three years to keep 'em healthy—that's all they ask!

PERENNIAL POTTING MIX

Here's how to make the perfect growing mix for all of your potted perennial plants and seedlings.

1 part sharp sand
1 part clay loam
1 part organic matter or
    professional planter mix

Per cubic foot of soil mixture, add:

1¹⁄₂ cups of Epsom salts
³⁄₄ cup of coffee grounds
    (rinsed)
12 eggshells (dried and
    crushed to a powder)

Blend all of the ingredients together, and use the mixture to make your perennials feel comfy and cozy in their new home.

Perennials for Pennies

Looking to fill your yard with a bounty of bloomers without breaking the bank? Midsummer's your last chance to sow perennial seeds and get plants sturdy enough to survive their first winter. Or, if you followed my advice in the previous chapter and sowed the seeds in early summer, your seedlings are probably ready to be transplanted to individual 2- or 3-inch-square pots about now. Use my Perennial Potting Mix (above), and your seedlings will have everything they need to grow sturdy and strong for beautiful blooms next year!

Spotlight on...

Daylilies

If you're searching for easy-care summer color, look no further than daylilies (*Hemerocallis*). These no-fail perennials produce clumps of grass-like leaves and clusters of showy, trumpet-shaped blooms that come in just about every color except true blue. As the name suggests, each flower opens for only one day. But good-quality hybrids produce lots of buds on each plant, so they can easily light up your midsummer yard for a month or more.

There are literally thousands of named daylilies to choose from, so narrow down your choices based on the flower form, bloom color, and height that you want. My advice? Buy plants in bloom, so you'll see exactly what you're getting. (These plants are tough enough to tolerate transplanting, even in full flower.)

Whichever variety you choose, give your plants full sun or light shade and average, well-drained soil. Most are hardy in Zones 3 to 9.

Weed 'Em and Reap

Ever hear the old saying, "One year's seeding means seven years' weeding"? Trust me, it's all too true! If you let just one weed ripen its blooms in your garden, it can produce hundreds or even thousands of seeds, and each of those seeds can live in the soil for years before it sprouts. It's easy to see the moral to this little story: Weed early, and weed *often!*

184

A Quick Snip Tip

Would you believe that a few minutes of your time can extend the bloom season of your perennials by weeks or even months each year? It's true! If you cut many early-summer bloomers back by half to two-thirds when their first flush of flowers fades, they'll bounce back with another round of blossoms in just a few weeks' time. Give this a try with catmints (*Nepeta*), coreopsis, golden marguerite (*Anthemis tinctoria*), red valerian (*Centranthus ruber*), and spike speedwell (*Veronica spicata*); it'll work great on many others, as well!

MIX & FIX

Yellow Jacket Trap

Are pesky yellow jackets spoiling your summer flower fun? Lure them to their doom with this sweet brew.

1 banana peel
1 cup of sugar
1 cup of vinegar
Water

Cut the banana peel into pieces and slip them into a 2-liter plastic soda bottle. Combine the sugar and vinegar in a separate container, then pour the mixture into the soda bottle. Add enough water to fill the bottle to within a few inches of the top, then hang it from a sturdy tree branch. Yellow jackets will fly in, but they won't get out!

Say Bye-Bye to Old Blooms

What's the best way to have a great-looking perennial garden in just five minutes a day? Spend that quality time keeping spent flowers picked off of your plants! Besides making your perennials look like a million bucks, this simple trick stops seeds from draining energy away from the plants as they form.

On perennials with leafy flower stems, like asters, pinch or snip off faded flowers just above a bud or leaf. When the lower buds are all done, cut the flowering stem down to the ground. Or, if the flowers bloom on bare stems (like hostas), prune the stems close to the ground when all of the flowers are finished.

The Root of the Matter

You know, sometimes the old ways are still the best. When my Grandma Putt wanted to make more of her favorite perennials, she'd use an old trick called "root cuttings," and I still use it today.

It's as simple as it sounds: Just dig up a piece of root in midsummer, cut it into 1- to 2-inch pieces, and plant the pieces in a 50-50 mix of sand and good soil. Keep the area moist, and soon, leaves will appear. By next spring, you can move the new plants to your garden. This trick works great with Oriental poppy (*Papaver orientale*) and bleeding heart (*Dicentra spectabilis*), as well as blanket flowers (*Gaillardia*), garden phlox (*Phlox paniculata*), and sea hollies (*Eryngium*), to name just a few.

No-Fail Drought Busters

If summer dry spells are common in your climate, do yourself a favor and get some mulch in your flower garden, *pronto!* Use stuff you already have around, if you can, such as homemade compost or chopped leaves from last fall's yard cleanup. Grass clippings are great, too, but don't apply them more than 1 inch deep at one time, because fresh clippings tend to heat up and may harm your plants. Whatever you use, a layer about 3 inches thick is about right for keeping the soil moist and cool for good root growth—your perennials will thank you for it!

SOS—Save Our Seeds!

I'm a big fan of growing perennials for seed, because it's a great way to get a whole lot of plants for very

Grandma Putt's
GREEN THUMB TIPS

Don't have time to whip up one of my terrific tonics to send perennial pests packin'? Then try this tip from Grandma Putt's bag of tricks: Just give those bad bugs a pinch! Yep—squashing a pest with your fingers (or dropping it into a cup of soapy water) has to be *the* quickest way to stop plant damage immediately. Plus, dead bugs don't breed, so you'll cut down on future damage at the same time!

little money. If you're really thrifty, you can take this trick one step further and get new perennials totally for *free*—just save seeds from the plants you already have! By midsummer, spring-flowering perennials are starting to ripen their seeds, so it's a good time to get busy collecting. Here's what to do:

Step 1: When the seedpods or seedheads begin to turn brown, snip them off into paper bags.

Step 2: Label the bags, then leave them (still open) in a warm, dry place for a week or two.

Step 3: Pick out the biggest pieces of chaff (bits of dried stems, leaves, and pods), then store the seeds in labeled paper envelopes in a cool, dry place. For best results, plant them within two years.

A Perennial Favorite

Whether you call 'em gayfeathers (*Liatris*), blazing stars, or just plain old liatris, these native wildflowers are real showstoppers! Their claim to fame is their feather-like flower spikes, which are covered with fuzzy flower heads in pinkish purple or white. But they do more than attract your eye—gayfeathers are magnets for birds and butterflies, and they also make great cut flowers.

You can count on gayfeathers to come back year after year with no help from you: no extra fertilizer, no special watering, and no division, either! In fact, the only reason you'd ever need to dig 'em up is if they outgrow their space; in that case, just divide the clumps in early spring or fall. Talk about easy!

MIX & FIX

CHAMOMILE MILDEW CHASER

If your flowering plants are looking gray and dusty, there's a good chance they've got powdery mildew. To send these funky fungi fleeing, apply this elixir at the first sign of trouble.

4 chamomile tea bags
2 tbsp. of Murphy's Oil Soap®
1 qt. of boiling water

Make a strong batch of tea by letting the tea bags steep in the boiling water for an hour or so. Once the tea cools, mix with the Murphy's Oil Soap®. Apply once a week with a 6 gallon hose-end sprayer.

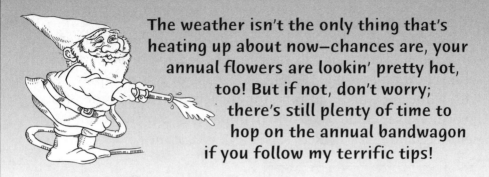

The weather isn't the only thing that's heating up about now—chances are, your annual flowers are lookin' pretty hot, too! But if not, don't worry; there's still plenty of time to hop on the annual bandwagon if you follow my terrific tips!

Color Your World

Ready to give your yard some knock-your-socks-off excitement? Then add annuals! There's just nothing that can beat these color-packed plants for adding sizzle to summer beds and borders. Here's how to brighten things up:

Gorgeous gold. To my mind, nothing says summer like bright yellow blooms. They look great with other rich colors, like ruby red and royal blue, but they're also super for pepping up pastel plantings. Some of the best bright yellow annual bloomers include marigolds (*Tagetes*), gloriosa daisy (*Rudbeckia hirta*), and sunflower (*Helianthus annuus*).

Awesome orange. Most folks probably don't think of orange flowers as their favorites, but once you see how great they look in your garden, you'll be hooked! Pair them with bright yellow and rich red, or create a can't-miss contrast with purple or blue

Ask Jerry

Q: Hey, Jer—I finally had a chance to dig a new flower bed this month. Is it too late to plant annuals for color this year?

A: Not at all! If you sow seeds of fast-growing annuals right now, you can still enjoy several months of color before Jack Frost makes a return appearance. Moss rose (*Portulaca grandiflora*), sweet alyssum (*Lobularia maritima*), pot marigold (*Calendula officinalis*), and love-in-a-mist (*Nigella damascena*) are a few best bets for midsummer sowing.

partners. Try marigolds here, too, or 'Profusion Orange' zinnias or 'Cosmic Orange' cosmos (*Cosmos sulphureus*), to name just a few.

Rousing red. When you're looking for pure flower power, toss some red-flowered annuals into your beds and borders. Mix 'em with yellow and orange for a kaleidoscope of color, or pair them with white and shades of pink for an elegant effect. Some of my favorite reds include 'Accent Red' impatiens, 'Supercascade Red' petunias, and 'Lady in Red' salvia (*Salvia coccinea*).

HANDY HERBAL FERTILIZER

Why bother buying fancy commercial fertilizers? If you've got comfrey (*Symphytum officinale*) in your yard, you have the fixin's for a nutrient-rich brew that *all* of your year-round bloomers will love.

5 to 10 comfrey leaves
1 qt. of water
Dishwashing liquid

Pack the comfrey leaves in a large flowerpot with at least one drain hole. Set another flowerpot—upside down this time—into a 5-gallon bucket. Place the leaf-filled pot on top of the upside-down pot, then set a brick on top of the leaves. As the leaves decompose, a brown liquid will appear in the bottom of the bucket. Add 1 tablespoon of this liquid to 1 quart of water, toss in a few drops of dishwashing liquid, and pour this around any plant that needs a quick nutrient boost.

Feeding Frenzy for Fantastic Flowers

Annuals tend to be plenty generous with their blooms, but remember—it takes *lots* of energy to keep that flower show going! Keep fertilizing every few weeks through the summer (my Handy Herbal Fertilizer at left is one super option), and you'll be guaranteed to have a yard full of fabulous flowers right up to the first fall frost.

Plan Ahead for Beautiful Biennials

Don't think your seed-sowing options are over just yet, 'cause midsummer's prime time for sowing biennials for next year's blooms. They'll sprout up quick in the warm soil, and you'll have lush, leafy plants by early fall—just in time to transplant them where you want them to flower next spring or summer. Best biennial bets for midsummer sowing include Canterbury bells (*Campanula medium*), forget-me-nots (*Myosotis*), foxglove (*Digitalis purpurea*), hollyhock (*Alcea rosea*), money plant (*Lunaria annua*), sweet William (*Dianthus barbatus*), and pansies (*Viola*).

Bountiful Bouquets from Your Backyard

When it comes to making stunning summer bouquets, annuals have a lot to offer! Besides blooming in an incredible range of colors, these dependable beauties actually grow *better* if you pick their flowers frequently. So when you gather blooms for indoor arrangements, you're actually doing both yourself and your plants a favor!

Grandma Putt's

GREEN THUMB TIPS

My Grandma Putt enjoyed experimenting with different ways to dry flowers, and she came up with a great trick that I still use today. You see, some blooms dry better when right-side-up, so instead of hanging them upside down, simply stand the fresh stems in a coffee can or tall, wide-mouthed jar. This works great with baby's breaths (*Gypsophila*), poppy (*Papaver*) seedheads, grains (like oats and wheat), and grasses, too.

If you want only a few flowers now and then, simply snip them from the plantings in your yard; otherwise, set aside a special bed just for your favorites. Here are some top-notch annuals that no cutting garden should be without: cosmos, prairie gentian (*Lisianthus russellianus*), snapdragon (*Antirrhinum majus*), statice (*Limonium sinuatum*), and zinnias.

Keep It Comin'

Sure, cosmos make fantastic cut flowers, but they have another thing going for them: Once you have cosmos in your garden, you'll never need to buy seeds a second time. Every summer, use yarn to mark plants with flowers in your favorite colors. When their seedheads turn brown, crumble them into a bowl, then scatter the seeds and chaff back in your garden. Every year, you'll have more flowers—*for free!*

Two Tips for the Good Guys

Way too many folks nowadays buy into the "only good bug is a dead bug" mindset. The truth of the matter is that many of the bugs we find in our flower gardens do no damage; in fact, some of those bugs are actually good guys. These "beneficials" either attack the bad bugs directly or lay their eggs on the bodies of the pests. They're nature's way of keeping the pest population under control. Beneficials will show up on their own—especially

FLOWER PEST PRIMER

Wondering what's bugging your bloomers? Here's a handy chart to help you identify the culprits in no time flat!

What You See	Who's to Blame
Distorted, sticky leaves, stems, and/or buds; leaves and/or buds that discolor and drop off	Aphids
Holes in leaves and/or flowers	Beetles, caterpillars, slugs, or snails
Winding tunnels between upper and lower leaf surfaces	Leaf miners
Small, sunken brown spots on leaves; distorted shoots and buds	Plant bugs
Silvery streaking on leaves; darkened buds that fail to open; streaking on flower petals	Thrips
Powdery black coating on leaves and/or stems	Sooty mold fungus, which lives on sticky "honeydew" released by aphids

if you keep sprays to a minimum—but you can encourage more of them to stick around in your yard by providing them with a happy home. One way is to plant lots of pollen- and nectar-rich annual flowers, such as cosmos, sunflowers (*Helianthus*), and sweet alyssum (*Lobularia maritima*). Give them a water source, too, by filling a shallow saucer with water and adding a few small rocks for landing sites. These two simple steps will go a long way toward attracting beneficials to your yard and keeping *all* your plants pest-free!

Spotlight on...

Marigolds

When you need easy-care midsummer flowers, marvelous marigolds (*Tagetes*) are where it's at! Their bright blooms come in shades of yellow, orange, maroon, and creamy white for a dazzling display of cheerful color in any sunny bed or border. Here are the four types you're likely to run across in garden centers and seed catalogs:

African or American marigolds (*T. erecta*): Double, 4- to 5-inch-wide flowers on 1½- to 3-foot-tall plants. Compact cultivars stay under 18 inches.

French marigolds (*T. patula*): Six- to 12-inch-tall plants with 1- to 2-inch-wide, single, semi-double, or double flowers.

Triploid marigolds: Crosses between African and French marigolds, with 1-foot-tall plants and single or double, 2- to 3-inch-wide flowers. They keep blooming even in hot weather.

Signet marigolds (*T. tenuifolia*): Mounding, 9- to 12-inch plants with lacy leaves and masses of tiny, ¾-inch-wide flowers.

Your Midsummer Strategy

Ever notice that some annuals stop blooming during the dog days of summer? Don't you dare pull them out, though! Just keep 'em watered, and be patient—they'll start flowering again when cooler weather arrives.

Cut and Dried

Beautiful blooms all through summer and fall—*and* winter, too? You bet! There's no better way to enjoy your annuals year-round than by drying your favorites for long-lasting indoor arrangements. Here's how:

Step 1: Gather flowers and seedpods in late morning, after all the dew has dried. Cut blooms at all different stages, from tiny buds to fully open flowers.

Step 2: Collect the stems into small bunches (about six stems in each), and wrap a rubber band around them near the cut ends.

Step 3: Hang the bundles in a warm, dry, dark place with good air circulation for fast drying. (The quicker your flowers dry, the better they'll hold their colors.)

Step 4: After one to three weeks, your flowers should be fully dry. Give them a spritz of hair spray to help them hold on to their petals, then use them in crafts or store them in tissue paper–lined boxes in a dry place.

MIX & FIX

ZINNIA SPOT SPRAY

If you're seeing gray spots on your zinnia leaves, whip up a batch of this simple solution.

**2 tbsp. of baby shampoo
1 tbsp. of baking soda
1 gal. of warm water**

Mix these ingredients together, and mist-spray your plants lightly once a week to keep funky fungi from zapping your zinnias!

Spotlight on . . .

Impatiens

Talk about being made for the shade! Impatiens (*Impatiens walleriana*) are a mainstay in many shady gardens, and with good reason: Just give 'em evenly moist soil, and they'll bloom full blast from early summer well into fall. That's one of the longest bloom times of any annual! Tuck them among hostas, ferns, and other perennials for spots of color; plant them in masses as a glorious groundcover; or enjoy them in pots on your deck or patio—there's simply no *bad* way to use 'em.

The typical impatiens have single, flat flowers in shades of red, pink, salmon, or white, but in the past few years, some exciting new shapes and colors have come on the market. I'm particularly partial to the "rosebud" types, like the 'Rose Parade' series; the petal-packed blooms do look just like miniature roses. New Guinea impatiens have larger, jewel-toned, single flowers over deep green, bronze, or variegated leaves. And African impatiens, such as golden yellow 'Blondie', have unusual hooded blooms.

All in Good Taste

Masses of bright blooms and great-looking leaves, too—that's what nasturtiums (*Tropaeolum majus*) are all about. Their fancy flowers come in shades of red, orange, yellow, pink, and cream, either as solid colors or with two-toned blooms, like those of 'Strawberries and Cream'. Besides being beautiful to look at, the peppery-flavored flowers and leaves of these foolproof annuals are mighty tasty, too!

Nasturtiums need full sun and do fine in average to poor soil. In rich, moist soil, the plants will look lush and leafy, but you'll get hardly any flowers— so hold off on the compost and fertilizer!

MIX & FIX

COMPOST BOOSTER TONIC

Whether you use it as a mulch or dig it into the soil to help hold water, you can never have too much compost! To keep your pile cookin' and the compost a-comin', try the following formula.

1 can of beer
1 can of regular cola (not diet)
1 cup of ammonia
1/2 cup of weak tea water*
2 tbsp. of baby shampoo

Mix all of the ingredients together and pour into a 20 gallon hose-end sprayer. Saturate your compost pile every time you add a new, foot-deep layer of ingredients to it.

*Soak a used tea bag and 1 teaspoon of dishwashing liquid in a gallon of warm water until the mix is light brown.

The Bucket Brigade

Want to put together the ultimate flower garden cleanup kit? All it takes is two things: a good pair of garden clippers and a basic 5-gallon, plastic bucket. Keep these two items by your back door, and carry them with you every time you head out to look at your annual flowers. While you're admiring the beautiful blooms, snip off the dead ones, and toss them into the bucket. Finish the tour with a trip to your compost pile, and toss in the contents of the bucket so it's empty for the next trip. There's no easier way to keep your annuals looking picture-perfect!

Fill 'Er Up

As you stroll around your yard, make it a point to pull any weeds as soon as you see 'em—especially in new beds. Keep a few extra annuals on hand to fill in the gaps that are left, and you'll stop pesky weed problems right in their tracks.

A Bounty of Bulbs

Summer bulbs sure don't get the same press that their early-rising counterparts do—and that's a darn shame. After all, summer-blooming bulbs have some of the biggest and most spectacular flowers you could ever ask for. So take a look at these great tips I've gathered, then see if you don't have the urge to get more bulbs growing in your yard!

Pack 'Em In

By this time, your spring-flowering bulbs have retreated back underground, leaving gaps in your otherwise perfectly planted beds and borders. No sense in letting those spaces go to waste, so here's what I want you to do: Hit your local garden center

Knock 'Em Dead Tonic

This tough tonic is all you need to wipe out a wide variety of garden pests.

6 cloves of garlic, chopped fine
1 small onion, chopped fine
1 tbsp. of cayenne pepper
1 tbsp. of dishwashing liquid
1 qt. of warm water

Mix all of these ingredients and let sit overnight. Strain out the solid matter, pour the liquid into a hand-held sprayer, and knock those pests for a loop.

MIX & FIX

for sales on leftover annuals. I recommend buying small transplants in cell packs (usually six per pack), if you can get them. Besides being cheaper, these smaller plants are easy to tuck into those "empty" spots without bugging your bulbs.

The Great Divide

When it comes to division, bearded irises are one of the oddballs; unlike most plants, they actually *prefer* to be divided in mid- to late summer. You see, they take a rest right after their big

Spotlight on...

Lilies

There's certainly nothing subtle about the big, beautiful blooms of lilies (*Lilium*). These classic summer bulbs flower in can't-miss colors like fiery orange, rousing red, and sunshine yellow, as well as pastel pinks, creams, and white. That means you're certain to find at least one that pairs perfectly with your favorite annuals and perennials.

Most lilies like full-sun sites, but there are some shade-lovers, too, including American Turk's-cap lily (*L. superbum*), Canada lily (*L. canadense*), Henry lily (*L. henryi*), and Japanese lily (*L. speciosum*). Good drainage is a must for all, so unless you have sandy soil, consider planting your lilies on a slight slope, or else build raised beds for them. These bloomers need lots of energy to strut their stuff, so be generous when you feed them. I've found that scattering a handful of 5-10-5 fertilizer around each clump in early spring, late spring, and midsummer does the trick. If you have wood ashes handy, give your lilies a dose of them, too: 1 pound for every 20 square feet of lily bed in spring.

flush of early-summer bloom, so this is the best time to divide crowded clumps and replant them before they get growing again.

Just lift the clumps with a spading fork, then break the rhizomes apart with your hands. Discard any pieces without buds (they won't grow), as well as any that have soft, rotten spots (signs of pesky pests known as iris borers). Replant the remaining rhizomes into compost-enriched soil, and you're back in business!

Plan a Hummingbird Feast

Filling your yard with flowers'll do more than attract attention from your neighbors; it'll attract hummingbirds as well! These winged wonders are especially fond of brightly colored blooms— red, orange, yellow, and hot pink. Good choices in this color range include Asiatic Hybrid lilies and gladiolus, as well as impatiens, nasturtium (*Tropaeolum majus*), snapdragon (*Antirrhinum majus*), and standing cypress (*Ipomopsis rubra*).

HUMMINGBIRD NECTAR

Hummers will visit a feeder all summer long, once they get the idea that it's filled with nectar. You can buy packets of nectar mix, but making your own is easy and inexpensive.

1 part white sugar (not honey, which hosts bacteria harmful to hummers)
4 parts water
A few drops of red food coloring (optional)

Boil the mix, and let it cool before filling the feeder. Once hummers start coming, decrease the solution to about 1 part sugar and 8 parts water. No, this isn't the old bait-and-switch tactic—there's a good reason for diluting the solution. Hummingbirds can sometimes suffer a fatal liver disorder if they get too much sugar. Replace the nectar every three days or so—every other day if temperatures are above 60°F. But first wash the feeder with soap and scalding water, and rinse thoroughly. Otherwise, the nectar and/or feeder can host hummingbird-harming bacteria.

MIX & FIX

Get Goin' with Begonias

Want to enjoy the biggest begonia blooms on the block? It's super-easy! You see, most tuberous begonias produce clusters of three flowers: one male flower flanked by two females. The female flowers have a swollen seed capsule right behind the petals, while the male doesn't. When the blooms are still small buds, pinch off the two female flowers. All the growing energy in that stem will go into making one huge bloom!

Bulbs That Make Scents

Sweet-smelling summer bulbs make some of the best—and most expensive—florist flowers. But did you know that you can save a bundle by growing these beauties right in your own back-yard? Peacock orchid (*Acidanthera bicolor*), Oriental Hybrid lilies, and tuberose (*Polianthes tuberosa*) are all good choices. Tuck a few into your vegetable garden for cutting; add them to beds and borders to scent your yard; or plant them in pots to perfume your porch, deck, or patio. For just pennies a bulb, you can have all the fragrant flowers you'll ever need!

Divine Vines and Groundcovers

Flowers, flowers everywhere—from over your head to the ground at your feet. When summer color is what you're after, you simply can't have too many vines and groundcovers growing in your yard. I have a bunch of top-notch tips to share with you for these versatile plants, so get ready to get growin'!

Social Climbers

There's just nothing like a fabulous flowering vine for dressing up a porch post or drab deck railing. I'm partial to clematis, myself—there's just somethin' about those big, beautiful blooms that can't be beat—but they *can* take a few years to look their best. No need to miss out while you're waiting for your clematis to fill in, though; pair it with a quick-climbing annual vine for loads of blooms in no time flat! Morning glories (*Ipomoea*) are a classic choice, but really, any annual vine will do the trick.

Mandevilla Magic

No matter where you live, you can bring a touch of the tropics to your yard—just plant a mandevilla! This gorgeous, fast-growing, twining vine flowers from early summer up to frost (even longer in frost-free areas) with huge, bright pink, trumpet-shaped blooms. It grows only 6 to 8 feet tall in most climates, so it's a perfect size for adorning arbors, posts, and trellises, and it's happy growing in pots on a deck or patio. In fact, growing it in containers is a great idea, because mandevilla is hardy only in Zones 9 to 11; elsewhere, you'll want to bring it indoors for the winter to enjoy as a houseplant.

Ask Jerry

Q: *I'd like to grow a vine over my deck to provide summer shade. Any ideas?*

A: You bet! In fact, I have several suggestions that should do the trick. Wisterias are simply stunning with beautiful blooms *and* lush leaves, but they take a *lot* of pruning. Dutchman's pipes (*Aristolochia*), chocolate vine (*Akebia quinata*), and hops (*Humulus lupulus*) are three other fast growers that'll provide lots of lovely leaves to keep you cool all summer long.

Say So Long, Weeds!

Groundcovers make great-looking edgings for paths and walkways, and they need a lot less trimming than turf grass to stay neat and tidy. But when weeds creep into your walkways, even the best groundcovers can't help; it's time for you to take control and get rid of those ugly weeds. It's easier than you think—just dump some salt on 'em, douse 'em with boiling water, or spritz 'em with my Wonderful Weed Killer (below). Within a day or two, the weeds will curl up and die, and you can easily pull them out.

Don't Worry About This Wort

St. John's wort (*Hypericum calycinum*) has been making quite a splash in the news the past few years, thanks to its herbal use for treating depression. The sunny yellow blooms of this gorgeous groundcover can make quite a splash in your yard as well, and they certainly spread good cheer wherever they grow!

In just one season, the plants grow 18 inches tall, but spread to 2 feet across, creating a carpet of bright green leaves dotted with bright blooms through much of the summer. This tough-as-nails perennial grows in full sun or light shade and does just fine in dry soil, so it's a winner for covering tough slopes where other plants just can't cut it!

MIX & FIX

WONDERFUL WEED KILLER

Nothing spoils the look of a formal garden quicker than weed-filled paths. Use this tonic to kill weeds in gravel walks, or in cracks between bricks or stones in walkways.

1 gal. of white vinegar
1 cup of table salt
1 tbsp. of dishwashing liquid

Mix all of the ingredients together until the salt has dissolved. Spray the solution on weeds, or pour it along cracks to kill weeds. Don't spray it on plants that you want to keep, and don't pour it on soil that you want to be able to garden in someday!

A Classy Grass

Ornamental grasses are one of the hottest things in gardening today, and with good reason: They're beautiful, tough, and practically problem-free!

Unfortunately, some bad apples in the bunch have given even well-behaved grasses a reputation for being weedy spreaders. Well, here's one grass that you'll never have to worry about: 'Karl Foer-

ster' feather reed grass (*Calamagrostis* x *acutiflora* 'Karl Foerster').
This gorgeous grass grows in noncreeping clumps of deep
green leaves, with 5-foot-tall, pinkish gray, summer plumes that
turn tan and last through much of the winter. Plant it in masses
as an easy-care groundcover, or use individual plants in beds and
borders or as accent plants. You'll be glad you did!

Glorious Container Gardens

There's simply nothin' finer than a collection of pretty potted plants to dress up a dull deck, porch, or patio. Containers give you a great opportunity to get up close and personal with your favorite bloomers, and they're mighty practical, too! Whether you use yours to showcase special plants, or simply for spots of summer color, I've got some handy hints for making the most of container gardens around your home.

Wondering About Watering?

It's a fact, folks: The smaller the pot, the more often you'll
need to water it! Bigger pots hold more growing medium, so they
also hold more moisture; small pots, on the other hand, may need
watering once or even twice a day to keep plants from getting
parched. If you *still* prefer to use single-plant pots, then try this
simple trick: Set a shallow saucer (about 1 inch deep) under each
one, and fill it to the brim each time you water. That'll give your
potted bloomers plenty of moisture to draw on during the heat of
the day, and they'll stay in tip-top shape all summer long.

202

Made for the Shade

Sure, container gardens are great for sunny sites, but they're practically *perfect* when it comes to bringing color to shady summer sitting areas! Forget about fighting with bone-dry soil that's riddled with tree roots; pots and planters provide top-notch growing conditions for all sorts of shade-lovers. Shady containers also need a whole lot less watering and feeding than those in the sun, so they're ideal for easy maintenance. Impatiens, begonias, coleus, caladiums, ferns, and hostas are just a few of the many fantastic flowering and foliage plants that can turn any shady site into a color-filled showplace.

MIX & FIX

APHID ANTIDOTE

To keep aphids and other pests off your favorite flowers, mix up a batch of this amazing antidote.

1 small onion, chopped fine
2 medium cloves of garlic,
  chopped fine
1 tbsp. of dishwashing liquid
2 cups of water

Put all of the ingredients in a blender, blend on high, and then strain out the pulp through cheesecloth or pantyhose. Pour the liquid into a hand-held sprayer, and douse your flowers at the first sign of aphid trouble.

Nighty Night, Mighty Mites!

Most folks aren't crazy about seeing spiders in their yard, but if you do find some, be glad—these good guys eat lots of pesky pests that would otherwise bug your bloomers. But spider *mites*—barely visible, spider-like creatures that suck the sap out of plant tissues—are definitely *not* a good thing! Leaf symptoms can range from a few yellow speckles to total browning, and when the browned leaves drop off, the whole plant gets weakened. Keeping container plants well watered can help prevent problems, but if you suspect spider mites are already at work, treat your plants with a soap-based spray or my Super Spider Mite Mix (below) to stop them in their tracks.

Keep 'Em Drinking

Flower-filled container plantings can sure suck up lots of water, which can be a real problem if you live where summer droughts bring watering restrictions. Well, here's a great trick that saves water *and* feeds your plants at the same time! Next time you cook vegetables, use the nutrient-rich water left in the pot (after it's cooled) to give your thirsty pots a drink.

Water Gardens to Go

Would you love to have a water garden, but lack the space, time, or money to take care of an in-ground pond? Well, then—why not make yourself a pond-in-a-pot! You can use pretty much any waterproof container, such as an old washtub or a wooden half-barrel with a plastic liner. In a shallow container (less than a foot deep), you can place a layer of garden soil in the bottom and plant directly into it; otherwise, grow your plants in individual pots and set them on bricks or rocks to keep them at the right depth. Either way, top the soil with gravel, then slowly add water. Once the water clears, you can add a small pump and/or a few fish for extra interest. What a cool way to beat the heat!

SUPER SPIDER MITE MIX

Spider mites are tiny, all right, but they get up to mite-y BIG mischief in your garden! When they show up, send 'em scurryin' with this floury remedy.

4 cups of wheat flour
½ cup of buttermilk (not fat-free)
5 gal. of water

Mix all of the ingredients together, and mist-spray your plants to the point of run-off. This mix will suffocate the little buggers without harming your flowers.

MIX & FIX

Jerry's Best Bets for...
Midsummer Sizzle

Asking me to pick my favorite bloomers for midsummer is like letting a kid loose in a candy store! There are so many winners to choose from, but I've managed to whittle down this list to the best of the best. Give any or all a try when surefire midsummer color is what you're searching for!

Trees

Amur maackia
  (*Maackia amurensis*)
Golden-rain tree
  (*Koelreuteria paniculata*)
Japanese pagoda tree
  (*Sophora japonica*)
Lily-of-the-valley tree
  (*Oxydendrum arboreum*)
Stewartias (*Stewartia*)

Shrubs

Big-leaved hydrangea
  (*Hydrangea macrophylla*)
Bottlebrush buckeye
  (*Aesculus parviflora*)
Bumald spirea
  (*Spiraea* x *bumalda*)
Bush cinquefoil
  (*Potentilla fruticosa*)
Butterfly bushes
  (*Buddleia*)

Carolina rose
  (*Rosa carolina*)
Cumberland azalea
  (*Rhododendron bakeri*)
Elderberries
  (*Sambucus*)
Hills-of-snow
  (*Hydrangea arborescens*)
Japanese spirea
  (*Spiraea japonica*)
Panicle hydrangea
  (*Hydrangea paniculata*)
Rosebay rhododendron
  (*Rhododendron maximum*)
Smoke bush
  (*Cotinus coggygria*)
Summersweet
  (*Clethra alnifolia*)
Swamp azalea
  (*Rhododendron viscosum*)
Sweet azalea
  (*Rhododendron arborescens*)
Virginia sweetspire
  (*Itea virginica*)

Perennials

Astilbes (*Astilbe*)
Balloon flower
  (*Platycodon grandiflorus*)
Bats-in-the-belfry
  (*Campanula trachelium*)

Bee balms (*Monarda*)
Blanket flowers (*Gaillardia*)
Border phlox
  (*Phlox paniculata* and *P. maculata*)
Campions (*Lychnis*)
Catmints (*Nepeta*)
Coreopsis (*Coreopsis*)
Daylilies (*Hemerocallis*)
Gayfeathers (*Liatris*)
Hollyhock (*Alcea rosea*)
Hostas (*Hosta*)
Pincushion flower
  (*Scabiosa caucasica*)
Purple coneflower
  (*Echinacea purpurea*)
Shasta daisy
  (*Leucanthemum* x *superbum*)
Speedwells (*Veronica*)
Stokes' aster
  (*Stokesia laevis*)
Yarrows (*Achillea*)

Annuals

Begonias (*Begonia*)
Celosias (*Celosia*)
Cosmos (*Cosmos*)
Floss flower
 (*Ageratum
 houstonianum*)
Flowering tobaccos
 (*Nicotiana*)
Four-o'clocks
 (*Mirabilis jalapa*)

Geraniums
 (*Pelargonium*)
Gloriosa daisy
 (*Rudbeckia hirta*)
Impatiens (*Impatiens*)
Lavatera
 (*Lavatera trimestris*)
Love-in-a-mist
 (*Nigella damascena*)
Love-lies-bleeding
 (*Amaranthus caudatus*)
Marigolds (*Tagetes*)
Nasturtium
 (*Tropaeolum majus*)
Petunias (*Petunia*)
Pot marigold
 (*Calendula officinalis*)
Rose periwinkle
 (*Catharanthus roseus*)
Salvias (*Salvia*)
Spider flower
 (*Cleome hasslerana*)

Strawflower
 (*Bracteantha bracteata*)
Sunflower
 (*Helianthus annuus*)
Verbenas (*Verbena*)
Zinnias (*Zinnia*)

Bulbs

Cannas (*Canna*)
Dahlias (*Dahlia*)
Gladiolus (*Gladiolus*)
Lilies (*Lilium*)
Lily-of-the-Nile
 (*Agapanthus*)
Peacock orchid
 (*Acidanthera bicolor*)
Summer hyacinth
 (*Galtonia candicans*)
Tuberose
 (*Polianthes tuberosa*)
Tuberous begonias
 (*Begonia*)

Vines

 Black-eyed Susan vine
 (*Thunbergia alata*)
Exotic love
 (*Mina lobata*)
Honeysuckles
 (*Lonicera*)
Hybrid clematis
 (*Clematis*)

Jackman clematis
 (*Clematis* x *jackmanii*)
Morning glories
 (*Ipomoea*)
Trumpet vine
 (*Campsis radicans*)

Groundcovers

Creeping thyme
 (*Thymus serpyllum*)
Dwarf Chinese astilbe
 (*Astilbe chinensis*
 'Pumila')
Kamschatka sedum
 (*Sedum kamtschaticum*)
'Karl Foerster' feather
 reed grass
 (*Calamagrostis* x
 acutiflora 'Karl Foerster')
St. John's wort
 (*Hypericum calycinum*)

CHAPTER 9

Late Summer: Let's Beat the Heat!

B y this time of year, most folks are getting pretty tired of taking care of their yard—but not *you!* Once you know the secrets of year-round gardening, your yard will be as flower-full during the dog days as it is earlier in the season. I've rounded up all my best tips for beating the heat and keeping your plants in great shape, so your year-round yard will be the showcase of the neighborhood!

Late summer's a time for light chores—mainly keeping things tidy and getting ready for the bigger projects you can do once early fall brings cooler weather and more reliable rainfall.

- Collect seeds from your favorite flowers to store for next year
- Keep dead flowers pinched off of annuals and perennials
- Watch out for pest and disease problems
- Keep after those weeds!
- Clip and tie climbing vines as needed

- Stop fertilizing
- Fill gaps in beds and borders with potted chrysanthemums or ornamental kale
- Plant bearded iris rhizomes and fall-flowering bulbs
- Divide and replant spring-flowering perennials
- Cut flowers for fresh or dry arrangements
- Choose sites for new gardens that you'll prepare in fall
- Make notes about what worked and what didn't

It beats me why more gardeners don't make the most of trees and shrubs for late-summer color. These fuss-free plants are some of the brightest and most dependable bloomers you'd ever want to see, so take some time to get to know 'em; you'll be glad you did!

Let This Son Shine

Now, here's a terrific little tree you don't run across every day! Seven-son tree (*Heptacodium miconioides*) is fairly new to the gardening scene, but I predict it has a bright future with folks looking for great late-season interest.

This honeysuckle relative grows 10 to 15 feet tall, with an amazing display of fragrant, creamy white flowers in late summer. As the blooms fall off, they reveal red seed capsules fringed with reddish pink, petal-like sepals. It looks like the whole tree is in flower again—in an entirely different color! This tree's stems also have interesting, peeling bark, so they're attractive all winter long, too. Rarely bugged by pests or diseases, seven-son tree blooms best in full sun, but can grow in partial shade as well. It may take a little time to track down this gem of a tree, but trust me—it'll be worth it!

Grandma Putt's

GREEN THUMB TIPS

My Grandma Putt was all for feeding her flowering plants generously, because she knew that making beautiful blooms takes lots of energy. But once the season turned to late summer, she cut off the food supply—and so should you! Even though the weather's still plenty warm, it's time for your trees and shrubs to think about getting ready for winter, and that means sending their energy down to their roots, instead of into new shoots. If you keep fertilizing, you run the risk of killing 'em with kindness, because tender new twigs are prime targets for getting nipped by fall frosts.

It's Cut and Dried

Now's a great time to pick hydrangea flowers to enjoy indoors all winter long. You won't believe how easy it is to dry them: Simply stand the cut stems in a bucket filled with an inch or so of water. As the water dries out, so will the blooms. They'll be fully dry in a week or two, and they'll look great for months on end.

SQUEAKY CLEAN TONIC

No matter what bad-guy bugs are buggin' your plants, this tough tonic'll stop 'em in their tracks.

1 cup of antiseptic mouthwash
1 cup of tobacco tea*
1 cup of chamomile tea
1 cup of urine
¹/₂ cup of Murphy's Oil Soap®
¹/₂ cup of lemon-scented dish-
washing liquid

Mix all of these ingredients in a large bucket, then pour into a 20 gallon hose-end sprayer, and apply to the point of run-off.

*Place half a handful of chewing tobacco in an old nylon stocking, and soak it in a gallon of hot water until the mixture is dark brown.

Crape Myrtle Madness

If you're searching for a tree with stunning late-summer color, look no further than crape myrtles (*Lagerstroemia*). These beauties have long been favorites in the Deep South, and thanks to busy plant breeders, gardeners as far north as Zone 6 can now enjoy them, too! Even if winter's cold kills off the tops, hardy cultivars like 'Hopi' and 'Natchez' can spring back from the roots and still bloom the same year, with big bunches of pink, red, purple, or white flowers that last well into the fall (especially if you snip off the spent clusters). In areas where the stems *don't* die back, they develop beautifully mottled bark that you can enjoy throughout the winter. And everywhere they grow, crape myrtles have fabulous fall color—usually in shades of red, orange, and/or purple. That's a whole lot of year-round *WOW* from just one terrific tree!

Trouble-Free Trees and Shrubs   Late Summer: Let's Beat the Heat!

209

Plant Parenthood

Butterfly bushes (*Buddleia*) are top-notch shrubs for summer and fall flowers, and they're great favorites of beautiful butterflies, of course. But these pretty plants can become pesky pests, too, if you don't watch out! Left untended, they'll drop hundreds of seeds, and you're liable to find dozens of baby bushes all over your yard. Don't think you have to do without 'em, though—just make it a habit to snip off all the spent flower clusters every few days. This'll keep them from making too many babies—*and* encourage the production of new blooms, too!

Spotlight on...

Rose-of-Sharon

Rose-of-Sharon (*Hibiscus syriacus*) has to be one of the most forgiving shrubs you can ever lay your hands on! It'll grow in full sun or partial shade in Zones 5 through 8, and while it loves evenly moist, humus-rich, well-drained soil, it'll put up with drought, heat, compaction, and even pollution. Rose-of-Sharon normally forms a bush about 6 to 8 feet tall and about 4 feet wide, but if you cut the side shoots off along the trunks, you can make it look like a small tree instead.

But rose-of-Sharon is more than just practical; it's also a true beauty for shrubby summer color, with large, hibiscus-like blooms in shades of red, pink, purple, and white. It used to be that rose-of-Sharon could make a pest of itself by making way too many seedlings, but if you stick with modern cultivars like 'Diana' (which doesn't set seed), that concern's a thing of the past. Enjoy this super shrub mixed with perennials and annuals for all-summer color, tuck it into a foundation planting, or enjoy it alone as an accent or as a hedge.

No doubt about it: Summer's heat and humidity can really do a number on your beautiful bloomers. But when you know how to pick perennials that actually *enjoy* the dog days—*and* the tricks for keeping all your beds and borders looking their best—your yard will be the envy of all your neighbors!

Seeing Red

If you'd love to attract hummingbirds to your yard (and who wouldn't?), I've got the perfect perennial for you! It's called cardinal flower (*Lobelia cardinalis*) and with good reason: Its late-summer bloom spikes are as rich a red as the brightest cardinal you've ever laid eyes upon. This stunning late bloomer is a veritable magnet for hungry hummers, and butterflies love it, too! So you're *guaranteed* a great show of wildlife right in your backyard!

Cardinal flower grows best in light shade and loves evenly moist soil, so it's a perfect choice for planting in low spots or along streams. For extra interest, try great blue lobelia (*L. siphilitica*), and its white-flowered cultivar 'Alba'. Mix 'em together, and you'll have yourself a red, white, and blue garden that'd make Uncle Sam proud!

Ask Jerry

Q: *Hey, Jer—I think I'm seeing spots! The leaves of my hollyhocks are covered with yellow dots, and the plants don't look too good. What's the problem?*

A: The problem, my friend, is a fungal disease called rust. If you look on the undersides of the leaves, you'll notice the rusty orange spores that give this dastardly disease its name. There's not much you can do at this point, except cut all of your hollyhocks right down to the ground, and destroy (don't compost) the debris. To prevent problems next year, dust the leaves with sulfur (make sure you get the undersides, too!) every two weeks in late spring and early summer.

Start a Bargain Bloomer Hunt

If you're planning to put in some new perennial beds this fall, it's not too early to start thinking about plant shopping. And you're in luck, because most nurseries and garden centers start their end-of-season sales right about now. Check possible pur-

Spotlight on...

Ferns

Hey, folks—if you're looking for great foliage plants to pair with your flowering perennials, it's time to make friends with fronds. In other words, add some ferns to your yard! These sturdier-than-they-look plants are perfect partners for all kinds of shade-garden favorites, such as spring wildflowers and hostas. There are dozens of fabulous ferns to try, but here are three foolproof favorites to get you on your way:

Autumn fern (*Dryopteris erythrosora*): The new spring fronds of this beauty are as bright as a copper penny, then gradually turn dark green through summer. In fall, the dot-like spore cases on the undersides of the evergreen fronds turn bright red, adding color all through the winter. Zones 5 to 9.

Japanese painted fern (*Athyrium niponicum* 'Pictum'): The graceful fronds of this low-growing fern are shaded with silvery gray and green and held on arching, wine-red stems. Zones 3 to 8.

Ostrich fern (*Matteuccia struthiopteris*): This super-hardy fern has bright green, feathery fronds that can grow up to 5 feet tall! Zones 2 to 7.

SUMMER

Late Summer: Let's Beat the Heat!　　Dependable Perennials

212

chases carefully to make sure they're not carrying any pest or disease problems—sick plants are no bargain at any price! When you bring your acquisitions home, keep them all in one spot so you can water them regularly. When it comes time to plant your new garden, you'll have all the plants you need—at a fraction of what you'd have paid just a few months ago!

Pile It On!

What would you say if I told you there's a no-sweat, no-dig way to have a fabulous perennial garden in less than one year? You'd better believe it, because it's true! Instead of digging *down*, just build your beds *up* in layers. Here's how:

Step 1: In late summer, stake out the site where you want your new bed, then cover the area with a 1-inch-thick layer of newspapers.

Step 2: Place a few rocks over the papers to hold them down, and soak the area thoroughly. Water again as needed over the next few weeks to keep the papers moist.

Step 3: In the fall, remove the rocks, then spread 6 to 8 inches of leaves over the area. Top that with 8 to 12 inches of good soil or compost.

Step 4: Over the winter, sit back, and let all of the ingredients settle in. Come spring, you'll have a loose, fluffy flower bed that'll be a joy for you to plant in—*and* for your perennials to grow in!

Consider This "Lily"

With a name like August lily (*Hosta plantaginea*), there's no doubt that this pretty perennial belongs in your late-summer landscape. Most hostas are best known for their handsome

FERN FOOD

To keep all of your outdoor ferns looking lush, give them a dose of this milky brew.

**2 cups of milk
2 tbsp. of Epsom salts**

Combine the milk and Epsom salts in a 20 gallon hose-end sprayer, and give your ferns a generous drink until they are saturated.

MIX
&
FIX

foliage, but August lily has been beloved by generations of gardeners for its large, pure white, trumpet-shaped blooms. They're fragrant as well, so they're as nice to smell as they are to look at.

August lily grows fine in light shade, but can also take full sun, and it's adaptable to anywhere from Zones 3 to 9. So no excuses—if you want to enjoy beautiful blooms in late summer, you *need* at least one August lily in your yard!

The Manure Cure

Late summer is a super time to lay in a supply of farm animal manure for next spring's perennial flowers. Here's how I keep mine weed-free—and almost odor-free—in the meantime!

Step 1: Spread a big tarpaulin out on the ground, and dump the manure on top. Fold up the tarp's edges around the pile.

Step 2: Lay another tarp across the top, and cut a few slits in it for ventilation. Add a few rocks, so that it stays put.

Step 3: Let it sit until next spring, and *presto*—you've got black gold! Use this great stuff to enrich the soil before you plant, or spread a few shovelfuls on the soil surface around existing perennials as a soil-enriching fertilizer.

CREATIVE COLOR COMBOS

Late-summer gardens are filled with warm colors, like glowing gold, rousing red, and rich orange. These handsome hues make for some stunning plant partnerships, so feel free to experiment, 'cause you can't go wrong! Here are a few ideas to get you started:

✿ Rich pink 'Eva Cullum' garden phlox (*Phlox paniculata*) with yellow 'Golden Fleece' goldenrod (*Solidago sphacelata*) and the compact, rich green foliage of 'Little Bunny' fountain grass (*Pennisetum alopecuroides*)

✿ Golden yellow false sunflower (*Heliopsis helianthoides*) with deep blue 'May Night' salvia (*Salvia x sylvestris*) and bright red 'Lucifer' crocosmia

✿ Tall, rosy pink Joe Pye weed (*Eupatorium purpureum*) with the white daisies of boltonia (*Boltonia asteroides*) and silvery blue Russian sage (*Perovskia atriplicifolia*)

Keep Perennials in Their Place

Keeping spent flowers picked off your perennials does more than just keep your yard looking tidy—it also keeps good plants from going bad! You see, some perennials set seed so freely that they can actually become your worst weed enemies. Fortunately, there's a simple solution; just make it a point to keep those faded flowers cleaned up. Here are a few perennials to pay special attention to, so they don't get away from you:

➜ Black-eyed Susans (*Rudbeckia*)

➜ Campions (*Lychnis*)

➜ Common yarrow (*Achillea millefolium*)

➜ Coreopsis (*Coreopsis*)

➜ Golden marguerite (*Anthemis tinctoria*)

➜ Hollyhock (*Alcea rosea*)

➜ Jupiter's beard (*Centranthus ruber*)

➜ Mulleins (*Verbascum*)

➜ Purple coneflower (*Echinacea purpurea*)

MIX
&
FIX

POWDERY MILDEW CONTROL

Late summer's prime time for your phlox to shine, so don't let messy mildew spoil the show! Try this terrific tonic for picture-perfect phlox every time.

4 tbsp. of baking soda
2 tbsp. of Murphy's Oil Soap®
1 gal. of warm water

Mix all of the ingredients together. Pour into a hand-held sprayer, and apply liberally, as soon as you see the telltale white spots on your phlox.

The Annual Parade

Sure, annuals are awesome for early and midsummer color, but to my mind, late summer's when these bloomers really hit their stride. Let's take a look at some of the best bets for sultry summer color, as well as some pointers for keeping the show going 'til fall.

Verbena There? Done That!

For pure flower power in late summer, it's tough to beat moss verbena (*Verbena tenuisecta*). This low-growing beauty is as tough as they come, laughing at drought and breezing through sultry summer weather without missing a beat. Each cluster of purplish or pink blooms is like a little bouquet in itself; altogether, they practically smother the 12- to 18-inch-tall carpets of moss-like foliage. In Zones 8 to 10, moss verbena acts like a perennial; elsewhere, enjoy it as a long-blooming annual for can't-miss color from early summer into fall.

The Kindest Cut

If summer's heat and humidity have gotten the best of your annual bloomers, don't give them up for lost. You can enjoy several more weeks of flowers if you treat 'em right, right now! Cut them

Grandma Putt's GREEN THUMB TIPS

Back when I was a boy, Grandma Putt often kept me busy by sending me out to pick the dead blooms out of her flower garden. She explained that snipping off spent blossoms kept the plants stronger, made them bloom better, and prevented them from making unwanted seedlings—and after years of doing this in my own yard, I know she was right! But we'd always make an exception for a few fast-growing annuals, like larkspur (*Consolida ambigua*), love-in-a-mist (*Nigella damascena*), and four-o'clocks (*Mirabilis jalapa*). If you let these drop their seeds, you'll have plenty of free filler flowers to plug up gaps in your beds and borders next summer.

back by about half, then dose them with a shot of Grandma Putt's super Summer Rejuvenating Tonic (below). They'll be back in bloom before you know it!

Don't Be Nervous About Mellies

Melampodium (*Melampodium paludosum*) may not have a catchy name, but hey—what really matters is how it grows, not what it's called. And once you see how this awesome annual can brighten up your summer gardens, you'll call it a real winner! The compact, 1-foot plants are covered with bright yellow, daisy-like blooms that keep coming from early summer until the first frost. In the Deep South, mellies are happiest growing in some shade; elsewhere, they bloom best in full sun. Heat? Hah! Drought? No sweat. These tough little plants put up with the toughest conditions you can throw at them—and they'll give you months of gorgeous color in return.

SUMMER REJUVENATING TONIC

Whenever Grandma Putt's carefully planned annual gardens started to look a little tired in late summer, she'd give 'em a good drink of this potent pick-me-up.

¼ cup of beer
1 tbsp. of corn syrup
1 tbsp. of baby shampoo
1 tbsp. of 15-30-15 fertilizer
1 gal. of water

Mix all of these ingredients, then slowly dribble the solution onto the soil around your annuals. Within two weeks, they'll be real comeback kids!

Butter 'Em Up!

"Floating flowers"? Yup, that's what my Grandma Putt used to call butterflies! These winged wonders add all kinds of extra beauty through the summer—especially if you entice them to your yard by planting the flowers they love. Butterflies feed on many different kinds of blossoms, but they're especially fond of blooms that are made up of tiny "florets," such as those of floss flower (*Ageratum houstonianum*), heliotrope (*Heliotropium arborescens*), Mexican sunflower (*Tithonia rotundifolia*), and

Brazilian vervain (*Verbena bonariensis*). Butterflies need moisture and minerals, too, so if you make 'em a mud puddle to drink from, they'll be happy to spend their summer brightening up your yard!

Spotlight on . . .

Sunflowers

Sum-, sum-, summertime means sun-, sun-, sunflowers! These annual classics don't just attract attention from everyone who sees them; they attract flocks of hungry birds, too. Best of all, they're a snap to grow! Simply sow the seeds outdoors after all danger of frost has passed, or start 'em indoors, in individual pots, four to six weeks before your last spring frost date.

Tough and trouble-free, annual sunflowers (*Helianthus annuus*) have no special problems, except that the tall annual kinds can blow over in strong winds. If that's a problem in your yard, check out some of the newer, more compact cultivars, such as 3-foot-tall 'Teddy Bear'. These beauties are much more in scale with smaller flower beds, and they're terrific for adding quick height to first-year perennial borders. There are even tiny sunflowers that are perfect for pots and planters: 'Big Smile' barely reaches 15 inches tall. Among the taller types, there's an amazing range of colors beyond the typical sunny yellow, like creamy white 'Italian White', maroon 'Moulin Rouge', and tangerine-orange 'Sonja'. Or try a mix of colors—you *won't* be disappointed!

A Bounty of Bulbs

When it comes to late-summer color, not too many folks think about bulbs—but they're really missing out. There are some spectacular surprises for this season, and a few bulb-related chores to do, too, so let's get busy!

Ask Jerry

Q: *My friend tells me there's a crocus that'll bloom right on a windowsill—without even being planted in soil! Is she just pullin' my leg?*

A: Nope—it's the truth! But we're not talking about an ordinary crocus here—we're talking about autumn crocus (*Colchicum autumnale*). This amazing bulb sends up leaves in the spring, then goes dormant again in early summer. The cupped, pink flowers appear separately, in early fall. The bulbs *can* bloom while still indoors, but they'll be weakened, so it's better to plant them as soon as you get them in late summer. Set 'em 3 inches deep in a sunny, well-drained spot, and you'll enjoy their awesome autumn blooms for years to come!

Go Bananas with Cannas

If you're looking to bring a touch of the tropics to late-summer beds and borders, you can't do better than cannas (*Canna* x *generalis*). These brassy beauties bear broad, 1- to 2-foot-long leaves that can be plain green, deep reddish purple, or showily striped with yellow or white. Through the summer, they send up strong stems that can be 2 to 6 feet tall, with huge, showy blooms in shades of red, yellow, pink, orange, or coral. Give these heat-lovers full sun and rich, moist soil, and you'll enjoy their lush and lovely beauty month after month. In Zone 7 and south, you can leave 'em in the ground through the winter; elsewhere, plan to dig up the roots after the tops are nipped by frost, and store 'em indoors in a cool place until next spring. Then plant 'em and look forward to their late-summer show!

Irises Made Easy

If you ordered bearded iris rhizomes earlier this year, they'll arrive in late summer as bare-root rhizomes with closely cropped leaves. These thick, fleshy rhizomes call for a slightly different planting strategy than most bulb relatives—you definitely *don't* want to cover them with soil! Here's how to get 'em growing:

Step 1: Dig a hole wide enough to hold each rhizome, then build up a ridge of soil in the center of the hole.

Step 2: Set the rhizome flat on top of the ridge, with the roots spread out to each side, so it is about even with the soil surface in the rest of the garden.

Step 3: Holding the rhizome in place with one hand, scoop soil back into each side of the ridge to cover the roots (but not the rhizome), and pack it down firmly.

Abracadabra!

Hey—where did those beautiful pink blooms come from all of a sudden? Is it magic? Nope—it's magic lily (*Lycoris squamigera*)! This astounding oddity sends up leaves in the spring just like a normal bulb, then dies back to the ground by midsummer. A few weeks later, it suddenly makes a return appearance, sending up 2-foot-tall stems topped with the prettiest pink trumpets you can imagine—and no leaves in sight. Magic lily is great for adding late-summer color to plain green groundcovers, and it's super for sprucing up foundation plantings and flower gardens, too. No matter where you grow it, you'll be delighted when it bursts into bloom each year without fail—I *guarantee* it!

ORGANIC BULB SNACK

No matter when you plant, your bulbs will thank you for a taste of this all-natural nutrient boost.

10 lbs. of compost
5 lbs. of bonemeal
1 lb. of Epsom salts

Mix the ingredients, then drop 1 tablespoon of the mixture into the bottom of each planting hole. Store any leftover Organic Bulb Snack in an airtight container to keep it nice and dry.

MIX & FIX

Folks call this time of year the "dog days," but that doesn't mean your yard has to *look* like a dog! You can still enjoy a boatload of blooms if you use my terrific tips for growing vigorous vines and glorious groundcovers.

Ask Jerry

Q: *I have a shady spot that could really use a groundcover, but I'm looking for something a little different from the usual ivy and vinca options. Can you give me any suggestions?*

A: You bet I can! I've got the perfect plant for you: dwarf Chinese astilbe (*Astilbe chinensis* 'Pumila'). It forms tidy carpets of ferny leaves no more than 4 inches tall, with the added attraction of 1-foot-tall, pink flower spikes in late summer. It's stunning for either moist or dry shade in Zones 4 to 8.

A Honey of a Vine

When you're looking for a long-blooming vine to brighten up your yard, honeysuckles (*Lonicera*) are a really sweet option! Here are three of the best:

Goldflame honeysuckle (*L. x heckrottii*): This evergreen or semi-evergreen vine grows 10 to 20 feet tall, with blue-green foliage. In late spring and summer, it bears lightly fragrant flowers that are pink outside and yellow inside. Zones 4 to 9.

Late Dutch honeysuckle (*L. periclymenum* 'Serotina'): Growing 15 to 20 feet tall, this beauty blooms from early summer up until frost, with crimson buds that open into fragrant, pink flowers that age to creamy yellow. Zones 5 to 9.

Trumpet honeysuckle (*L. sempervirens*): Evergreen or semi-evergreen leaves on 10- to 20-foot vines, plus showy scarlet, sweet-scented blooms from late spring into fall. 'John Clayton' is bright yellow. Zones 4 to 9.

Divine Vines and Groundcovers Late Summer: Let's Beat the Heat! SUMMER

221

A Match Made in Heaven

Looking to get a bit more bang for your buck from spring-flowering groundcovers? It's easy to do—just pair 'em up with some late-blooming bulbs, like autumn crocus (*Colchicum autumnale*), showy crocus (*Crocus speciosus*), and magic lily (*Lycoris squamigera*). The groundcover will mask the bulb leaves as they die back in early summer, then support the blooms as they appear in late summer and early fall. It's a no-fail way to get twice the excitement from the same amount of garden space!

Spotlight on...

Morning Glories

Glory, glory—it's the season for marvelous morning glories (*Ipomoea*)! These quick-climbing, twining vines positively thrive in hot weather, blooming their fool heads off with dozens of new flowers every single day.

Growing great-looking morning glories is practically a no-brainer; just give 'em lots of sun and well-drained soil, plus some netting or a trellis to climb on. And don't be in any hurry to sow their seeds in spring. For best results, wait to sow until all chance of frost is past and the soil is warm (about the time you set out tomato and pepper plants). Keep the soil moist, and the seeds'll sprout up in the blink of an eye!

Thanks to busy plant breeders, amazing new morning glories appear every year. Two of my current favorites are 'Mt. Fuji Mix' (*I. nil*), with multi-colored blooms over silver-splashed leaves, and the classic 'Heavenly Blue' (*I. tricolor*), with stunning sky blue blossoms. Once you've tried these for yourself, I encourage you to experiment with a few of the latest and greatest offerings each spring. You simply can't go wrong with these foolproof flowering vines!

Lush and lovely—that's all there is to say about late-summer container plant-ings! Well, maybe not *all* there is to say: I've also got some super secrets for filling those pots with knock-your-socks-off color, *and* for keeping them looking great during the dog days!

Fabulous Fountain Grass

Container gardens are more than just plants plunked into pots—they're a place to let your creativity shine! And there's no better way to create attention-grabbing containers than by mak-ing the most of exciting and unusual annuals and perennials. With that in mind, I've got just the gem for you: purple fountain grass (*Pennisetum setaceum* 'Rubrum'). This gorgeous grass is ideal for adding height to container groupings, with arching, maroon foliage and purplish pink, brushy "foxtails" atop 4-foot stems. Purple fountain grass is a perfect part-ner for both pastels (pink and white flowers are particularly pretty) and bright blooms (such as compact orange zin-nias or cherry red petunias).

POTTED PLANT PICNIC

Container plants need lots of ener-gy to stay chock-full of flowers, so whatever you do, don't skimp on the fertilizer! Here's a meal your potted plants are sure to appreciate.

2 tbsp. of brewed black coffee
2 tbsp. of whiskey
1 tsp. of fish emulsion
$\frac{1}{2}$ tsp. of unflavored gelatin
$\frac{1}{2}$ tsp. of baby shampoo
$\frac{1}{2}$ tsp. of ammonia
1 gal. of water

Mix all of the ingredients together and feed to each of your potted plants once a week.

Plan Ahead for the Big Chill

Even though winter seems a long way off right now, late

Glorious Container Gardens | Late Summer: Let's Beat the Heat!

223

summer's the right time to think about brightening those dull days with potted plants. I'm particularly partial to bringing herbs indoors, because they taste and smell just as good as they look. To enjoy your favorites all winter long, take some time during this season to pot them up; rosemary, tarragon, and thyme are three good candidates. Leave the potted herbs outdoors for the next month or so (don't forget to water them), then bring 'em indoors before Jack Frost comes a-callin'!

Light Up Your Nights

What could be more relaxing than spending summer evenings out on your deck or patio, chatting with friends or simply watching the stars? Enjoying beautiful blooms and pleasing perfumes at the same time! When you fill your container gardens with night-flowering plants, you can add a whole new level of excitement to outdoor entertaining. Here are a few best bets for the night shift:

Angels' trumpet (*Datura inoxia*): Six-inch-long, pure white, richly fragrant trumpets bloom from midsummer until frost.

Four-o'clocks (*Mirabilis jalapa*): These bushy plants have colorful, trumpet-shaped, fragrant blooms that open in late afternoon.

Night phlox (*Zaluzianskya capensis*): Clustered, maroon buds open at dusk into starry, white flowers with a delightful vanilla-sweet scent.

Grandma Putt's
GREEN THUMB TIPS

There's nothing like flower-filled hanging baskets to dress up your home, but these aerial containers take some special care to stay in top shape. They can dry out in a flash on hot summer days, and once that happens, it can be tough to get them thoroughly watered again. But my Grandma Putt had a great trick for perking up parched baskets: She'd just dunk them in an old washtub filled with water, and let 'em soak for a half-hour or so. A kiddie pool works just as well, if you have one—and it's large enough to let you soak several baskets at one time.

Jerry's Best Bets for...
The Dog Days

Ready to add a kaleidoscope of color to your late-summer landscape? Well, then, I've got just what you need: a rundown of some of the very best bloomers to brighten up this sultry season!

Trees

Chastetrees (*Vitex*)
Crape myrtles
 (*Lagerstroemia*)
Golden-rain tree
 (*Koelreuteria paniculata*)
Japanese pagoda tree
 (*Sophora japonica*)

Shrubs

Bluebeard
 (*Caryopteris* x
 clandonensis)
Butterfly bushes
 (*Buddleia*)
Glossy abelia
 (*Abelia* x *grandiflora*)
Oak-leaved hydrangea
 (*Hydrangea quercifolia*)
Plum-leaved azalea
 (*Rhododendron
 prunifolium*)
Rose-of-Sharon
 (*Hibiscus syriacus*)
Summersweet
 (*Clethra alnifolia*)

Perennials

August lily
 (*Hosta plantaginea*)
Balloon flower
 (*Platycodon grandiflorus*)
Bee balms
 (*Monarda*)
Black-eyed Susans
 (*Rudbeckia*)
Boltonia
 (*Boltonia asteroides*)
Bugbanes (*Cimicifuga*)
Catmints (*Nepeta*)
Common rose mallow
 (*Hibiscus moscheutos*)
Coreopsis (*Coreopsis*)
Daylilies (*Hemerocallis*)
Fall astilbe (*Astilbe
 taquetii* 'Superba')
False dragonhead
 (*Physostegia virginiana*)
False sunflower
 (*Heliopsis helianthoides*)
Flaxes (*Linum*)
Frikart's aster
 (*Aster* x *frikartii*)

Garden phlox
 (*Phlox paniculata*)
Gayfeathers (*Liatris*)
Hostas (*Hosta*)
Inula (*Inula helenium*)
Joe Pye weeds
 (*Eupatorium*)
Ligularias (*Ligularia*)
Pearly everlasting
 (*Anaphalis margaritacea*)

Perennial lobelias
 (*Lobelia*)
Perennial sunflowers
 (*Helianthus*)
Pincushion flowers
 (*Scabiosa*)
Russian sage
 (*Perovskia atriplicifolia*)
Sneezeweed
 (*Helenium autumnale*)
Stokes' aster
 (*Stokesia laevis*)
Turtleheads
 (*Chelone*)

Annuals

Angels' trumpets (*Datura*)
Begonias (*Begonia*)
Castor bean
    (*Ricinus communis*)
Celosias (*Celosia*)
Cosmos (*Cosmos*)
Floss flower (*Ageratum
    houstonianum*)
Flowering tobaccos
    (*Nicotiana*)
Four-o'clocks
    (*Mirabilis jalapa*)
Geraniums (*Pelargonium*)
Gloriosa daisy
    (*Rudbeckia hirta*)
Impatiens (*Impatiens*)
Lavatera
    (*Lavatera trimestris*)
Love-lies-bleeding
    (*Amaranthus caudatus*)
Marigolds (*Tagetes*)
Nasturtium
    (*Tropaeolum majus*)
Night phlox
    (*Zaluzianskya capensis*)
Petunias (*Petunia*)
Rose periwinkle
    (*Catharanthus roseus*)
Salvias (*Salvia*)

Spider flower
    (*Cleome hasslerana*)
Strawflower
    (*Bracteantha bracteata*)
Sunflower
    (*Helianthus annuus*)
Verbenas (*Verbena*)
Zinnias (*Zinnia*)

Bulbs

Cannas (*Canna*)
Crocosmias
    (*Crocosmia*)
Dahlias
    (*Dahlia*)
Gladiolus
    (*Gladiolus*)
Lilies (*Lilium*)
Naked ladies
    (*Amaryllis
    belladonna*)
Peacock orchid
    (*Acidanthera
    bicolor* var.
    byzantinus)
Peruvian daffodil
    (*Hymenocallis
    narcissiflora*)
Red spider lily
    (*Lycoris radiata*)

Vines

Clematis (*Clematis*)
Cup-and-saucer vine
    (*Cobaea scandens*)
Honeysuckles (*Lonicera*)
Moon vine (*Ipomoea alba*)
Morning glories (*Ipomoea*)
Trumpet vine
    (*Campsis radicans*)

Groundcovers

Dwarf Chinese astilbe
    (*Astilbe chinensis*
    'Pumila')
Lantanas (*Lantana*)
Liriopes (*Liriope*)
Plumbago
    (*Ceratostigma
    plumbaginoides*)
Two-row stonecrop
    (*Sedum spurium*)
'Vera Jameson' sedum
    (*Sedum* 'Vera Jameson')

PART 4

FALL IN LOVE WITH AUTUMN

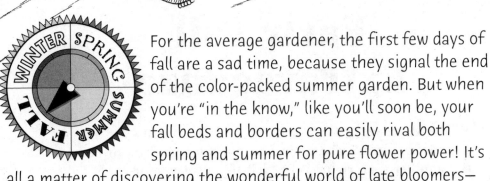

For the average gardener, the first few days of fall are a sad time, because they signal the end of the color-packed summer garden. But when you're "in the know," like you'll soon be, your fall beds and borders can easily rival both spring and summer for pure flower power! It's all a matter of discovering the wonderful world of late bloomers—asters, mums, and the like—plus knowing which annuals and perennials are generous enough to keep going well into the cooler season. It's a glorious time for bulbs, as well—not just in planting them for next spring, but for the beautiful autumn blooms of dahlias, fall-flowering crocuses, and many more. There's nothing like the warm soil, cooler temperatures, and more abundant rainfall this season has to offer to bring out the best in your plantings.

Of course, fall isn't *just* about flowers. With a collection of carefully chosen trees and shrubs, you'll enjoy a whole new level of landscape excitement: eye-popping fall color and fantastic fruits, too. So let's get started!

CHAPTER 10

Early Fall Extravaganza

The days are getting shorter, and the nights are getting cooler—so it's about time to put your gardens to bed for another year, right? WRONG! If you play your cards right, you can have a color-filled yard all the way through fall. So don't give up now—there are still plenty of exciting bloomers to choose from for this pleasin' season.

Early fall's a terrific time to be out in your yard, 'cause it's warm enough to be pleasant, but not as sultry as summertime. So take advantage of the wonderful weather this season to get caught up on your yard work—and to get ready for winter's return, too.

- Plant potted trees and shrubs in your yard
- Keep watering during dry spells
- Watch out for pest and disease problems
- Start preparing new beds and borders

- Plant new perennials, or transplant clumps
- Set out fall-flowering plants such as chrysanthemums, ornamental cabbages, and pansies
- Plant spring-flowering bulbs
- Divide summer-blooming perennials
- Gather flowers for fresh bouquets and for drying
- Protect annuals and container gardens from early frosts
- Move biennial and perennial seedlings into your gardens

As cold weather approaches, things start slowing down as far as trees and shrubs are concerned—but don't call it quits: There are still some late-season surprises left! Let's take a look at a few choice late bloomers, as well as some tips for keeping all your trees and shrubs in tip-top shape.

Celebrate Fall with Little Ben

Benjamin Franklin tree (*Franklinia alatamaha*) may be one of the last trees to bloom, but you know what they say—good things come to those who wait! While you're waiting, there's still plenty to enjoy in the form of glossy, deep green leaves on a slow-growing tree that only reaches 10 to 20 feet tall. In late summer and early fall, the flowers finally appear—large, saucer-shaped, lightly fragrant, pure white blooms with golden yellow centers. Then, as the blooms are finishing up, the leaves turn amazing shades of orange, purple, and red—WOW!

This little-known beauty thrives in acidic soil and partial shade (or a half day of sun) in Zones 5 to 8. Good drainage is a must, but the soil shouldn't dry out totally, either, so be prepared to water during dry spells. A generous layer of mulch will also help keep this trouble-free tree in all its glory.

Grandma Putt's

GREEN THUMB TIPS

Grandma Putt really loved her roses, so she made a habit of snipping off the faded flowers all through the summer to encourage more blooms. Come fall, though, she'd put her pruners away—and so should you! Letting your roses form "hips" (fruits) tells them to stop growing and get ready for cold weather, so they'll get through the winter better. The colorful hips look pretty, too—plus, they make tasty winter treats for hungry birds.

Pots Are Perfect for Fall Planting

Nowadays, most trees and shrubs are sold in containers—and that's good for both you *and* your plants! You see, potted trees and shrubs have a lot less transplant stress than bare-root or field-dug plants, so you can set 'em out just about any time (except the middle of summer and the dead of winter). But early fall's the ideal season to plant, because the cool air and warm soil encourage root growth, instead of leafy growth.

The Appeal of Abelia

Shrubs are super for giving your yard year-round interest, but most don't stay in bloom for more than a few weeks. Well, here's a winner that'll attract attention—and butterflies, too—from midsummer through midfall: glossy abelia (*Abelia* x *grandiflora*). This honeysuckle relative forms spreading clumps of shiny, deep green leaves that turn purplish red in fall, plus clusters of funnel-shaped, pink blooms over a period of two months or more. Try glossy abelia as a long-flowering, informal hedge, or tuck it into a foundation planting or flower bed; I *guarantee* you'll love it as much as I do!

Dependable Perennials

The season may be slowing down, but the perennials just keep on comin'! These late bloomers have had all summer to soak up the sun, so they tend to be on the tall side—and that makes 'em perfect for the back of a border, or as screens around a deck or patio. Here are my best bets for this season.

Awesome Autumn Anemones

Looking for showy flowers to liven up your fall garden? Then anemones are the answer! Chinese anemone (*Anemone hupehensis*), Japanese anemone (*A.* x *hybrida*), and grape-leaved anemone (*A. tomentosa*) all come in shades of pink and white and are hardy from Zones 4 to 8. They sprout up later than most perennials, so they're good buddies for spring-flowering bulbs; once the bulbs start dying back, the anemones quickly fill their space. Toward the end of the growing season, fall anemones make perfect partners for other late bloomers like glossy abelia (*Abelia* x *grandiflora*), asters, and monkshoods (*Aconitum*).

This Begonia Won't Be-goin' Just Yet

If you're lucky enough to have a shady site with moist soil, here's a real gem for you! Each year, hardy begonia (*Begonia grandis* subsp. *evansiana*) sends up 30-inch-tall clumps of wing-shaped leaves topped with arching clusters of pink or white flowers from late summer through fall. Unlike most begonias, which shrivel away at the slightest touch of frost, hardy begonia can survive the winters outdoors as far north as Zone 6—or even in Zone 5, if you give it a sheltered site and a thick blanket of leaves for the winter.

Ask Jerry

Q: *I'd really like my yard to be more colorful in fall, but most of the "autumn-flowering" perennials I plant end up blooming in late summer—several weeks before I want them to! Any advice?*

A: The answer's right at the tips of your fingers: Just give 'em a pinch! Next year, in early to midsummer, pinch or snip off the top few inches of each stem tip. That'll delay blooming by a few weeks, so you'll have beautiful blooms to enjoy just when you need 'em!

Be a Super Sale Shopper

Here's a super money-saving tip: Buy potted perennials at end-of-the-season sales, then bring them home and divide them *before* planting. By next spring, you'll have two, three, four, or even more new perennials for less than the normal price of one clump!

To Sedum Is to Love 'Em!

Now, here's what I like: a plant with a name that says it like it is! 'Autumn Joy' sedum is everything its name suggests—and lots more, too. This tough-as-nails perennial makes neat, 18- to 24-inch-tall clumps of fleshy, gray-green leaves that look great all through the growing season—enough to make it worth growing, even if it never bloomed! But it *does* bloom, too, with broccoli-like bud clusters opening into bright pink flowers from late summer into early fall, then turning brick red and lasting through winter. Give 'Autumn Joy' sedum full sun and well-drained soil, and believe you me—you'll find this problem-free perennial as much of a joy to grow as I do!

A Star for the Shade

Hey, shade gardeners—I've got a real beauty of a late bloomer for you! Black cohosh (*Cimicifuga racemosa*) forms shrubby clumps of foliage about 4 feet tall and wide, accented with 6- to 8-foot-tall, spiky, white, late-summer-to-early-fall flowers that glow like candles in even the shadiest site. This has got to be one of the ultimate no-maintenance perennials—pests and diseases are

CREATIVE COLOR COMBOS

Welcome fall with a blast of bright color, or try a pastel palette for a softer scene—either way, autumn-flowering perennials and partners give you lots of options! Here are a few combos to get you inspired:

✿ Bright yellow 'Fireworks' goldenrod (*Solidago rugosa*) and rosy pink purple coneflower (*Echinacea purpurea*) backed by flame grass (*Miscanthus* 'Purpurascens')

✿ Royal purple 'Purple Dome' New England aster (*Aster novae-angliae*) with the rich yellow fall foliage of Arkansas bluestar (*Amsonia hubrectii*)

✿ White boltonia (*Boltonia asteroides*) and pink 'September Charm' Chinese anemone (*Anemone hupehensis*) with glossy abelia (*Abelia* x *grandiflora*)

no problem, and even old clumps rarely need division. Just plant black cohosh in a shady site with humus-rich soil, then forget about it (except to enjoy those amazing fall flowers)!

Rejuvenating Your Perennials: It's as Easy as 1, 2, 3!

Early fall is prime time for dividing overgrown summer-flowering perennials, so don't let this season slip by! Give the clumps

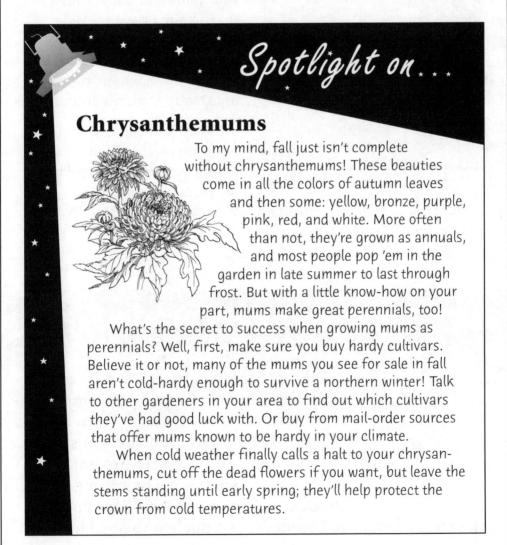

Spotlight on . . .

Chrysanthemums

To my mind, fall just isn't complete without chrysanthemums! These beauties come in all the colors of autumn leaves and then some: yellow, bronze, purple, pink, red, and white. More often than not, they're grown as annuals, and most people pop 'em in the garden in late summer to last through frost. But with a little know-how on your part, mums make great perennials, too!

What's the secret to success when growing mums as perennials? Well, first, make sure you buy hardy cultivars. Believe it or not, many of the mums you see for sale in fall aren't cold-hardy enough to survive a northern winter! Talk to other gardeners in your area to find out which cultivars they've had good luck with. Or buy from mail-order sources that offer mums known to be hardy in your climate.

When cold weather finally calls a halt to your chrysanthemums, cut off the dead flowers if you want, but leave the stems standing until early spring; they'll help protect the crown from cold temperatures.

you plan to divide a thorough watering about an hour or so ahead of time, then follow these three simple steps:

Step 1: Cut all the top growth of the clump back by half, then dig up the roots with a spade, spading fork, or shovel.

Step 2: Gently tease or break apart the clump with your hands, or cut it with a sharp knife or spade. Make sure each new piece has at least one bud or stem and some roots. Soak the pieces in my Dandy Division Tonic.

Step 3: If the new divisions are on the small side, pot them up. Otherwise, replant the pieces into compost-enriched soil, and give 'em a good drink to settle the soil. By next spring, they'll be rarin' to grow!

MIX & FIX

DANDY DIVISION TONIC

When dividing perennials, soak the best-rooted pieces in this tonic for about 10 minutes just before replanting them.

1 can of beer
¹/₄ cup of instant tea granules
2 tbsp. of dishwashing liquid
2 gal. of water

When you're finished planting, dribble any leftover tonic around the newly set divisions.

The Annual Parade

Fall is a fabulous time in the flower garden as your annuals celebrate the return of cooler weather with a blast of bright color. You still have several weeks to enjoy 'em, so what are you waiting for? Check out these terrific tips for making the most of early fall annuals, and put 'em to good use!

Make the Most of Cosmos

Here's an awesome summer-and-fall annual that no garden should be without: cosmos (*Cosmos bipinnatus*). This no-fail flower thrives in any sunny, well-drained spot, and its showstopping, pink or white daisy-like flowers are just beautiful in bouquets.

Most cosmos grow 3 to 5 feet tall: a perfect height for the middle or back of a bed or border. But cosmos often need support, so if staking isn't your thing, stick with dwarf cultivars, such as 2-foot-tall 'Sonata'. Snipping off the dead flowers regularly will keep your cosmos blooming like gang-busters right up until frost.

Keep Those Bloomers Comin'

Who says you have to say "sayonara" to your favorite flowers, just because Jack Frost is on his way? With a little planning on your part, you can enjoy beautiful blooms all winter long, too! Simply take a few minutes in early fall to collect cuttings of your favorite annual bloomers, then keep the small plants on a sunny windowsill or under lights through the winter. Come spring, you can take cuttings from *those* cuttings, and you'll have lots more of your favorites to fill your yard with color—for *free!* Begonias, geraniums (*Pelargonium*), and impatiens are three of the easiest annuals to root, but this super secret works great on a wide variety of annuals. So go ahead and experiment!

RHUBARB PEST REPELLENT TONIC

Are bad bugs getting the best of your fall flowers? Here's a potent plant tonic that'll say "Scram!" to just about any kind of pest you can think of.

3 medium-size rhubarb leaves
¼ cup of dishwashing liquid
1 gal. of water

Chop up the rhubarb leaves, put the pieces in the water, and bring it to a boil. Let the mixture cool, then strain it through cheesecloth to filter out the leaf bits. Mix in the dishwashing liquid. Apply this terrific tonic to your plants with a small hand-held sprayer, and kiss your pest problems good-bye!

MIX & FIX

Spotlight on...

Salvias

Sure, everyone knows the classic summer-garden star, scarlet sage (*Salvia splendens*)—but that's just the tip of the iceberg! Here are three top-notch choices that soak up the sun all summer, then put on a fabulous show in fall.

Anise sage (*S. guaranitica*): Upright, 4- to 6-foot-tall stems clad in deep green leaves and topped with spikes of deep blue blooms all through summer and fall.

Mexican bush sage (*S. leucantha*): Shrubby clumps of 4- to 5-foot-tall, fuzzy, white stems with narrow, sage-green leaves and spikes of reddish purple flowers in late summer and fall.

Pineapple sage (*S. elegans*): This hummingbird favorite bears bright red fall blooms on 3- to 5-foot-tall stems, with bright green leaves that smell just like fresh pineapple—yum, yum!

All three are perennials in Zones 7 to 10, but they make great annuals everywhere else—*and* they're easy to overwinter indoors as cuttings from year to year. Just give 'em full sun and well-drained soil, then stand back and wait for the end-of-the-season spectacular to start!

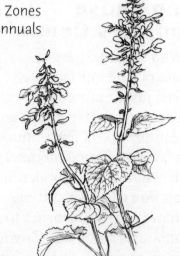

A Bounty of Bulbs

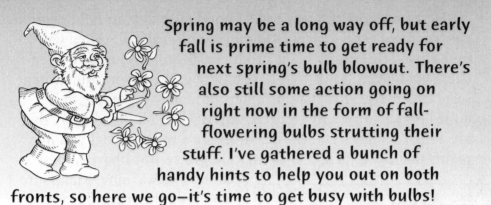

Spring may be a long way off, but early fall is prime time to get ready for next spring's bulb blowout. There's also still some action going on right now in the form of fall-flowering bulbs strutting their stuff. I've gathered a bunch of handy hints to help you out on both fronts, so here we go—it's time to get busy with bulbs!

Think Pink

Want to put your fall garden in the pink? I've got a pair of late-blooming bulbs that'll brighten up any year-round yard—*guaranteed!*

Autumn crocus (*Colchicum autumnale*): One-foot-tall, strap-like leaves appear in spring and die back in early summer. Goblet-shaped, 6-inch-tall, pink blooms appear separately in early fall.

Showy crocus (*Crocus speciosus*): Grass-like, 6-inch-tall leaves shoot up in spring, then the plant goes dormant by early summer. In early fall, rosy purple blooms grow to 6 inches tall.

Both of these bulbs thrive in sunny or lightly shaded sites with well-drained soil. They're perfect for planting among low-growing perennials, or for adding autumn color to green groundcovers.

Ask Jerry

Q: *I saw some bulbs for sale a few weeks ago labeled "saffron crocus." Is there any connection between these bulbs and the spice called saffron?*

A: There certainly is! If you had bought and planted those saffron crocus (*Crocus sativus*) bulbs back in late summer, you'd now have pretty purplish flowers in your garden. The small red parts (called stigmata) in the center of each bloom are the source of saffron—a costly spice used to add yellow coloring and delicate flavoring to foods. You can pick the red stigmata, dry them, add them to your favorite dishes—*and* save yourself a bundle in the process!

238

Do the Chive Jive

Here's a wonderful way to add good taste to your fall flower garden: grow garlic chives (*Allium tuberosum*)! Also called Chinese chives, this pretty plant produces spreading clumps of slender, bright green leaves that have a light garlic flavor—super in a salad or stir-fry. From late summer into fall, you'll enjoy the added bonus of sweetly scented, starry, white bloom clusters that are 12 to 18 inches tall. Garlic chives are a must-have if you like plants that are as practical as they are pretty. But I have to pass along one warning: Make sure you keep the spent flowers pinched off, because if you don't, you'll quickly find seedlings sprouting up where you don't want 'em!

MIX & FIX

ANIMAL PEST PREVENTION POTION

Tired of pesky critters digging up your newly planted bulbs? Send 'em scurryin' with a whiff of this potion.

1 cup of ammonia
¹/₂ cup of dishwashing liquid
¹/₂ cup of urine
¹/₄ cup of castor oil

Mix all of these ingredients in a 20 gallon hose-end sprayer, and thoroughly saturate all of the animal runs and burrows you can find.

Bulb Buyers Beware!

Bulb displays are starting to show up in garden centers right about now, so don't delay—buy your bulbs today! Shopping early will give you the best selection, and you'll get the plumpest, healthiest bulbs before they dry up from sitting out in the open. As you choose your bulbs, avoid any that have mushy, gray spots on them, or that feel much lighter than the others; unhealthy bulbs are no bargain at *any* price!

Party Hardy with Cyclamen

Listen up, fall gardeners—I've got a real beauty of a bulb for you! Hardy cyclamen (*Cyclamen hederifolium*) looks as delicate as a pampered houseplant, but it's actually tough enough to survive outdoors as far north as Zone 5. It turns the seasons upside down, sending up dainty pink or white blooms in early fall, *before* its heart-shaped, silver-and-green leaves appear in mid- to late fall. Then those lovely leaves stick around all winter and spring before disappearing in early summer. That's a total of 10 months of beauty from one little bulb!

Spotlight on...

Dahlias

When long-blooming bulbs are what you're after, dahlias are the answer! No matter where you live, dashing dahlias can fill your yard with fabulous flowers in practically every color of the rainbow, from midsummer all the way until frost. The blooms range from 1 inch to 1 foot across, and they come in lots of different forms: daisies, pom-poms, powder puffs, and more! And the plants themselves can be anywhere from 1 to 7 feet tall, so you can fit them into all parts of your yard: beds, borders, foundation plantings, and even pots.

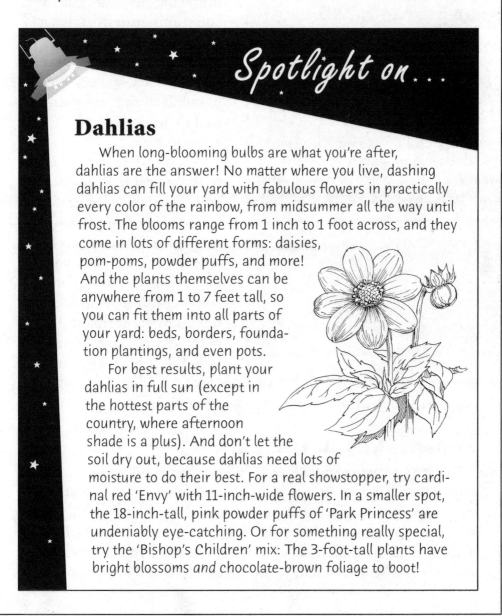

For best results, plant your dahlias in full sun (except in the hottest parts of the country, where afternoon shade is a plus). And don't let the soil dry out, because dahlias need lots of moisture to do their best. For a real showstopper, try cardinal red 'Envy' with 11-inch-wide flowers. In a smaller spot, the 18-inch-tall, pink powder puffs of 'Park Princess' are undeniably eye-catching. Or for something really special, try the 'Bishop's Children' mix: The 3-foot-tall plants have bright blossoms *and* chocolate-brown foliage to boot!

240

Keep This Spider Beside Ya

Red spider lily (*Lycoris radiata*) may be a late bloomer, but believe you me—it's worth waiting for! This classic Southern favorite sends up strap-like leaves that last from midfall to early summer, then the leafless flowering stems appear from late summer to frost. Each sturdy, 12- to 18-inch-tall stalk is topped with a cluster of bright red, spidery-looking blooms that are *guaranteed* to attract lots of attention!

If you'd like to add some of these beauties to your own yard (they can grow as far north as Zone 6, if you give 'em a sheltered site), take my advice: Place your order in early spring for shipment in June, as soon as the bulbs go dormant. Later-planted bulbs usually survive, but it may take them a few years to settle in. Why waste time waiting, when you can enjoy their beautiful blooms the same year?

MIX & FIX

ANTI-EARWIG ELIXIR

Earwigs—those long, dark, beetle-like pests with wicked-looking pincers on their nether end—love to chew holes in dahlias, mums, and other fall flowers. Chase 'em away with this simple spray.

1 whole head of garlic, chopped
2 drops of dishwashing liquid
Water

Place 1 cup of water and the garlic in a blender, and purée until smooth. Strain, then add the dishwashing liquid to the remaining liquid. Add enough water to make 1 quart of spray. Apply to earwig-infested flowers with a hand-held sprayer to send these pests a-packin'.

Snowflakes in the Fall

There's a spring snowflake (*Leucojum vernum*) and a summer snowflake (*L. aestivum*), so you just know there has to be an autumn snowflake (*L. autumnale*), too! It's smaller than its showier relatives—reaching just 4 inches or so, with pinkish white, bell-shaped blooms—but it's a winner if you're looking for something a little different to round out your fall flower options!

After a long, sultry summer, your vines are probably looking pretty lush right about now. But there's more to enjoy than just good-looking leaves—fall is prime time for many flowering vines, too! Many great groundcovers and grasses come into their own in this season, too, so let's check out some top-notch choices for your early fall yard.

Clematis Keep On Comin'

As far as perennial vines are concerned, it's tough to beat the clematis clan for color all through the growing season! Species like anemone clematis (*Clematis montana*) are among the first to bloom in spring, then the colorful, large-flowered hybrids take over for summer. Many of those hybrids keep on going right into fall—and some other species come into play, too, to end the season with a bang. Here are two more beautiful late bloomers that make clematis the vines of choice for smart year-round gardeners:

Sweet autumn clematis (*C. terniflora*): In early fall, the 30-foot vines of this climber are covered with thousands of small, white, fragrant flowers. This is a vigorous vine, so be sure to give it a sturdy support, and to prune the whole plant close to the ground in spring. Zones 4 to 9.

Ask Jerry

Q: Hey, Jer—I really want to grow moon vine (*Ipomoea alba*), but it starts to bloom so late in the season, I barely get a half-dozen flowers before the vines get nipped by frost. Any advice?

A: If you want blooms earlier in the season, you need to give your moonflowers a jump start in spring. Sow the seeds indoors in peat pots, two or three weeks before your last frost date, and move 'em out to the garden in early summer. They'll get growing in a jiffy and be in bloom before you know it!

242

'Radar Love' golden clematis (*C. tangutica*): Here's a clematis with a difference: bright *yellow* blooms! Sow the seeds indoors in early spring, and you'll enjoy several weeks of late-summer and fall blooms on 8-foot vines the very same year. Zones 5 to 9.

MIX & FIX

FLOWER FLEA FLUID

"Flower fleas" was Grandma Putt's name for leafhoppers. When she spotted any of these feisty little guys bugging her best bloomers, she'd let 'em have it with this powerful stuff.

1 cup of tobacco tea*
1 tbsp. of baby shampoo or dishwashing liquid
1 qt. of water

Mix all of these ingredients together in a hand-held sprayer, and apply liberally to leaves until they are dripping wet on both sides.

*Place half a handful of chewing tobacco in an old nylon stocking, and soak it in a gallon of hot water until the mixture is dark brown.

You'll Love This Voluptuous Vine!

With a name like "exotic love," it's easy to guess that there's nothing subtle about this eye-catching climber! Also called firecracker vine, *Mina lobata* explodes with sprays of tubular blooms in late summer and fall. Red buds open to orange flowers that age to yellow, with all three colors visible in every single cluster. WOW! Climbing to 15 feet, this easy annual vine makes a dynamite display in any sunny, well-drained site.

It's a Vine in Time for Tea

Looking for something *really* different? I've got the perfect climber for you: cup-and-saucer vine (*Cobaea scandens*). This speedy grower shoots up to 20 feet in height, with honey-scented, 3-inch, cupped blooms surrounded by a saucer-like, green ruff at the base. The flowers normally don't appear until early to midfall, but starting the seeds indoors in midspring gives them a head start for earlier blossoming. Purple flowers are

most common, but 'Key Lime' has pale green to cream blooms—ideal for evening gardens!

Get the "Lead" Out!

If you're as crazy about blue flowers as I am, you know how tough it is to find true-blue blooms. Well, for early fall, look no further than leadwort (*Ceratostigma plumbaginoides*)! This gorgeous groundcover creates 1-foot-tall carpets of deep green leaves that turn burgundy red in fall, plus cobalt blue blooms from late summer through fall. Give it a spot with well-drained soil and partial shade, and plan on mowing the whole patch to the ground in early spring to keep it tidy. In return, you'll get the most beautiful blue blooms you could ever wish for—at a time of year when you can really enjoy 'em!

Don't Be Leery of Liriope

Southern gardeners call it monkey grass; Northerners know it as lilyturf, or simply liriope. By any name, it's a tough-as-nails groundcover that's truly tough to beat! *Liriope muscari* grows in slow-spreading tufts, with slender, evergreen leaves all year and spikes of small, purple-blue blooms in late summer and fall. It's hardy in Zones 6 to 9. *L. spicata* is similar, but it's slightly hardier (Zones 5 to 9) and a much faster spreader. Both can grow in anything from full sun to full shade, tolerate tough, root-filled soil under mature shade trees, and laugh at heat and drought—everything you could ask of a year-round groundcover!

Grandma Putt's **GREEN THUMB TIPS**

Tired of people and pets wearing a path through your plants? When Grandma Putt and I planted new groundcovers, she made sure we left spaces for the well-worn paths our family and visitors already used. That's a great way to nip problems in the bud! But if a path appears *after* planting, do what Grandma did—go with the flow, and lay some stepping stones there to keep folks from compacting the soil and trampling your plants in the process!

A Classy Grassy Groundcover

Grasses aren't just for lawns anymore—they're also some of the greatest garden plants you can get your hands on! And no doubt about it: One of my most favorite groundcover choices from this group is fountain grass (*Pennisetum alopecuroides*). Hardy in Zones 5 to 9, this 2- to 3-foot-tall perennial looks fantastic planted in masses, filling sunny sites with tidy, long-lived mounds of arching, bright green leaves. Bushy, pinkish or cream-colored flower spikes appear in late summer and early fall, then turn tan and last until the end of fall. 'Moudry' is a showy selection with black flower spikes, but watch out for this one: It'll spread seeds all over your yard if you don't snip off *all* of the spent blooms!

MIX & FIX

DOG-BE-GONE

Digging dogs can destroy a good-looking groundcover patch quick as a wink. To keep Fido away from his favorite digging spots, liberally apply this mix to the soil.

**2 cloves of garlic
2 small onions
1 jalapeño pepper
1 tbsp. of cayenne pepper
1 tbsp. of Tabasco® sauce
1 tbsp. of chili powder
1 qt. of warm water**

Chop the garlic, onions, and jalapeño pepper finely, then combine with all of the remaining ingredients. Let the mix sit for 24 hours, then sprinkle it on any areas where dogs are a problem.

Sow Your Wild Oats

Sure, there are lots of gorgeous ornamental grasses for sunny sites—but what about you shade gardeners? Well, I've got a great grass for you, too: wild oats (*Chasmanthium latifolium*). This clump-former isn't all that eye-catching in spring or summer, but be patient; in fall, it sends up 2- to 3-foot-tall stems topped with flat, scaly "spikelets" that dangle from the slender flower stalks like so many unwary fish. The leaves and spikelets age to coppery brown as fall goes on, then stick around to grace your yard through most of the winter, too—nice!

Spotlight on...

Miscanthus

Searching for a special plant to accent a bed, border, or foundation planting with year-round interest? The ornamental grasses known as miscanthus are definitely worth a second look! These high-impact sun-lovers form fountain-like clumps of arching foliage that look great from early summer through most of the winter, plus feathery fall flower heads that are sure to attract attention for months on end.

The miscanthus you're most likely to find at your local garden center is Japanese silver grass (*Miscanthus sinensis*). It is generally hardy in Zones 5 to 9 and grows 4 to 6 feet tall. There are dozens of cultivars to choose from. 'Cosmopolitan' has green leaves with white edges, while 'Cabaret' has green edges and a white center stripe. Porcupine grass (*M. sinensis* 'Strictus') has yellow bands across its leaves; it is similar to zebra grass (*M. sinensis* 'Zebrinus'), but much less likely to need staking. While most miscanthus have good fall foliage color, flame grass (*M.* 'Purpurascens') is especially showy, changing from green to bright orange to deep purplish red before turning copper-colored through winter.

Jerry's Best Bets for...
Awesome Autumn Blooms

Don't think for a minute that fall's the time to start giving up on your garden! With a little help from the plants on this list, you can still enjoy a bounty of early autumn bloom for weeks to come.

Trees

Benjamin Franklin tree
(*Franklinia alatamaha*)
Crape myrtles
(*Lagerstroemia*)

Shrubs

Bluebeard (*Caryopteris* x *clandonensis*)
Bush clover (*Lespedeza thunbergii*)
Butterfly bushes (*Buddleia*)
Glossy abelia
(*Abelia* x *grandiflora*)
Japanese bush clover
(*Lespedeza japonica*)
Shrub bush clover
(*Lespedeza bicolor*)

Perennials

Asters (*Aster*)
'Autumn Joy' stonecrop
(*Sedum* 'Autumn Joy')

Azure monkshood
(*Aconitum carmichaelii*)
Azure sage (*Salvia azurea*)
Blanket flower
(*Gaillardia* x *grandiflora*)
Boltonia
(*Boltonia asteroides*)
Border phlox
(*Phlox paniculata*)
Bugbanes (*Cimicifuga*)
Chinese anemone
(*Anemone hupehensis*)
Chrysanthemums
(*Chrysanthemum*)
False sunflower
(*Heliopsis helianthoides*)
Gayfeathers (*Liatris*)
Goldenrods (*Solidago*)
'Goldsturm' black-eyed
Susan (*Rudbeckia fulgida* 'Goldsturm')
Grape-leaved anemone
(*Anemone tomentosa*)

Hardy ageratum
(*Eupatorium coelestinum*)
Hardy begonia
(*Begonia grandis* subsp. *evansiana*)
Japanese anemone
(*Anemone* x *hybrida*)
Joe Pye weed
(*Eupatorium fistulosum*)
Late-flowering hosta
(*Hosta tardiflora*)
Nippon daisy
(*Nipponanthemum nipponicum*)
Obedient plant
(*Physostegia virginiana*)
Pearly everlasting
(*Anaphalis cinnamomea*)
Rose mallows (*Hibiscus*)
Russian sage
(*Perovskia atriplicifolia*)
Shining coneflower
(*Rudbeckia nitida*)
Showy stonecrop
(*Sedum spectabile*)
Sneezeweed
(*Helenium autumnale*)
Stokes' aster
(*Stokesia laevis*)
Turtleheads (*Chelone*)
'Vera Jameson' sedum
(*Sedum* 'Vera Jameson')
Yellow corydalis
(*Corydalis lutea*)

Annuals

Angels' trumpets (*Datura*)
Begonias (*Begonia*)
Castor bean
    (*Ricinus communis*)
Celosias (*Celosia*)
Cosmos (*Cosmos*)
Floss flower (*Ageratum
    houstonianum*)
Flowering tobaccos
    (*Nicotiana*)
Four-o'clocks
    (*Mirabilis jalapa*)
Geraniums (*Pelargonium*)
Gloriosa daisy
    (*Rudbeckia hirta*)
Impatiens (*Impatiens*)
Lavatera (*Lavatera trimestris*)
Love-lies-bleeding
    (*Amaranthus caudatus*)
Marigolds (*Tagetes*)
Nasturtium
    (*Tropaeolum majus*)
Ornamental cabbage
    (*Brassica oleracea*)
Pansy (*Viola* x *wittrockiana*)
Petunias (*Petunia*)
Pot marigold
    (*Calendula officinalis*)
Rose periwinkle
    (*Catharanthus roseus*)
Salvias (*Salvia*)
Spider flower
    (*Cleome hasslerana*)

Strawflower
    (*Bracteantha bracteata*)
Sunflower
    (*Helianthus annuus*)
Sweet alyssum
    (*Lobularia maritima*)
Verbenas (*Verbena*)
Zinnias (*Zinnia*)

Bulbs

Autumn crocuses
    (*Colchicum*)
Autumn snowflake
    (*Leucojum autumnale*)
Curly chives (*Allium
    senescens* 'Glaucum')
Garlic chives
    (*Allium tuberosum*)
Guernsey lily
    (*Nerine bowdenii*)
Hardy cyclamen
    (*Cyclamen hederifolium*)
Prairie onion
    (*Allium stellatum*)
Red spider lily
    (*Lycoris radiata*)
Saffron crocus
    (*Crocus sativus*)
Showy crocus
    (*Crocus speciosus*)

Vines

Cup-and-saucer vine
    (*Cobaea scandens*)
Exotic love (*Mina lobata*)
Golden clematis
    (*Clematis tangutica*)
Hybrid clematis (*Clematis*)
Late Dutch honeysuckle
    (*Lonicera periclymenum*
    'Serotina')
Moon vine (*Ipomoea alba*)
Morning glories (*Ipomoea*)
Sweet autumn clematis
    (*Clematis terniflora*)

Groundcovers
and Grasses

Flame grass (*Miscanthus*
    'Purpurascens')
Fountain grass (*Pennisetum
    alopecuroides*)
Heather (*Calluna vulgaris*)
Japanese silver grass
    (*Miscanthus sinensis*)
'Karl Foerster' feather reed
    grass (*Calamagrostis* x
    acutiflora 'Karl Foerster')
Leadwort (*Ceratostigma
    plumbaginoides*)
Liriopes (*Liriope*)
Oriental fountain grass
    (*Pennisetum orientale*)
Pampas grass
    (*Cortaderia selloana*)
Purple moor grass
    (*Molinia caerulea*)
Ravenna grass
    (*Saccharum ravennae*)
Switch grass
    (*Panicum virgatum*)
Wild oats (*Chasmanthium
    latifolium*)

CHAPTER 11

A Celebration of Color—Midfall

Forget about ending the growing season with barely a whimper! When you put my favorite midfall tips and tricks to work, your yard will positively EXPLODE with spectacular color all the way through autumn.

While you're out enjoying the autumn splendor of your well-planned yard, remember that you must still attend to a few chores. Midfall's a great time to look back on the successes of this year, to get things ready for winter, and to plant bloomers for next year as well!

- Plant container-grown trees, shrubs, perennials, and vines
- Keep watering during dry spells
- Cut down perennials that are no longer blooming
- Divide or transplant over-grown perennials
- Jazz up fall beds and borders with cool-season annuals like pansies and ornamental cabbage
- Pull out tender annuals that have been nipped by frost
- Keep planting spring-flowering bulbs
- Fertilize plantings of established bulbs
- Dig tender summer bulbs, such as dahlias, for indoor storage
- Prepare new beds for planting next spring
- Keep an eye out for pest and disease problems
- Watch out for weeds, too!

The warm days and crisp nights of midfall are just the ticket for bringing out the best fall leaf colors in deciduous trees and shrubs. So don't miss out on Mother Nature's bounty: By choosing plants with fabulous autumn foliage, you can easily pack another month or more of eye-catching color into your year-round yard!

Presto, Change-O!

Whether they're wearing their spring and summer greens or their multi-colored autumn coats, trees and shrubs give our yards some mighty fine color. But do you remember from high school biology class why those leaves change color? No? Well, here's a quick refresher course to get you in the know.

The green color comes from chlorophyll, the sub-

Grandma Putt's GREEN THUMB TIPS

Long after her neighbors put their garden hoses away, my Grandma Putt would keep watering all the way through fall dry spells. Fall is prime time for good root growth, she told me, so keeping the soil moist is important for all plants. But it serves another purpose, too: making sure that evergreen trees and shrubs have plenty of water in their leaves before drying winter winds come along. Thanks to Grandma's fall watering secret, I've never yet lost one of my evergreens to winter damage—and you won't either!

stance that helps plants convert light, water, and carbon dioxide into food. As trees and shrubs prepare for winter dormancy, they stop producing chlorophyll, which lets other leaf colors come through. In other words, the bright golds, oranges, and reds were there in the leaves all the time; they were just masked by the green!

Go for the Gold

If you're thinking about adding a shade tree to your yard, this is the perfect season to get the job done! And when it comes down to just which tree it should be, you can't do better than my personal favorite: the ginkgo (*Ginkgo biloba*). This top-notch tree is a true beauty all year long, but its real claim to fame is its fall

Spotlight on . . .

Maples

When it comes to knock-your-socks-off fall color, maples (*Acer*) are among the best of the best. These terrific trees come in a wide range of shapes, sizes, and colors, so you're sure to find one that'll look just great in your yard. Here are three of my own favorites for year-round interest:

Coralbark maple (A. *palmatum* 'Sango-kaku'): Growing only 15 feet tall, this spectacular small tree offers light green spring and summer leaves, bright yellow fall color, and glowing red twigs for winter color. Zones 6 to 9.

Paperbark maple (A. *griseum*): A small to medium-sized tree (about 30 feet tall) with pale green spring leaves, bluish green summer foliage, bright red fall color, and cinnamon brown, peeling bark for winter interest. Zones 5 to 7.

Red maple (A. *rubrum*): A classic shade tree that grows up to 60 feet tall, with red flowers in spring, deep green summer leaves that turn bright red or orange in fall, and silvery gray bark in winter. Zones 3 to 9.

display, when the fan-shaped, bright green leaves turn a glowing golden yellow hue.

Great-looking ginkgos are tough as nails: They can adapt to a wide range of sunny sites in Zones 3 through 8, and pests and diseases are never a problem. Just make sure that you buy a *male* form, such as 'Autumn Gold' or 'Princeton Sentry', because the females produce stinky, messy fruits you can do without!

Don't Trash 'Em!

It never fails: Every fall, some folks insist on raking their leaves into trash bags and setting them out with the garbage. Talk about throwing money away! You see, fall leaves provide a bounty of top-notch organic matter for improving your soil, mulching your gardens, and more—all for *free*. So keep those bagged leaves in an out-of-the-way spot in your yard for later use, or create a temporary bin from flexible wire fencing to corral loose leaves until you're ready to use 'em. When your neighbors are blowing their hard-earned pay on bags of mulch and compost next spring, you'll have a handy supply right in your own backyard, ready to use!

SHRUB PEST PREVENTER

Fend off funky fungi and other wintertime nasties with this truly excellent elixir.

1 cup of baby shampoo
1 cup of antiseptic
**   mouthwash**
1 cup of tobacco tea*
1 cup of chamomile tea
Warm water

Mix the shampoo, mouthwash, and teas in a bucket, and then add 2 cups of it to a 20 gallon hose-end sprayer, filling the balance of the sprayer jar with warm water. Overspray your shrubs until they are dripping wet whenever the temperature is above 50°F.

*Place half a handful of chewing tobacco in an old nylon stocking, and soak it in a gallon of hot water until the mixture is dark brown.

The Sweet Smell of Success

Hey—where's that cotton-candy smell coming from? Has the circus come to town? Nope—it's courtesy of the katsura tree

(*Cercidiphyllum japonicum*)! This spectacular shade tree is a real beauty, with heart-shaped leaves that are purplish in spring, blue-green in summer, and glowing yellow in fall. While it's worth growing this gem just for these features, you get an added bonus: The fall leaves have a wonderful sweet, caramel-like scent that'll fill your yard with fragrance for several weeks each year. Mmmm!

Dependable Perennials

There's nothing like the cooler weather of fall to bring out the best in your late-blooming perennials! The colors are richer and the blooms themselves last longer, so there's still lots of beauty to go around. Let's take a look at a few fabulous late bloomers for this season, then check out some top-notch tips for making next year's garden even better!

Let's Get the Blues

The fluffy blue blooms of floss flower (*Ageratum houstonianum*) are a winner for long-lasting color, but you have to replant this annual each spring to enjoy its beautiful blossoms each summer and fall. Well, here's a way to have the fun *without* all the work: Just plant hardy ageratum (*Eupatorium coelestinum*) once instead!

This no-fail fall perennial thrives in partial shade and average to moist soil in Zones 6 to 10. It spreads by creeping roots, but don't worry: Dividing the clump every year or two will keep it from spreading out of bounds. To my mind, you simply can't have too much hardy ageratum because it's a top-notch cut flower, and it's a favorite with butterflies, too!

Sow Now for Spring

Lots of perennials are easy to start from spring-sown seeds—but what about those less-than-cooperative kinds? It turns out that some perennials (bulbs, too) need to chill out for a bit *before* warm weather gets 'em growing. It's easy to give them what they want: Simply sow the seeds now, then leave the pots outside for the winter. (If you have a cold frame, that's ideal; otherwise, set them in a basement window well or against the foundation of your house.) They'll go through the usual freezing and thawing cycles, then sprout up in spring when mild weather returns. Anemones, bleeding hearts (*Dicentra*), columbines (*Aquilegia*), lilies (*Lilium*), and primroses (*Primula*) are just a few of the bloomers that appreciate this special treatment.

Foliage Favorites for Fall

When you think of fall foliage color, trees and shrubs are the plants that come to mind—but don't forget about perennials, too! Some garden favorites that are prized for their pretty flowers also offer colorful fall leaves. Balloon flowers (*Platycodon grandiflorus*) and bluestars (*Amsonia*), for instance, turn a glowing golden hue, while bergenias and leadwort (*Ceratostigma plumbaginoides*) change from bright green to a rich red. Combine these beauties with late-blooming perennials, and your beds and borders will positively pop with color all through the fall!

Ask Jerry

Q: *I don't believe it—I just saw goldenrod (Solidago) for sale at my local garden center! Why would anyone want to plant this pesky weed in their yard?*

A: Because it's actually a great garden plant, that's why! Sure, goldenrods have a bad reputation for causing hay fever, but that couldn't be further from the truth; the real culprit is the green-flowered ragweed (*Ambrosia*), which blooms at the same time. Smart gardeners know it's safe to plant goldenrods for fall garden color, so go ahead and give any of the new cultivars a try—18-inch 'Golden Fleece' and 4-foot 'Fireworks' are two of the best.

254

Toad-ally Awesome

Now, here's a perennial you don't see in everyone's yard—and maybe you should! Toad lilies (*Tricyrtis*) don't have the most appealing name, but they're definitely appealing for jazzing up

Spotlight on...

Asters

A year-round flower garden simply isn't complete without a few asters for fall color! These classic late bloomers are bedecked with dozens or even hundreds of daisy-like blooms in white or shades of blue, purple, or pink, on bushy plants that are anywhere from 1 to 5 feet tall.

The two most common fall bloomers are New York aster (*Aster novi-belgii*) and New England aster (*A. novae-angliae*), but there are lots of great hybrids and selections, too. 'Alma Potschke' is a real stunner, with large, bright pink blooms, while 'Purple Dome' is a compact variety with rich purple-blue flowers. These asters are hardy in Zones 4 to 9 and appreciate full sun and moist, but well-drained soil. To keep them from flopping (and to get lots more blooms, as well), cut the plants back by one-third in late spring or early summer.

Love asters, but have a shady garden? There are some great choices for you, too! Blue wood aster (*A. cordifolius*) and white wood aster (*A. divaricatus*)—both hardy in Zones 4 to 8—are two late-blooming wildflowers that'll do a truly bang-up job of brightening your fall yard!

shady sites. These clump-formers send up graceful, arching stems in spring, clad in rich green leaves that are sometimes marked with curious brown spots. In late summer and fall, upward-facing white, purple, or yellow flowers appear along the upper part of each stem, creating a great show at a time when not much else is happening. The intricately spotted blooms are worth a close look, so grow toad lilies in humus-rich soil next to a path or bench; that way, you can admire them up close on your fall garden strolls.

Time to Make Your Bed

Now that summer's sultry heat is just a memory, it's time to get busy preparing new areas for next year's fabulous flower gardens. Just follow these simple steps now, and next spring, you'll have a bed of loose, fluffy soil that *all* of your bloomers will love!

Step 1: Sprinkle flour or lime to mark the outline of your new flower garden, then cut around that outline with a sharp spade to create a crisp edge.

Step 2: Make parallel cuts, 6 to 8 inches apart, across the entire bed. When you're done, your plot will look kind of like a piece of lined notebook paper.

Step 3: Start turning over the soil, work-

MIX & FIX

BEDTIME SNACK

Fall is a fine time to break new ground, because the soil has all winter to digest slow-acting amendments. This rich mixture works miracles in heavy clay!

25 lbs. of gypsum
10 lbs. of natural organic garden food (either 4-12-4 or 5-10-5)
5 lbs. of bonemeal
2 lbs. of Epsom salts

Mix all of these ingredients together, then apply them to every 100 sq. ft. of soil with your hand-held broadcast spreader. Work them into the soil and cover with a thick blanket of leaves, straw, or other organic mulch.

ing along one strip at a time. Keep going until you're tired, then take a break for the day. You've earned a rest!

Step 4: When you've dug up the whole plot, chop up any surface clumps, then spread a 2-inch-thick layer of chopped leaves or compost over the whole area. Come spring, the soil will be in perfect shape for planting!

Ask Jerry

Q: *I could have sworn I saw a shasta daisy (Leucanthemum x superbum) in full bloom as I was driving through town today—but how can that be? I thought shastas only flowered in the summertime!*

A: What you saw is actually a shasta relative known as nippon daisy (*Nipponanthemum nipponicum*). This trouble-free perennial has the same yellow-centered, white-petaled blooms, but it blooms a whole lot later—usually mid- to late fall. What a great way to extend the daisy season!

The Annual Parade

Jack Frost is about ready to make his return appearance, but plenty is going on where your annual flowers are concerned! There's still time to plant some super-hardy annuals for color this year, and some chores need to be done to help get things ready for spring. So c'mon—let's get goin'!

Cabbage for Color? You Bet!

When it comes to cool-weather color for your flower gardens, it's tough to beat ornamental cabbages and kales (*Brassica oleracea*). But it's not flowers you'll grow them for: It's their colorful foliage! Cabbages have broad leaves with wavy edges, while kales have narrower, jagged-edged leaves; on both, the blue-green background is heavily splashed with white, purple, or pink. You'll see them for sale starting in late summer, in small cell packs or in larger individual pots. Small plants are fine if you get 'em in the ground right away, but in most cases, you're better off buying a few full-size plants as you find room for them. That way, you'll get instant results—and you'll be *guaranteed* a great show all fall!

S.O.S.— Save Our Seeds

Before you give up on this year's garden, why not save some of your best bloomers for next year? By this time, most annuals have lots of seeds that are ripe for the plucking. To gather them, simply tap or shake them into paper envelopes (a separate one for each different kind of seed, please), label them, then set them in a dry place. Come spring, you'll have lots of seeds to sow, without having to dig into the piggy bank!

Grandma Putt's GREEN THUMB TIPS

My Grandma Putt liked to enjoy her annuals as long as possible, so we'd usually wait until *after* a hard frost to pull out the dead annuals and toss them onto the compost pile. But she always made two exceptions: She'd insist that we clean up the impatiens and begonias *before* frost. I found out why when I neglected her advice in my own garden: Once nipped by frost, these juicy-stemmed plants turn into slimy mush that's no fun to handle!

Plan Ahead for a Spring Fling

Want to get a jump on your spring garden? Then sow seeds of hardy annuals now! Once you get this year's frost-nipped annuals cleaned up, simply scatter seeds over the empty spaces and rake them lightly into the soil. They'll sprout up quicker than even the earliest spring-sown seeds—you'll be *amazed* at the results! Great candidates for fall sowing include larkspur (*Consolida ajacis*), spider flower (*Cleome hassleriana*), and sweet alyssum (*Lobularia maritima*), to name just a few; feel free to try others, too.

Ask Jerry

Q: *Years ago, we could only find pansies for sale in spring, but now I notice that many places are selling them in fall, too. Are these different from regular spring pansies?*

A: The answer is: yes and no! Yes, these "winter pansies" are different from spring-planted pansies. They'll take as much sun as you can give 'em, and they'll bloom all through the cold season, providing a bunch of color for months on end. The flowers of winter pansies are a little smaller than those of their spring cousins, but otherwise, they have the same cheerful faces—just what you need to get through a long, dull winter!

A Bounty of Bulbs

Bulbs in fall? You bet! If you want a great show next spring, now's the time to get new bulbs in the ground. It's also the season for digging up tender bulbs for indoor storage over the winter. There are even a few bulbs coming into bloom just now, too—so let's take a look at some of my favorite tips for these darling Dutch dandies!

What's in a Name?

Now here's a pretty little bulb with a bit of an identity crisis! It's called winter daffodil (*Sternbergia lutea*), but it doesn't bloom in winter, like the name suggests, or even in spring, like you'd expect from a normal daffodil. Instead, it sends up its bright yellow blooms in fall. And no—they don't look like daffodils: They're more like crocuses! Regardless of what you call this little-known bulb, it's a real winner for late-season color in any yard. Just keep in mind that the secret to success with winter daffodils is a site with excellent drainage—the bulbs can't stand soggy soil! Other than that, just let 'em be, and enjoy those bright blooms each fall without fail.

Glad to Keep Ya

If you love the big, beautiful blooms of common glads (*Gladiolus* x *hortulanus*) as much as I do, you're sure to have lots of 'em in your garden. And if it's the first time you've grown them, you probably have lots of questions about keeping 'em, too! While they're commonly known as tender bulbs, they're actually able to survive winter temperatures as low as 0°F, as long as they're protected with a 3- to 6-inch layer of mulch. But to be on the safe side, most folks dig up their glads whenever the foliage begins to turn yellow, or when it has been killed by frost. Leave the tops attached until they become brittle, then gently break them off, along with the loose scales and the withered corms from the preceding year. Spread out the plump corms in shallow boxes or paper grocery bags, and keep them in a dry place between 40° and 50°F until spring.

BULB BREAKFAST

Don't spend a fortune buying special bagged fertilizer for your bulbs! Just whip up a batch of this marvelous mix.

10 lbs. of compost
5 lbs. of bonemeal
2 lbs. of bloodmeal
1 lb. of Epsom salts

Blend all of the ingredients together in a wheelbarrow. Before setting out your bulbs, work this hearty breakfast into every 100 sq. ft. of soil in your bulb beds and borders. Or drop 1 tablespoon of this mixture into the bottom of each planting hole. Store leftover Bulb Breakfast in an airtight container to keep it nice and dry.

TLC for Tender Bulbs

Glads aren't the only bulbs that you should think about taking indoors for the winter—there are several other tender bulbs that need a little special attention this time of year. Here's the scoop on four more bulbs that appreciate coming in from the cold, plus some tips for keeping 'em comfortable:

Caladiums: Cut off the frost-nipped tops, then dig up the tubers, and place them in a dry area for a week or two. Store them in dry sand, vermiculite, or peat moss at 45° to 50°F.

Cannas: Dig up the clumps after light frost has blackened the leaves, and cut the tops back to 6 inches. Set the clumps in boxes of barely damp vermiculite or peat moss. Store them in a dry place at 40° to 50°F.

MIX & FIX

BULB CLEANING TONIC

When you remove your bulbs, corms, and tubers from the ground in fall, wash them with this tonic.

2 tbsp. of baby shampoo
1 tsp. of hydrogen peroxide
1 qt. of warm water

Mix these ingredients in a bucket, and give your bulbs a bath. Just be sure to let them dry thoroughly before you put them away for the winter—otherwise, they'll rot.

Dahlias: Once frost has darkened the leaves, cut the stems close to the soil level, and dig up the clumps. Let them sit in a dry, shady spot for a day or two, then place the tubers upside down in barely moist sand or vermiculite at 40° to 50°F.

Tuberous begonias: Lift the plants *before* frost strikes, keeping some soil around the bulbs, and set them in a dry spot indoors. When the foliage wilts, cut it off, then store the bulbs in dry sand at about 50°F.

Keep 'Em High and Dry

Fall is prime time for bulb planting, so what are you waiting for? While you're deciding where to set out new bulbs, remember this rule of thumb: A sunny, well-drained site is always your best bet. Bulbs will rot in soggy soil, so avoid planting them in areas of your yard that are prone to flooding, like at the bottom of a slope, or in a low spot.

Top-Notch Troweling

Nowadays, you can walk into any garden center and find an amazing array of bulb-planting tools to choose from. Well, I've tried 'em all, and believe you me: I've never found one that can beat a regular old garden trowel! You'll feel the same, once I fill you in on a little secret Grandma Putt taught me. Instead of holding your trowel like a spoon, grab the handle so the inner curve of the blade faces you, pointing downward. Then stab straight into the soil like you're using an ice pick. Pull back on the handle to open a pocket in the soil, tuck in a bulb, remove the trowel, and pat the soil down. Grandma could plant a whole lot of bulbs pretty darn quick with this trick—and so can you!

Ask Jerry

Q: *Hey, Jerry—any tips for figuring out which end is up when planting bulbs? Or doesn't it matter?*

A: With some bulbs, it's anyone's guess, but for most, there's a definite difference! The top of the bulb comes to a point, while at the base, there's usually some sign of roots, or the flat plate that the roots grow out of. Setting a bulb upside down won't kill it, but the new shoot'll have to put more energy into righting itself, and that can weaken the bulb.

Hole-y Cow—What a Great Idea!

Have more than a handful of bulbs to plant? Instead of digging dozens of individual holes, things will go a whole lot quicker if you dig one larger hole that can hold several bulbs. Simply use a trowel or spade to dig out the planting area to the proper depth, then place the bulbs in neat, evenly spaced patterns, and replace the soil. (*Hint:* If you place the soil you dig out onto a sheet of plastic, it'll be easy to dump the dirt back in the hole when it comes time for refilling!)

DEEP THOUGHTS

Not sure how low to go with your fall-planted bulbs? Check the chart below for all the answers!

Bulb	Recommended Depth
Checkered lily (*Fritillaria meleagris*)	4–5"
Crocuses (*Crocus*)	3–4"
Crown imperial (*Fritillaria imperialis*)	6–8"
Daffodils (*Narcissus*)	5–7"
Drumstick allium (*Allium sphaerocephalon*)	4–5"
Dutch hyacinth (*Hyacinthus orientalis*)	4–6"
Dutch iris (*Iris* Dutch Hybrids)	4–6"
Giant onion (*Allium giganteum*)	7–8"
Glory-of-the-snow (*Chionodoxa luciliae*)	3–4"
Grape hyacinths (*Muscari*)	3–4"
Grecian windflower (*Anemone blanda*)	3–4"
Lilies (*Lilium*)	3 times the diameter of the bulb
Siberian squill (*Scilla siberica*)	3"
Snowdrop (*Galanthus nivalis*)	3–4"
Striped squill (*Puschkinia scilloides*)	3"
Summer snowflake (*Leucojum aestivum*)	4–5"
Tulips (*Tulipa*)	6–8"
Wood hyacinth (*Hyacinthoides hispanica*)	3"

Layering's the Answer

Psst! Want to learn the secret to getting two—or even three times—the blooms in the same amount of space? You won't believe how easy it is—*if* you use my fantastic layering trick! All you do is dig one hole about 8 inches deep, then plant several layers of bulbs in the same spot. Here's how:

Step 1: Set the bulbs of the latest bloomers you've chosen (usually late tulips or lilies) in the bottom of the hole.

Step 2: Replace enough soil to barely cover the tips of those bulbs, then set in the next layer (early and midseason tulips are a good choice, and so are daffodils).

Step 3: Repeat the process of adding more soil, then setting in the top layer of smaller bulbs (perhaps a mix of snow crocuses for extra-early color and squills for a little later color).

Step 4: Finish with a mulch of leaves, shredded bark, or wood chips, plus a scattering of moth crystals over the top to help keep critters away.

Bulbs by the Bunch

The biggest mistake most folks make when planting bulbs? Scattering them all over the place! Come spring, the result is easy to see: sparse dots of color that really don't amount to much. Trust me—whether you're planting 20 bulbs or 200, you'll always

---

BULB BATH

To keep your bulbs bug-free, treat them to a nice warm bath before putting them into their planting bed.

2 tsp. of baby shampoo
1 tsp. of antiseptic mouthwash
1/4 tsp. of instant tea granules
2 gal. of warm water

Mix all of the ingredients in a bucket, then carefully place your bulbs into the mixture. Stir gently, then remove the bulbs one at a time and plant them. When you're done, don't throw the bath water out with the babies. Your trees, shrubs, and evergreens would love a little taste, so don't let it go to waste.

MIX & FIX

get the biggest bang for your gardening buck by growing 'em in groups. A half-dozen bulbs is a bare minimum for each group, but you know what they say: the more, the merrier!

Bulb Buddies for Shrubs

Running out of room in your beds and borders for bulbs? Never fear—spring-blooming bulbs are super for sprucing up the space around the base of mature shrubs where the grass tends to be sparse and scrawny. They'll get all the sun they need in spring, then go dormant by the time the shrubs leaf out for summer.

Vamoose, Varmints!

Hey—what's going on? You carefully planted a bunch of bulbs yesterday, and today, they're scattered all over your yard! Don't blame your dog or the kids down the street—squirrels are probably the culprits.

It's not the bulbs themselves that these pesky critters are after; it's the loose, fluffy soil that seems to draw them like a magnet.

To keep squirrels from upending your bulbs, lay chicken wire over the area immediately after planting, and cover it with mulch. Remove the wire anytime the following year; squirrels don't seem to bother established bulbs.

Forcing's the Issue

When autumn leaves are falling, it's time to start thinking about some treats for the dull days of winter. Buy a few extra

MIX & FIX

GOPHER-GO TONIC

Having problems with gophers getting after your bulbs? I've had amazing results with this tonic, and so have others who've tried it!

4 tbsp. of castor oil
4 tbsp. of dishwashing liquid
4 tbsp. of urine
Warm water

Combine the castor oil, dishwashing liquid, and urine in ½ cup of warm water, then stir the mix into 2 gallons of warm water. Pour it over any gopher-infested areas.

spring-flowering bulbs, and follow my simple pointers for tricking them into blooming several months early—a technique called forcing. Here's how:

Step 1: Place a piece of screening over drain holes in a clay or plastic pot before adding soil. Half-fill the pot with good-quality houseplant potting soil, then gently place the bulbs on top of the soil, leaving just $1/2$ inch or so between them.

Step 2: Add more potting soil, until just the tips of the bulbs are visible. Drench the soil thoroughly after planting to settle the bulbs and soil.

Step 3: I like to bury my prepared bulb pots 6 to 8 inches deep in my garden and mark the spot with bamboo stakes. Some of my friends prefer to park their pots in the garage or an unheated porch. If you do that, make sure the pots stay dark and damp, and keep the temperature between 40° and 50°F.

Ask Jerry

Q: *I know you say to buy bulbs as early as possible, but it seems I never get around to planting them until late fall. Is it okay to keep 'em laying around until I'm ready?*

A: Yep—it's always best to buy 'em early, and then get 'em in the ground right away. But if that's not convenient, it's fine to store 'em in a cool place (50° to 60°F) until you have time to plant.

Step 4: After 10 weeks, it's time to dig up or bring in your bulbs. Put the pots in your basement or in a dimly lit room that's cooler than 65°F.

Step 5: When the foliage is about 3 inches tall, place the plants in direct sunlight, and keep them moist. As soon as the blossoms appear, take the plants out of direct sunlight so they will last longer. Keep them in a cool place; turning back the thermostat at night suits forced bulbs just fine. With proper care, the flowers should last 7 to 10 days.

Divine Vines and Groundcovers

Most folks don't think much about vines and groundcovers for fall, and that's a darn shame. Take my advice and make the most of these awesome autumn beauties in your year-round yard—you'll be glad you did! Here are some of my very best tips to help you on your way.

Jeepers, Creeper!

If you'd like to deck your walls with fabulous fall color, look no further than Virginia creeper (*Parthenocissus quinquefolia*)! This vigorous native vine is a snap to grow in shade or sun, and it looks great all through the growing season. The rich green, five-fingered leaves are perfect for providing summer shade over an arbor, and they're great for dressing up wooden fences and walls, too. And in fall, you'll get a fantastic display of color: usually bright red in full-sun sites and a mix of pastel yellow, orange, and pink in shady sites.

Be Careful with Clingers

Vines are tailor-made for dressing up dull walls, but I should pass along one warning: It's never a good idea to

MIX & FIX

WINTERIZING TONIC

To head off trouble next spring, zap cutworms and other bad bugs with this tonic.

1 cup of Murphy's Oil Soap®
1 cup of tobacco tea*
1 cup of antiseptic mouthwash
Warm water

Mix the Murphy's Oil Soap®, tobacco tea, and mouthwash in a 20 gallon hose-end sprayer, filling the balance with warm water. Saturate your lawn and garden, and they'll be rarin' to grow come spring!

*Place half a handful of chewing tobacco in an old nylon stocking, and soak it in a gallon of hot water until the mixture is dark brown.

let English ivy (*Hedera helix*), Boston ivy (*Parthenocissus tricuspidata*), or other clinging vines climb directly on house walls. Their clinging roots can cause pitting on aluminum siding, and they'll hang on tightly to *any* surface if you try to remove them. Sure, you can pull or cut down the vines themselves, but you'll be left with thousands of tiny "holdfasts" stuck to the siding, and it's almost impossible to get rid of them!

Spotlight on . . .

Switch Grass

Are you new to the world of ornamental grasses? Or are you looking for an out-of-the-ordinary variety to add multi-season interest to your yard? Either way, I've got the perfect plant for you: switch grass (*Panicum virgatum*)!

This top-notch native grass can spread by creeping roots, but normally stays in distinct clumps, so you don't need to worry about it taking over your yard. Switch grass is mighty adaptable, too: It grows in sun or in light shade, and it can take just about any soil, from dry to wet, in Zones 4 through 9. The upright leaves are typically green or gray-green, but some special cultivars come in other colors: 'Heavy Metal', 'Dallas Blues', and 'Cloud Nine' have beautiful powder-blue foliage, while 'Shenandoah' has reddish purple leaf tips. All switch grasses have fantastic fall color, too— usually yellow, but red, orange, and purple are also possible. The 3- to 6-foot-tall plants look equally good planted alone as accents, combined with perennials in borders, or grown in groups as large-scale groundcovers. In fact, I can't imagine a *bad* way to use 'em!

Jerry's Best Bets for...
Fantastic Fall Color

When it comes to filling your yard with year-round color, flowers aren't the only game in town—look to the leaves, too! Including plants with colorful fall foliage is a sure way to create a landscape that looks as spectacular in autumn as it does in spring and summer.

Trees (Red or Burgundy)

Amur maple
(*Acer tataricum* subsp. *ginnala*)
Ashes (*Fraxinus*)
Benjamin Franklin tree
(*Franklinia alatamaha*)
Bradford pear
(*Pyrus calleryana*)
Chinese pistache
(*Pistacia chinensis*)
Chinese tallow tree
(*Sapium sebiferum*)
Crape myrtles
(*Lagerstroemia*)
Flowering dogwood
(*Cornus florida*)
Full-moon maple
(*Acer japonicum*)
Japanese maple
(*Acer palmatum*)
Kousa dogwood
(*Cornus kousa*)

Northern red oak
(*Quercus rubra*)
Red maple (*Acer rubrum*)
Scarlet oak
(*Quercus coccinea*)
Serviceberries (*Amelanchier*)
Smoke bush
(*Cotinus coggygria*)
Sour gum (*Nyssa sylvatica*)
Sourwood
(*Oxydendrum arboreum*)
Sweet gum
(*Liquidambar styraciflua*)

Trees (Yellow, Gold, or Orange)

Birches (*Betula*)
Chinese pistache
(*Pistacia chinensis*)
Chinese tallow tree
(*Sapium sebiferum*)
Fringe trees (*Chionanthus*)
Gingko (*Ginkgo biloba*)
Japanese flowering cherry
(*Prunus serrulata*)
Japanese zelkova
(*Zelkova serrata*)
Katsura tree
(*Cercidiphyllum japonicum*)
Korean mountain ash
(*Sorbus alnifolia*)

Redbuds (*Cercis*)
Sargent cherry
(*Prunus sargentii*)
Snakebark maple
(*Acer capillipes*)
Striped-bark maple
(*Acer pensylvanicum*)
Sugar maple
(*Acer saccharum*)
Tulip tree
(*Liriodendron tulipifera*)
Witch hazels (*Hamamelis*)

Shrubs (Red or Burgundy)

American cranberry bush
(*Viburnum trilobum*)
Barberries (*Berberis*)
Burning bush
(*Euonymus alatus*)
Chokeberries (*Aronia*)
Cotoneasters
(*Cotoneaster*)

Doublefile viburnum
(*Viburnum plicatum* var.
tomentosum)
Fothergillas (*Fothergilla*)
Highbush blueberry
(*Vaccinium
corymbosum*)
Koreanspice viburnum
(*Viburnum carlesii*)
Linden viburnum
(*Viburnum dilatatum*)
Oak-leaved hydrangea
(*Hydrangea quercifolia*)
Prairie rose (*Rosa setigera*)
Red-osier dogwood
(*Cornus stolonifera*)
Royal azalea
(*Rhododendron s
chlippenbachii*)
Staghorn sumac
(*Rhus typhina*)
Sweet azalea
(*Rhododendron
arborescens*)
Tea viburnum
(*Viburnum setigerum*)
Virginia sweetspire
(*Itea virginica*)

Shrubs
(Yellow, Gold,
or Orange)

Beautyberries (*Callicarpa*)
Fothergillas (*Fothergilla*)
Japanese kerria
(*Kerria japonica*)

Korean rhododendron
(*Rhododendron
mucronulatum*)
Red-vein enkianthus
(*Enkianthus
campanulatus*)
Rugosa rose (*Rosa rugosa*)
Spireas (*Spiraea*)
Summersweet
(*Clethra alnifolia*)
Swamp azalea
(*Rhododendron
viscosum*)
Virginia rose
(*Rosa virginiana*)
Winterberry
(*Ilex verticillata*)

Perennials, Vines,
and Groundcovers
(All Colors)

Balloon flower
(*Platycodon
grandiflorus*)
Bergenias (*Bergenia*)
Bluestars (*Amsonia*)
Boston ivy
(*Parthenocissus
tricuspidata*)
Culver's root
(*Veronicastrum
virginicum*)
Flame grass
(*Miscanthus
'Purpurascens'*)

Fountain grass
(*Pennisetum
alopecuroides*)
Hostas (*Hosta*)
Japanese anemone
(*Anemone* x *hybrida*)
Leadwort (*Ceratostigma
plumbaginoides*)
Monkshoods (*Aconitum*)
New England aster
(*Aster novae-angliae*)
New York aster
(*Aster novi-belgii*)
Peonies (*Paeonia*)
Solomon's seals
(*Polygonatum*)
Switch grass
(*Panicum virgatum*)
Virginia creeper
(*Parthenocissus
quinquefolia*)
Wild oats (*Chasmanthium
latifolium*)
Wintercreeper
(*Euonymus fortunei*)
Wisterias (*Wisteria*)

CHAPTER 12

Late Fall: Don't Give Up Yet!

S ure, there's lots of fun stuff to do indoors this time of year, what with getting ready for the holidays and all. But if you've used my top tips for creating a year-round landscape, your outdoor space can still look great in late fall—and on into the winter, too! Let's take a look at some super plants for interest during this season, as well as some tips for getting ready for winter flower fun.

Take advantage of those remaining mild fall days to get your garden cleaned up and ready to grow like gang-busters once spring returns!

- Do a final weeding in beds and borders
- Finish planting hardy bulbs for spring color
- Dig up and store any remaining tender bulbs before the ground freezes
- Plant bare-root shrubs and roses
- Rake fallen leaves and add them to your compost pile, or shred them for use as mulch

- Pull out frost-killed annuals and use them to start a new compost pile
- Prepare new beds and borders for planting next spring
- Keep watering during dry spells (especially around evergreen trees and shrubs)
- Once garden chores are done, clean, sharpen, and store your tools
- Drain garden hoses and hang them for storage
- Hit end-of-the-season sales to stock up on garden supplies for next year

By this time of year, the tree and shrub show turns from colorful leaves to bright berries, beautiful bark, and engaging evergreens. Believe it or not, there are also a few hardy varieties that *start* blooming now— how's that for turning the seasons upside down? Here's a bunch of my best tips for making the most of all your options for this fall season!

Which Hazel? This One!

Fabulous foliage, flowers, *and* fragrance in late fall? You bet! Just plant a Virginia witch hazel (*Hamamelis virginiana*) in your yard. This great native tree is a true late bloomer—sometimes flowering at the same time as its green leaves turn bright gold, and sometimes after the leaves have dropped. Either way, you'll enjoy the sweet scent as it perfumes your whole property! Virginia witch hazel grows in sun or partial shade and adapts to average soil just about anywhere in Zones 4 to 9.

Berry Nice Ideas

When it comes to color in fall and winter, berries simply can't be beat! Creating a berry-beautiful display takes some planning—and a bit of luck, too—but the results are worth it. Here are some tips to

Ask Jerry

Q: *I'd swear I just saw a cherry tree in bloom today, but it's almost wintertime! Is it just mixed up—or am I?*

A: Don't worry about your sanity, my friend—it's entirely possible you *did* see a cherry blooming in November! Specifically, you saw fall-flowering cherry (*Prunus* x *subhirtella* 'Autumnalis'). This wonderful small tree is a little tricky to find, but it's definitely worth tracking down for year-round interest. The pink buds open into pale pink blooms during mild spells from late fall through early spring. It has pretty bark and great fall foliage color, too!

help you get the most from these fabulous fruiting plants:

→ Before you buy plants for their berries, check to see if they need a pollinator (in other words, if you need to plant both a male and a female variety to get fruit). Bayberries (*Myrica*) and hollies (*Ilex*) are two common examples of berry-makers that need pollinators.

→ Berries show up best when you give them a good background. Evergreen trees and shrubs are great for showing off white and bright orange fruits, while deep red and purple berries look good against a lighter wall or fence.

→ Keep in mind that birds love berries as much as people do! One way to fool them is to plant varieties with yellow fruits, instead of the reds that birds tend to home in on. Keeping berry-bearing shrubs close to your house—especially near a door you use often—can help discourage timid birds from feasting on your fruits.

A Purple Haze for Chilly Days

Sure, everyone thinks of berries as being red, but they can come in every color of the rainbow—and then some! Take beautyberries (*Callicarpa*), for instance: They've got the most perfectly purple berries you could ever imagine! They have pretty pink summer flowers, too, but their amazing berries are their claim to fame from fall through much of the winter. Beautyberries produce fruit on young stems only, so snip out a few of the

Grandma Putt's
GREEN THUMB TIPS

What's the very best fertilizer you can give leafy plants? *Other leaves!* Here's a super-easy recipe for making "leaf mold," courtesy of Grandma Putt: Simply gather dry, shredded leaves into plastic garbage bags, and moisten them slightly. Close the bags and stack them in a corner of your yard. By spring, you'll have a generous supply of humus-rich leaf mold to feed all your bloomers!

Trouble-Free Trees and Shrubs　　　Late Fall: Don't Give Up Yet!

273

oldest stems at the base of the plant each spring, or simply cut the whole shrub to the ground once every few years. It'll bounce back better than ever!

Spotlight on...

Viburnums

If I could have only one type of berry-bearing shrub in my yard, I'd choose viburnums (*Viburnum*), hands down! They come in all shapes and sizes to fit almost any site—from 4-foot dwarf European cranberry bush (*V. opulus* 'Compactum') to 12-foot tea viburnum (*V. setigerum*). Most bloom in spring or early summer, with clustered, white blooms that mature into red, orange, or blue berries by late summer or fall. Deciduous viburnums usually have fantastic fall leaf colors, too, in shades of red, purple, and orange, while evergreen varieties have handsome foliage all winter.

There are dozens of viburnums to choose from, but one I'd never be without is called 'Onondaga' (*V. sargentii*). It grows about 6 feet tall, with deep red new leaves that are red-tinged green in summer and bright red in fall. Its large clusters of reddish buds open into pinkish white flowers in early summer, then produce glossy red berries that last all the way to spring for a spectacular winter display—WOW!

As a group, viburnums are generally hardy in Zones 5 to 8, and they'll adapt to full sun or partial shade and average soil. They're fairly trouble-free, too—they just need a little trimming now and then to stay tidy.

Let's Get Hip!

Roses aren't just for summer color anymore! When you choose roses that have showy fruits (called hips), you can enjoy them practically year-round. Here's a checklist of some of the best bets for eye-catching winter color:

- ✔ 'Alba Semiplena'
- ✔ 'Belle Poitevine'
- ✔ 'Bonica'
- ✔ 'Dart's Dash'
- ✔ 'Frau Dagmar Hartopp'
- ✔ 'Hansa'
- ✔ 'Rosa Mundi'
- ✔ Apple rose (*Rosa pomifera*)
- ✔ Red-leaved rose (*R. glauca*)
- ✔ Rugosa rose (*R. rugosa*)
- ✔ Virginia rose (*R. virginana*)

MIX & FIX

ROSE ROUSIN' ELIXIR

To get bare-root roses off to a rip-roarin' start, give 'em a taste of this magical mixer before you plant.

1 tbsp. of 5-8-5 or 5-10-5 garden fertilizer
1 tbsp. of baby shampoo
1 tbsp. of corn syrup
1 gal. of warm water

Mix these ingredients together in a bucket, and soak the roots in the solution overnight. When you're done, sprinkle this mixture around all your other rosebushes, too—they'll love you for it!

Rose Grower's Graft Guidelines

If you want to get a jump on next spring's rose show, late fall's a great time to get bare-root roses in the ground. Most times, the roses you buy will be grafted plants—the top growth of a desirable rose growing on the roots of another rose. You can tell when you look at the base of the plant, 'cause grafted roses have a knobby-looking area just above the roots. It's important to know where the graft union is, since it'll tell you how deep to set the plant in the ground. In the North (Zone 6 and colder), set the graft union 3 inches below the soil surface. In the South, set it 1½ inches *above* the soil line.

Believe it or not, there's still action in the flower garden this time of year—*if* you've had the foresight to include some true late bloomers to round out the season. Check out these tips for getting all you can out of your year-round yard and garden.

Mum Magic

Colorful and cold-hardy, hybrid chrysanthemums are classic favorites for early fall color all across the country. But don't forget to check out some of the lesser-known mums, too, like the three below—they'll extend the season all the way up to winter!

'Sheffield Pink' chrysanthemum: Single, apricot pink, yellow-centered daisies bloom for weeks atop 1-foot-tall stems from mid- through late fall. Tough as nails and drought-tolerant, too!

'Mei-Kyo' chrysanthemum: Bushy, 2-foot-tall plants with double pink blooms in late fall. If you haven't had luck overwintering other mums, give this one a try!

Gold-and-silver chrysanthemum (*C. pacificum*): Actually, you'll grow this mostly for its 1-foot-tall mounds of silver-edged leaves, but the bright yellow, late fall buttons are showy as well.

Ask Jerry

Q: *I enjoyed growing perennials in pots on my deck this summer, and I'd like to have them there again next year. Do they need any special care to make it through the winter?*

A: In mild-winter areas (roughly Zone 7 and south), it may be enough to bring your potted perennials up next to the house, close to the foundation. In cooler areas, dig a trench in your vegetable garden and sink the pots into the soil, up to their rims; for extra protection, cover them with a foot or so of leaves.

A Tip from the Pros

Since most folks don't spend much time outside at this time of year, it just makes sense to bring the blooms *indoors!* Snip a bit of whatever looks good, then bring everything inside to create a bountiful bouquet. Don't forget to pick some leaves, too: Adding leaves helps separate the blooms and show each one off to its advantage. Plus, you don't need as many flowers to fill your container!

But don't think of leaves simply as fillers; they can add a lot of interest in their own right. Variegated or colored leaves can rival the brightest blooms, for instance, while others can add scent or beautiful texture. Some of my favorite foliage plants for fresh fall arrangements include heucheras, lady's mantle (*Alchemilla mollis*), lamb's ears (*Stachys byzantina*), and lavenders, as well as ornamental grasses and ferns.

Grandma Putt's

GREEN THUMB TIPS

It's tempting to cut down everything in your garden after frost, but if you take Grandma Putt's advice and leave some of the seedheads standing, you'll have more to look at during the winter. Without their colorful petals, seedheads have a subtle beauty all their own. Plus, they catch falling snowflakes, creating fun snow sculptures that change with each flurry. Standing seedheads can also provide a natural source of seeds to attract winter birds to your garden without the bother of filling feeders!

A Classy Aster

If you like your flowers tall enough to look you right in the eye, I've got a doozy of a late bloomer for you: Tatarian aster (*Aster tataricus*). This big 'un grows up to 6 feet tall, with sturdy stems that never need staking. They're topped by large clusters of small, but abundant lavender-purple daisies with yellow centers from mid- to late fall—perfect for those Thanksgiving Day table decorations! Tatarian aster thrives in full sun and average to moist soil in Zones 3 to 9.

Debris Dilemma

We all know how important it is to clean up our flower gardens at the end of the growing season, but how we should get rid of the debris is an ongoing debate. Should you burn it, bury it, or add it to your compost pile?

Some folks compost everything, while others won't compost anything at all, for fear of spreading pests, pathogens, and seeds all through their yard. I fall somewhere between the two—I burn material that is definitely disease- or insect-ridden (as well as woody stalks that are almost certain to harbor borers), and try to compost everything else that looks reasonably safe.

The Path to Success

Tired of slogging through wet, muddy paths in your flower gardens? Then this is a great time to roll out the red carpet—or any other color carpet, for that matter! Cut old carpeting and rugs into strips, and lay them down in your garden between your flower beds. Top them with some bark mulch, and you've got a great-looking (and weed-free) pathway.

FLOWER BED BONANZA

After fall cleanup, spray all of your perennial beds with this mixture.

1 can of beer
1 can of regular cola (not diet)
¹/₂ cup of dishwashing liquid
¹/₂ cup of tobacco tea*

Mix all of the ingredients together in a bucket, then apply liberally with a 20 gallon hose-end sprayer.

*Place half a handful of chewing tobacco in an old nylon stocking, and soak it in a gallon of hot water until the mixture is dark brown.

MIX & FIX

A Bounty of Bulbs

Things are winding down now as far as the bulb action goes, but there are still a few chores to do to get ready for spring. Here are some tips to make your tasks a little easier—as well as some pointers for enjoying late bloomers, both indoors and out!

Weather Watch

All of your best-laid garden plans can be washed down the drain if you don't consider the weather. Don't attempt to dig, seed, weed, or plant without first seeing if Mother Nature is going to cooperate. Believe you me, you don't want her to wash out, blow out, burn out, or freeze out all of your hard work!

➜ When the leaves drop early, the Indian summer will be short, and the winter will be mild.

➜ If the crickets sing in the chimney, it will be a long winter.

➜ When the leaves fall late, winter will be hard.

➜ If the earthworms leave their homes in the ground, a heavy rain is on the way.

➜ When the hornets' nests are fat and low, winter will be cold.

➜ When the hawks fly low, there will be much snow.

Ask Jerry

Q: *It's not even wintertime yet, and some of my bulbs are starting to poke their noses out of the soil! Is there anything I should do to protect them?*

A: Don't worry about it; this is common with a few hardy bulbs—especially grape hyacinths (*Muscari*) and Madonna lilies (*Lilium candidum*). Their leaf tips might get a little tattered, but don't worry: The flowers will be just fine next year.

➜ If the moss on the north side of the tree dries up in the fall, it will be a mild winter.

➜ When the clouds in the sky look like horses' tails, frost is coming.

Pretty in Pink

At this time of year, a flower doesn't have to be big and bold to be a welcome sight! The small, pale pink blooms of hardy cyclamen (*Cyclamen cilicium*) look mighty delicate, but they're tough enough to appear in the cold days toward the end of fall. Even when the lightly scented flowers are gone, the silver-mottled green leaves stick around all winter, making a pretty winter groundcover for a shady, sheltered site in Zones 6 to 9. Give this great little cyclamen a try—and be prepared for lots of comments from curious visitors who see it in your yard!

Grandma Putt's GREEN THUMB TIPS

My Grandma Putt always joked that she liked to baby her tender bulbs—and you should do the same! No, it doesn't mean you have to burp them or change their diapers; just do what Grandma did, and give 'em a good dusting with medicated baby powder before you put them away for winter storage. They'll make it through the cold months in tip-top form and be rarin' to grow come spring!

Pack 'Em a Lunch

Treat all your fall-planted bulbs to an organic lunch by sprinkling on a mixture of 10 pounds of compost, 5 pounds of bonemeal, and 1 pound of Epsom salts per 100 square feet of soil. For an extra treat, add up to 15 pounds of fireplace ashes to the mix. This will give them a nutritional boost that's good to grow on!

Divine Vines and Groundcovers

Fall is a fine time to enjoy vibrant vines and glorious groundcovers—*if* you follow my advice for choosing the best late-season lovelies available. It's also time to get ready for the big chill, so I've got tips to help you get through the winter in fine style.

Ice-Fighting Options

In many parts of the country, snow is just one of Old Man Winter's nasty tricks: Icy paths and pavement can be a real pain, too. Most folks get around this by tossing a lot of salt around—but come spring, you may find that the beds and borders adjoining salt-treated driveways and walkways are full of dead plants! To prevent this deadly damage, treat your beds with my Winter Walkway Protection Tonic (at left). Or, stick with old-fashioned ice-fighters like sawdust, sand, or ashes. You'll still get good traction—and your plants will stay healthy and happy!

What a Grape Idea!

If you like your plants to be as hardworking as they are good-looking, check out ornamental grapes (*Vitis*) the next time you need a vine to dress up a fence or arbor. Besides providing cooling summer shade, grapes are great for knock-your-socks-off fall color. And when you prune them, you've got the fixings for plenty of grapevine

MIX
&
FIX

WINTER WALKWAY PROTECTION TONIC

To keep the grass and groundcovers around your walks and driveways in good shape during the winter, first sprinkle the areas liberally with gypsum. Then apply this tonic.

1 cup of dishwashing liquid
1/2 cup of ammonia
1/2 cup of beer

Mix all of these ingredients in a 20 gallon hose-end sprayer, and then apply the mixture over the gypsum.

Divine Vines and Groundcovers Late Fall: Don't Give Up Yet!

FALL

281

wreaths. Here are three of my favorite grapes to get you started:

Crimson glory vine (*V. coignetiae*): Large, broad, leathery green leaves that turn rich shades of red, purple, and orange in fall. Zones 5 to 8.

Teinturier grape (*V. vinifera* 'Purpurea'): Rich purple foliage all summer, turning bright red in fall. Small clusters of purple grapes, too—but they're not tasty. Zones 6 to 9.

Variegated grape (*V.* 'Variegata'): Broad, white-splashed green leaves all through the growing season. Zones 6 to 9.

Spotlight on...

English Ivy

If there's one word I'd use to describe English ivy (*Hedera helix*), it's *versatile!* Set young plants fairly close to each other (about 6 inches apart), and they'll quickly knit together into a deep green carpet that makes a great evergreen groundcover for even the deepest shade. Or set a single plant against a vertical surface that it can grab on to—like a tree trunk or a stone wall—and it'll be upward bound in a flash!

English ivy thrives in humus-rich, well-drained soil, and it can adapt to either acid or alkaline conditions. It's a winner for partial or full shade—especially those tough, root-filled sites under mature trees. The vigorous vines can quickly smother more delicate companions, so it's smart to keep English ivy in beds by itself. Plan to mow or trim around it a few times a year, too, to keep it from creeping out of bounds. Other than that, English ivy needs practically no care.

The kinds you're most likely to find for sale include 'Baltica', 'Bulgaria', and 'Thorndale', all of which have deep green foliage and are hardy in Zones 4 to 9. Or, for something a little showier, try 'Goldheart', with bright yellow-centered leaves.

Jerry's Best Bets for...
The Late Show

Late fall's got all kinds of fun in store for the adventurous year-round gardener! Lingering fall foliage, along with late-blooming flowers and bright berries, are just what the doctor (Doctor Baker, that is) ordered to keep winter woes at bay. Try one of the great late plants on the list below, or try a bunch—trust me, you'll be glad you did!

Trees with Late Fall Flowers

Fall-flowering cherry
    (*Prunus* x *subhirtella*
    'Autumnalis')
Sasanqua camellia
    (*Camellia sasanqua*)
Virginia witch hazel
    (*Hamamelis virginiana*)

Trees with Red Fruits

American holly
    (*Ilex opaca*)
Chinese pistache
    (*Pistacia chinensis*)
Crabapples (*Malus*)
English holly
    (*Ilex aquifolium*)
Hawthorns (*Crataegus*)
Korean mountain ash
    (*Sorbus alnifolia*)

Trees with Orange or Yellow Fruits

American holly
    (*Ilex opaca*)
Crabapples (*Malus*)
English holly
    (*Ilex aquifolium*)
European mountain ash
    (*Sorbus aucuparia*)

Shrubs with Red Fruits

American cranberry bush
    (*Viburnum trilobum*)
Barberries (*Berberis*)
Blue holly
    (*Ilex* x *meserveae*)
Cotoneasters (*Cotoneaster*)
European cranberry bush
    (*Viburnum opulus*)
Heavenly bamboo
    (*Nandina domestica*)
Japanese aucuba
    (*Aucuba japonica*)
Linden viburnum
    (*Viburnum dilatatum*)
Moyes rose (*Rosa moyesii*)
Prairie rose (*Rosa setigera*)
Red chokeberry
    (*Aronia arbutifolia*)
Red-leaved rose
    (*Rosa glauca*)

Rugosa rose (*Rosa rugosa*)
Smooth sumac
    (*Rhus glabra*)
Staghorn sumac
    (*Rhus typhina*)
Tea viburnum
    (*Viburnum setigerum*)
Virginia rose
    (*Rosa virginiana*)
Winterberry
    (*Ilex verticillata*)

Shrubs with Orange or Yellow Fruits

Blue holly
    (*Ilex* x *meserveae*)
European cranberry bush
    (*Viburnum opulus*)
Firethorns (*Pyracantha*)
Linden viburnum
    (*Viburnum dilatatum*)
Winterberry
    (*Ilex verticillata*)

Shrubs with Blue, Purple, or White Fruits

Beautyberries
(*Callicarpa*)
Japanese fatsia
(*Fatsia japonica*)
Northern bayberry
(*Myrica pensylvanica*)
Sapphireberry
(*Symplocos paniculata*)
Snowberry
(*Symphoricarpos albus* var. *laevigatus*)

Late-Blooming Perennials

Azure monkshood
(*Aconitum carmichaelii*)
Chrysanthemum
(*Dendranthema weyrichii*)
Gold-and-silver chrysanthemum
(*Chrysanthemum pacificum*)
Korean chrysanthemum
(*Chrysanthemum* x *koreanum*)
'Mei-Kyo' chrysanthemum
(*Chrysanthemum* 'Mei-Kyo')

October daphne
(*Sedum sieboldii*)
'Raydon's Favorite' aster
(*Aster oblongifolius* 'Raydon's Favorite')
Shining coneflower
(*Rudbeckia nitida*)
Tatarian aster
(*Aster tataricus*)

Annuals Still in Bloom

Edging lobelia
(*Lobelia erinus*)
Flowering tobaccos
(*Nicotiana*)
Garden verbena
(*Verbena* x *hybrida*)
Johnny-jump-up
(*Viola tricolor*)
Pansy
(*Viola* x *wittrockiana*)
Pot marigold
(*Calendula officinalis*)
Swan River daisy
(*Brachyscome iberidifolia*)
Sweet alyssum
(*Lobularia maritima*)

Late-Blooming Bulbs

Cyclamen
(*Cyclamen cilicium*)
Italian arum
(*Arum italicum* 'Marmoratum')
Ornamental onion
(*Allium thunbergii*)
Winter daffodil
(*Sternbergia lutea*)

Vines and Groundcovers with Bright Berries

Hypericums
(*Hypericum*)
Japanese skimmia
(*Skimmia japonica*)
Partridgeberry
(*Mitchella repens*)
Porcelain vine
(*Ampelopsis brevipedunculata*)
Wintergreen
(*Gaultheria procumbens*)

PART 5

WOW!
WONDERFUL
WINTER
BLOOMERS

What's the best way to send your wintery woes on their way? A nice stroll through a beautiful garden! Best of all, you don't have to travel to the tropics to see beautiful blooms and lovely leaves during the big chill; they can be right outside your door.

I'll be honest with you, folks: Planning a wonderful winter garden is a bit trickier than it is for spring, summer, or fall. But when you know what to look for, you'll be astonished by all of your exciting options: evergreen foliage, colorful bark, bright berries, and even fragrant flowers. As I've worked on my own yard, I've learned a lot about what makes for *real* winter interest, and I can't wait to share my best secrets with you. So c'mon, folks—let's get you goin' on your own winter wonderland!

CHAPTER 13

Early Winter Wonderland

I t's sad to see, but the last act of any gardening year is putting your yard to bed for the winter. Some folks hardly give it any thought, but in many cases, it's just as important as all the TLC you gave your plants during the growing season. Read on for the tips, tricks, and tonics to get it done the fast, fun, and easy Jerry Baker way.

Now's the time to finish up those last-minute cleanup chores—*and* to think ahead for next year's bloomers, too!

- Finish up your notes on what worked well this year

- Jot down ideas about what you want to change or add in the upcoming year

- Start ordering seeds for next year's flower beds and borders

- Finish planting hardy bulbs in the South

- Give your perennial gardens a winter snack

- Once the ground freezes, apply a good, protective winter mulch

- Check stored bulbs and tubers, and discard any that show signs of rot

- Finish cleaning and storing your garden tools

- Water evergreens until the ground freezes, then use antidessicant sprays to prevent winter damage

- Pot up amaryllis (*Hippeastrum*) bulbs for gorgeous midwinter blooms indoors

When winter rolls around, it's easy to see how important trees and shrubs are for adding off-season landscape interest. Beautiful berries, interesting bark, and eye-catching evergreen foliage—all of these features are invaluable for livening up your yard during dull winter days. With that in mind, I've gathered up a bunch of my best tips for putting together a great-looking winter landscape anyone would envy!

Winter Beauty Is Only Skin Deep

Most folks don't give much thought to bark when they're choosing trees and shrubs for their yard—and that's a darn shame! When the leaves are gone and flowers are just a memory, the bark's what you're left to look at for several months out of the year. So take my advice, and look for these fabulous bark features before you select your next new tree or shrub:

Eye-catching color. Once you start checking out bark with an eye toward winter interest, you'll be amazed at all the colors it can come in: every shade of brown, of course, but also black, gray, green, orange, purple, red, and white, too!

Grandma Putt's GREEN THUMB TIPS

Thanks to lush leaves and beautiful blooms, it's easy to have a yard that looks great during spring, summer, and fall. But when winter rolls around, that's when it's time for your yard to take shape—literally! When I was a boy, Grandma Putt would point out to me all the different shapes trees and shrubs can take on: rounded, pyramidal, vase-shaped, weeping, and so on. She knew—and now you do, too—that including plants with distinctive shapes is a can't-miss trick for livening up any winter landscape!

Interesting textures. Trunks and twigs come in a wide variety of textures, as well. They can be glossy and as smooth as glass, marked with horizontal or vertical stripes or ridges, or deeply divided into square or diamond-shaped chunks.

Peeling bark. I'll admit that it can take a little getting used to seeing bark peeling off of healthy trees! But once you get comfortable with the sight, you'll appreciate how much interest it can add to winter stems. On some plants—like lacebark pine (*Pinus bungeana*)—it flakes off in chips to reveal lighter patches underneath; in others—such as paperbark maple (*Acer griseum*)—it peels off in paper-thin strips that glow with color when the sun shines through them.

BYE-BYE BIRDIE BREW

This timely tonic will keep pesky birds from eating the berries on your trees and shrubs before you have time to enjoy them!

1 tbsp. of baby shampoo
1 tbsp. of ammonia
1 gal. of water

Mix these ingredients together, and spray the potion on your trees and shrubs when they are full of berries. Reapply after each rain.

Have a Holly-Jolly Winter!

Deep green foliage and bright red berries make evergreen hollies (*Ilex*) a favorite for winter landscapes—and with good reason! But there's a whole other group of hollies that can pep up your yard during the off-season—namely, the deciduous hollies. The best known of the bunch is winterberry (*I. verticillata*) and its hybrids. Hardy in Zones 4 to 9, it forms a dense shrub that grows best in average to moist, acid soil in full sun or light shade. 'Red Sprite' is a compact selection (to 4 feet) with particularly long-lasting red berries. 'Winter Red' is similar, but grows to 8 feet tall; its counterpart, 'Winter Gold', has yellow berries. As with evergreen hollies, only the female plants produce fruit, so you must plant one male (such as 'Apollo' or 'Jim Dandy') for every five or so female winterberries!

Winter Tool Wrap-Up

Yep, I've said this before, but it's worth repeating: When it's time to put your yard to bed for the winter, it's also time to put your tools to rest. If you just throw them in a box in the garage without taking a few minutes to clean and prepare them, you'll have a real mess on your hands come spring. Here's how to wrap things up:

- Sand, prime, and paint rusted surfaces on any and all tools and power equipment.
- Oil springs, nuts, bolts, gears, and levels with WD-40®.
- Wipe down your garden hose, electrical cords, and rubber or plastic tool parts with Armor All®.
- Sharpen tool edges and paint metal parts with rust-resistant paint.
- Seal wood handles with a good water-sealing product.
- Clean, drain, and separate all your pressure sprayers and hose-end sprayers.

Grandma Putt's
GREEN THUMB TIPS

Here's a dilemma: When do you prune shrubs that you're growing for their berries? Whether you trim them before or after bloom, you're still going to lose some of the fruits you might have been able to enjoy through the winter. Well, my Grandma Putt came up with a smart solution I just have to share with you: Prune 'em just as soon as the birds finish eating the berries! (Yep, even if it's during the winter.) That'll give you the best possible show each year, while still letting you keep your shrubs in good trim.

Here's a Screwy Idea

Here's a super winter shrub with a twist—well, actually, lots of twists! Corkscrew hazel (*Corylus avellana* 'Contorta'), also called Harry Lauder's walking stick, grows about 6 feet tall and wide, with curiously curled stems that make an attention-grabbing winter accent for any yard. The branches look great in arrangements, too, by the way! Just be sure to snip out any straight stems right at the base of the plant, so they don't spoil the effect. Corkscrew hazel grows in sun or light shade and can adapt to either average or dry soil in Zones 4 to 8.

Appealing Camellias

If you're a warm-climate gardener searching for winter beauty, camellias belong at the top of your list. These large shrubs offer evergreen foliage, which is a nice plus, but their real claim to fame is their wonderful *winter* blooms! Sasanqua camellia (*Camellia sasanqua*) actually starts flowering in fall and continues through winter, while common camellia (*C. japonica*) generally begins in early winter and keeps going through early spring. The bowl-shaped blooms are usually 3 to 4 inches across and can be white, pink, or red. Both of these beauties are rated as hardy in Zones 7 to 9, but common camellia tends to be a bit touchier about the cold, so it's smart to give it a wind-sheltered site.

Their Bark Has a Real Bite!

Bright-barked shrubs are one of the very best investments you can make for your year-round landscape. Unlike berries, which can fall prey to hungry birds, colorful bark is

Rosy Clean-Up Elixir

Late fall to early winter is the best time to get a jump on the insects and diseases that like to plague roses. So after your bushes have shed their leaves, but before you mulch them for the winter, spray 'em thoroughly with this terrific tonic.

1 cup of baby shampoo
1 cup of antiseptic mouthwash
1 cup of tobacco tea*

Place all of these ingredients in a 20 gallon hose-end sprayer, and douse each rosebush from top to bottom.

*Place half a handful of chewing tobacco in an old nylon stocking, and soak it in a gallon of hot water until the mixture is dark brown.

sure to stick around all through the winter months. And since young stems tend to have the best color, the regular pruning they prefer will help keep these shrubs in good size for just about any spot.

It's hardly surprising that the best of the barkers are the shrubby dogwoods (*Cornus*). My all-time favorite of the bunch is 'Elegantissima' red-twig dogwood (*C. alba*) because its white-splashed leaves look great all through the growing season, then the red stems show off in winter. 'Silver and Gold' is also variegated, but has bright yellow twigs instead of red ones. Plant 'em together, and you're *guaranteed* a real year-round spectacle!

Ask Jerry

Q: *Every winter, some of my evergreen trees and shrubs end up with ugly browned leaf tips. Is this some kind of disease problem?*

A: Don't worry about dastardly diseases—what you're dealing with is called winter damage. It happens when winter winds draw water out of the leaves, and the roots can't take up more from the frozen ground. Watering your evergreens well *before* the soil freezes will go a long way toward preventing this problem. For extra protection, treat your trouble-prone plants with an antidesiccant spray, such as my Weatherproof™, to help prevent water loss in the first place.

Dependable Perennials

Perennials for winter interest? Sure thing! No, we're not talking about flowers now—but wait until you see how much off-season interest good-looking leaves and showy seedheads can add to your yard. Here's the lowdown on some wonderful winter beauties, plus some bonus tips for keeping all of your beds and borders in prime form.

These Perennials Keep Their Heads

Want to get double—or even triple—the impact from your flowering perennials? Then choose those with good-looking seed-heads that last well into winter! Instead of just a few weeks of beautiful blooms each summer, you'll get month after month of good color *and* interesting structure to boot! Plus, their seeds provide welcome food for winter birds. Here are eight great choices for super winter seedheads—there are lots of others, too.

Astilbes (*Astilbe*)

'Autumn Joy' sedum (*Sedum* 'Autumn Joy')

Bee balms (*Monarda*)

Black-eyed Susans (*Rudbeckia*)

Joe Pye weeds (*Eupatorium*)

Purple coneflower (*Echinacea purpurea*)

Sea hollies (*Eryngium*)

Siberian iris (*Iris sibirica*)

Grandma Putt's **GREEN THUMB TIPS**

When I first started gardening on my own, I'd carefully cover my perennials with a thick layer of mulch each winter—only to find that the mulch had packed down and actually smothered the plants I wanted to protect. I finally remembered a trick Grandma Putt used to use, and suddenly, my mulch madness was a thing of the past! Simply lay old cornstalks or some woody brush over the beds *before* you add the mulch. That'll keep the mulch from resting right on the plants—and your perennials will be able to breathe under their warm winter blanket!

Three Steps to Super Garden Success

When the gardening year finally comes to a close, most folks are about ready to call it quits. But you're not done quite yet! I want you to rally your energy one more time and follow these simple steps to ensure a ready, willing, and able flower garden next season:

Step 1: Clean it up. By doing a serious end-of-season cleanup job, you'll limit the distribution of weed seeds; help control both insects and diseases; *and* save yourself time next spring, when there's lots of other work to do.

Step 2: Start a compost pile. If any of you who read, watch, or listen to me on a regular basis don't have some form of composting going on in your yard, then it's not because I haven't tried to persuade you. Now, please, get one going today!

Step 3: Drain any wet areas. If too much water settles in your garden, now's the time to begin to raise your garden beds, dig a runoff trench, or lay a drain tile in the problem area.

SLEEPYTIME MULCH TONIC

When Old Man Winter is just around the corner, you should tuck your beds in with a thick blanket of mulch. This mixture feeds the mulch that slowly feeds your garden.

1 can of beer
1 can of regular cola (not diet)
1 cup of baby shampoo
1/2 cup of ammonia
1/4 cup of instant tea granules

Mix all of these ingredients in a small bucket, pour the mixture into a 20 gallon hose-end sprayer, and saturate the mulch in flower beds, around shrubs, and beneath trees.

Some Like It Cold

While *people* prefer to bundle up at the drop of the thermometer, your *plants* will be much happier if you don't cover them up until *after* the ground freezes. Why wait so long? Because your real enemy isn't chilly temperatures; it's those midwinter thaws that cause the ground to shift, resulting in root damage. Unprotected plants that are heaved out of the soil can die from exposure, or they may just dry out. Likewise, unseasonable warm spells can cause dormant buds on unprotected plants to start growing, and they'll be killed by the next freeze. But if you mulch soon after the ground freezes, you'll keep the ground colder, lessening the chance of heaving during a warm spell.

Give Critters the Cold Shoulder

Need another reason to hold off on mulching? Well, if you cover up your beds and borders while the soil's still warm, you'll create a snug-as-a-bug home for mice, voles, and other animal pests. Even when the ground outside the garden is frozen solid, they'll be able to tunnel easily among your plants, and they'll happily snack on all the sweet and juicy perennials and bulbs you left for them. Yikes! To avoid turning your gardens into a free-for-all winter buffet, make sure your garden soil is frozen before you mulch; by that time, the critters should have found somewhere else to make their winter homes.

MIX & FIX

FROZEN FEED

To give your perennials a welcome winter snack and a rip-roarin' start in spring, wait until the ground freezes, then apply this mixture.

25 lbs. of garden gypsum
10 lbs. of garden fertilizer
    (4-2-4 or 5-10-5)
5 lbs. of bonemeal

Mix all of the ingredients together, then spread the mixture evenly over your beds and borders. This amount will cover 100 sq. ft.

Evergreen Gems for Flower Beds

When folks talk about evergreen foliage, what comes to mind? Trees and shrubs, right, like pines, spruces, and hollies? Believe it or not, there are evergreen *perennials,* too—and they're every bit as good as trees and shrubs for bringing welcome color to dull winter landscape. Here are three true-green choices to wet your whistle.

Bearsfoot hellebore (*Helleborus foetidus*): One- to 2-foot-tall stems clad in deeply divided, leathery leaves and topped with clusters of pale green, bell-shaped blooms from late winter through midspring. Zones 5 to 9.

Bergenias (*Bergenia*): Low-growing clumps of rounded, leathery, bright green leaves that often take on purplish or reddish tones in winter, plus clusters of red, pink, or white flowers in spring. Zones 3 to 9.

Gladwyn iris (*Iris foetidissima*): Typical iris-shaped blooms appear in early summer, but they're a nondescript grayish blue. The

Spotlight on...

Italian Arum

Here's a perky little plant that definitely has things backwards! Italian arum (*Arum italicum* 'Pictum') emerges from below-ground tubers in fall, producing an 18-inch-tall clump of awesome, arrow-shaped, deep green leaves that are veined and marbled with creamy white streaks. It looks for all the world like you left one of your tropical houseplants outside for the winter!

In mid- to late spring, Italian arum sends up greenish white, hooded flowers that nestle below the leaves. As summer approaches, the leaves die down, until the only parts left standing are the stalks of green-turning-to-red berries in mid- to late summer—what a show!

Italian arum thrives in Zones 5 to 9, in a site with winter and spring sun and summer shade. It loves humus-rich soil and lots of moisture, so keep it well mulched with compost, and water it during spring dry spells.

real showstopper is the resulting seedpods, which split open in fall to reveal bright orange-red seeds—and the strap-shaped evergreen leaves, too, of course! Zones 6 to 9.

Divine Vines and Groundcovers

The calendar year's coming to a close, but with well-chosen vines and groundcovers, the garden color just keeps on comin'! Here's the lowdown on several winter beauties, along with some tricks for keeping 'em in top-notch form.

Fine Vines for Winter Fun

With the holiday season close at hand, it's time to deck the walls (and fences and arbors, too) with evergreen vines! Ivies (*Hedera*) are the most obvious choice, but there are others, too:

Ask Jerry

Q: *Hey, Jer—any tips for taking care of ornamental grasses right about now?*

A: Warm-season (late-blooming) grasses usually hold up well through the winter, so enjoy 'em now and wait until spring to whack 'em back hard. Those that bloom earlier (called cool-season grasses) resent the harsh haircut that keeps warm-season types looking tip-top, but most still benefit from an annual trim. So, cut blue fescue (*Festuca glauca*), blue oat grass (*Helictotrichon sempervirens*), and other cool-season grasses back by about a third of their height, either in early winter or in early spring, before they begin growing. Or do what I do—just comb out any dead leaves with your fingers!

Wintercreeper (*Euonymus fortunei*) is another that's hardy in Zones 4 to 9. Warm-climate gardeners (Zone 8 and south) have several more options, including Armand's clematis (*Clematis armandii*), cross vine (*Bignonia capreolata*), Carolina jessamine (*Gelsemium sempervirens*), and confederate jasmine (*Trachelospermum jasminoides*).

One extra piece of advice: Plan on giving any evergreen vine a site that's sheltered from the prevailing winds. In cold climates particularly, tall vines exposed to drying winter winds can develop browned leaves that are tough to tidy up without a tall ladder!

Get an Edge with Sedges

They *look* like grasses, and they *grow* like grasses, but sedges (*Carex*) are in a class by themselves. Many of these gorgeous grass relatives have evergreen foliage, which makes them a must-have for winter gardens. There are lots of super sedges to select from in all kinds of colors: from the deep green, mop-top mounds of 'The Beatles' to the yellow-pinstriped leaves of 'Evergold' to the rusty orange, upright tufts of Buchanan sedge (*C. buchananii*). Sedges generally grow best in shady spots with soil that's on the moist side, but they're pretty adaptable. Best of all, most don't even need a yearly trim; just plant 'em once and enjoy 'em for years to come!

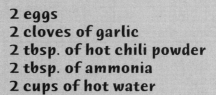

ALL-PURPOSE VARMINT REPELLENT

Are hungry critters making your winter gardens into their own private salad bar? Grandma Putt swore by this stuff for getting rid of just about any kind of unwelcome animal that came down the pike—and it still works like a charm for me!

2 eggs
2 cloves of garlic
2 tbsp. of hot chili powder
2 tbsp. of ammonia
2 cups of hot water

Mix all of these ingredients in a bucket, let the mixture sit for three or four days, and then paint it on fences, trellises, and wherever else unwanted varmints are venturing.

Jerry's Best Bets for...
Beautiful Bark

When early winter rolls around, it's time for your trees and shrubs to show their true colors—and their shapes, too! In the lists below, I've included some of the best choices for terrific twigs and trunks, as well as some with especially eye-catching shapes. For more options for trees and shrubs with interesting forms, turn back to "Jerry's Best Bets for Shapely Silhouettes" on page 14.

Trees with Attractive Bark

American yellowwood
 (*Cladrastis kentukea*)
Amur chokecherry
 (*Prunus maackii*)
Beeches (*Fagus*)
Benjamin Franklin tree
 (*Franklinia alatamaha*)
Chinese fringe tree
 (*Chionanthus retusus*)
Chinese paper birch
 (*Betula albosinensis*)
Coral-bark maple
 (*Acer palmatum*
 'Sango-kaku')
Crape myrtles
 (*Lagerstroemia*)
David maple (*Acer davidii*)
Gingko (*Ginkgo biloba*)
Golden weeping willow
 (*Salix alba* 'Tristis')
Himalayan birch
 (*Betula jacquemontii*)
Japanese flowering cherry
 (*Prunus serrulata*)
Japanese maple
 (*Acer palmatum*)
Japanese pagoda tree
 (*Sophora japonica*)
Japanese red pine
 (*Pinus densiflora*)

Kousa dogwood
 (*Cornus kousa*)
Lacebark elm
 (*Ulmus parviflora*)
Lacebark pine
 (*Pinus bungeana*)
Paperbark cherry
 (*Prunus serrula*)
Paperbark maple
 (*Acer griseum*)
Paper birch
 (*Betula papyrifera*)
Persian ironwood
 (*Parrotia persica*)
Persimmons
 (*Diospyros*)
River birch
 (*Betula nigra*)
Seven-son tree
 (*Heptacodium
 miconioides*)
Shagbark hickory
 (*Carya ovata*)

Snakebark maple
 (*Acer capillipes*)
Stewartias (*Stewartia*)
Strawberry tree
 (*Arbutus unedo*)
Striped maple
 (*Acer pensylvanicum*)
Sycamore
 (*Platanus occidentalis*)
Three-flower maple
 (*Acer triflorum*)
'Whitespire' birch
 (*Betula platyphylla* var.
 japonica 'Whitespire')

Shrubs with Showy Stems

Blueberries (*Vaccinium*)
Brooms (*Cytisus*)
Burning bush
 (*Euonymus alatus*)
Buttonbush
 (*Cephalanthus
 occidentalis*)
Cinnamon clethra
 (*Clethra acuminata*)
Ghost bramble
 (*Rubus biflorus*)
Hardy orange
 (*Poncirus trifoliata*)
Japanese clethra
 (*Clethra barbinervis*)

Japanese kerria
 (*Kerria japonica*)
Oak-leaved hydrangea
 (*Hydrangea quercifolia*)
Red-osier dogwood
 (*Cornus stolonifera*)
Red-twig dogwood
 (*Cornus alba*)

Red-twig willow
 (*Salix alba* var. *vitellina*
 'Chermesina')
Virginia rose
 (*Rosa virginiana*)
Wingthorn rose
 (*Rosa sericea* subsp.
 omeiensis f. *pteracantha*)
Winter jessamine
 (*Jasminum nudiflorum*)
Yellow-twig dogwood
 (*Cornus stolonifera*
 'Flaviramea')

Trees and Shrubs with Horizontal Branching

Atlas cedar
 (*Cedrus atlantica*)
Black gum
 (*Nyssa sylvatica*)
Dawn redwood
 (*Metasequoia
 glyptostroboides*)
Doublefile viburnum
 (*Viburnum plicatum*
 var. *tomentosum*)
Eastern white pine
 (*Pinus strobus*)

Flowering dogwood
 (*Cornus florida*)
Golden larch
 (*Pseudolarix
 amabilis*)
Japanese red pine
 (*Pinus
 densiflora*)
Kentucky coffee tree
 (*Gymnocladus
 dioica*)
Kousa dogwood
 (*Cornus kousa*)
Pagoda dogwood
 (*Cornus alternifolia*)
Pin oak
 (*Quercus palustris*)
Rockspray cotoneaster
 (*Cotoneaster
 horizontalis*)
Scots pine
 (*Pinus sylvestris*)
White oak
 (*Quercus alba*)

Trees and Shrubs with Curled or Contorted Stems

Burning bush
 (*Euonymus alatus*)
Contorted European beech
 (*Fagus sylvatica*
 'Tortuosa')
Contorted Hankow willow
 (*Salix matsudana*
 'Snake')
Contorted mulberry
 (*Morus australis*
 'Unryu')
Contorted quince
 (*Chaenomeles speciosa*
 'Contorta')
Corkscrew hazel
 (*Corylus avellana*
 'Contorta')

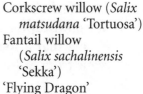

Corkscrew willow (*Salix
 matsudana* 'Tortuosa')
Fantail willow
 (*Salix sachalinensis*
 'Sekka')
'Flying Dragon'
 hardy orange
 (*Poncirus trifoliata*
 'Flying Dragon')
'Lavender Twist'
 weeping redbud
 (*Cercis canadensis*
 'Covey')
'Rocky Creek' holly
 (*Ilex crenata* 'Rocky
 Creek')
Twisted larch
 (*Larix kaempferi*
 'Diane')
Zig-zag camellia
 (*Camellia japonica*
 'Unryu')

CHAPTER 14

Make the Most of Midwinter

Most folks don't bother giving their yard a second thought during the depths of winter—and it's *their* loss. Once you know about all the exciting ways to jazz up your midwinter landscape, it's easy to fill your yard with colors, textures, and forms that'll make you *want* to be outside—or at least enjoy the view from indoors!

Your gardens should be under a snug blanket of mulch—and maybe even snow by now—and that pretty much puts a damper on digging, weeding, and so on. But there's still plenty to do if you want to get a jump start on the best year-round yard you've ever had!

- Order new seeds for the upcoming season's annuals and perennials
- Take a good look at your yard—both from the street and from indoors looking out—and figure out where you could use more plants for winter interest
- Sketch out plans for new flower beds and borders, so you'll be ready to plant come spring
- Check stored bulbs, and discard any that show signs of rot
- Cut back ornamental grasses that start looking a bit tattered
- Watch for perennials pushed out of the ground by frost
- Start bringing potted bulbs indoors for forcing

Whether your winter yard tends to be white with snow or brown with dead grass, evergreen trees and shrubs are invaluable for providing welcome color. There are still plenty of bright berries to enjoy, as well, and even some blooms busting out in the warmer parts of the country. So c'mon—let's take a good look at some perfect plants for your own winter wonderland!

Meet Your Greens

No two ways about it: Not all evergreens are created equal! When we think of elegant evergreens for winter color, we usually think of the rich greens of plants like spruces (*Picea*) and pines (*Pinus*). But other trees and shrubs touted as evergreen—such as arborvitaes (*Thuja*) and false cypresses (*Chamaecyparis*)—can be amazingly variable. Some varieties hold their color well, while others turn yucky colors that do little or nothing to improve the look of your yard.

These color changes have a lot to do with how severe winters are in your area, so take my advice: Bundle up on the next nice day and head out to your local botanical garden or arboretum for a stroll. Take note of which evergreens are holding their own at this

Grandma Putt's GREEN THUMB TIPS

I've said it before, but it bears repeating: If you want beautiful berries in your winter landscape, check to see if your chosen plant needs a buddy *before* you put it in the ground. Hollies (*Ilex*) and bayberries (*Myrica*) are just two shrubs that need partners for a good show: female plants to set fruit and male plants to provide the pollen. But what if you have room for only *one* shrub? Do what my Grandma Putt did, and set a male and female plant in the same hole! You'll be guaranteed a bountiful crop of berries every year—and a nice, bushy-looking shrub, too!

time of year—*and* which ones look the worse for wear. When it comes time to add more evergreens to your own yard, you'll know which plants to choose for glorious winter greens!

Evergreens—and Then Some!

Sure, evergreens are great for winter color—but don't forget everblues, evergolds, and everpurples, too! Trees and shrubs with anything-but-green foliage really perk things up this time of year, especially when you pair 'em with bright berries, colorful bark, and interesting ornamental grasses and groundcovers. Here are a few of my personal favorites to get you inspired:

Everblues: Blue atlas cedar (*Cedrus atlantica* f. *glauca*), 'Blue Star' juniper (*Juniperus squamata*), Colorado blue spruce (*Picea pungens* f. *glauca*)

Evergolds: Golden thread-leaved false cypress (*Chamaecyparis pisifera* 'Filifera Aurea'), 'Collen's Gold' arborvitae (*Thuja occidentalis*), 'Francis Mason' abelia (*Abelia* x *grandiflora*)

Everpurples: 'P.J.M.' rhododendron, 'Scarletta' fountain leucothoe (*Leucothoe fontanesiana*), grape hollies (*Mahonia*), heavenly bamboo (*Nandina domestica*)

Ask Jerry

Q: *I forgot to clean and oil my garden tools when I put them away last fall, and now they're getting rusty. Help!*

A: It's easy to get your rusty tools clean again, simply by rubbing them with a soap-filled steel wool pad dipped in kerosene or turpentine. (Be sure to do this in a well-ventilated area and wear gloves.) Finish the job by briskly rubbing the tools with wadded-up aluminum foil, and they'll shine like new!

Berry-Nice Bird Feeders

Don't be surprised if birds ignore your berried shrubs for a long time, then feast on them in mid- to late winter. Berries of hollies (*Ilex*) and junipers (*Juniperus*), for example, are simply not tasty to birds until they have been frozen and thawed several times, and actually begin to ferment. Some wildlife experts suspect that birds enjoy the alcohol that is present in well-weathered berries! Spray your shrubs with my Bye-Bye Birdie Brew (see page 288) to help keep these winged wonders away for a few more weeks, or simply let your feathered friends have their fun and enjoy their antics!

Spotlight on...

Hollies

When it comes to beautiful berries *and* outstanding foliage, evergreen hollies (*Ilex*) have to be the winners, hands down! Here are three of the best:

American holly (*I. opaca*): A 15- to 30-foot native holly with olive green foliage and dull red berries. Not the showiest of the bunch, but a little hardier than most other tree-size hollies. Some of the named selections, such as 'Jersey Knight' and 'Jersey Princess', can make a good winter display. Zones 5 to 9.

Blue holly (*I. x meserveae*): These shrub-sized hybrids have glossy, deep green leaves, deep purple stems, and glossy berries. They are a good choice for cooler areas. Zones 4 to 7.

Foster's holly (*I. x attenuata*): A group of hybrids well adapted to warm climates, with 'Foster #2' being the best of the bunch; it grows 20 to 30 feet tall and has glossy, medium-green leaves, plus deep red berries. (You'll need to plant the male 'Foster #4' as well to get fruit.) Zones 6 to 9.

Hollies grow best with full sun or partial shade in evenly moist, but well-drained, acidic soil. Give 'em a sheltered site whenever possible—the northern side of a building is usually best!

Build a Backyard Bird Sanctuary

For many folks, the whole idea of growing trees and shrubs with bright berries is to *attract* winter birds. But berries meet only one of their needs, so if you'd like to have a winter landscape that's literally for the birds, plan on adding the following features to your yard in the upcoming year:

→ Birds need lots of food, so besides berries, be sure to include seed-producing perennials as well as plenty of feeding stations.

→ A supply of fresh water for drinking and bathing is a must all year round, but it's *especially* important in winter!

→ A mix of trees, shrubs, and vines—both deciduous and evergreen—provides birds with welcome shelter from marauders, and safe places for nest-building, too.

Be Clever with Evergreens

Want to perk up your deck or patio for the winter? Snip some evergreen boughs—berried branches, too—and tuck them into pots and planters you've left outdoors for the season. Voilà—instant impact!

DEER BUSTER EGG BREW

If you notice that deer are starting to nibble on your winter landscape, protect the plants with this potent brew.

2 eggs
2 cloves of garlic
2 tbsp. of Tabasco® sauce
2 tbsp. of cayenne pepper
2 cups of water

Put all of the ingredients in a blender and purée. Allow the mixture to sit for two days, then pour or spray it all over and around the plants you need to protect. Reapply every other week or so, or after rain or snow, to keep the odor fresh.

MIX & FIX

Peerless Pieris

305

If you have good luck growing azaleas and rhododendrons, it's time to think about adding another elegant evergreen to your year-round yard: Japanese pieris (*Pieris japonica*). Talk about four-season interest—rich green foliage and sprays of red, pink, or cream-colored flower buds all winter, opening to bell-like blooms in spring, plus reddish new growth that ages to green through the rest of the growing season. It definitely earns its keep!

This slow-growing shrub eventually reaches about 8 feet tall and wide, so don't make the common mistake of tucking it into a tight corner or a narrow foundation planting—*unless* you choose a compact cultivar, such as pure white 'Cavatine' or rosy red 'Valley Valentine'!

A Honey of a Honeysuckle

Flowers in January? You bet! Winter honeysuckle (*Lonicera fragrantissima*) is one of the first shrubs to bust into bloom after New Year's with small, but intensely scented, white flowers over a period of several weeks. The plant itself isn't especially showy, so don't give it a prominent place; instead, pair it with other shrubs in a grouping near a door you use often, so you'll enjoy the scent as you pass by!

Ask Jerry

Q: *I saw the prettiest little rhododendron the other day—a compact, bushy plant totally covered in good-looking, deep green leaves. But when I looked at it closely, I saw a fuzzy brown coating on the undersides of the leaves. Is this some rare rhododendron disease?*

A: I can see why you'd wonder, but trust me—the plant you saw was in perfect health! That fuzzy brown stuff (folks in the know call it "indumentum") is a dead giveaway for a Yaku rhododendron (*Rhododendron yakushimanum*). If you check back in spring, you'll see that the new leaves look like they're completely covered in suede, but eventually, the indumentum wears off the leaf tops. Spring also brings pink buds that open to clusters of apple-blossom pink blooms. It's a true beauty—and at only 3 to 4 feet tall, it'll fit in just about any yard!

Spotlight on...

Crabapples

I used to think crabapples (*Malus*) were well named, 'cause nothing made me crabbier than dealing with their large, messy fruits and ugly, disease-damaged leaves. Well, thanks to busy hybridizers, all that's now a thing of the past! I wouldn't be without at least one crabapple in my yard, and you shouldn't, either.

Of course, most folks think of crabapples for their spring flowers, and that's fine; turn back to "Let's Get Crabby" on page 80 for some of my top picks for pretty blooms. But when you're looking for winter impact, it's the *fruits* you need to think about. In my experience, varieties with the smallest fruits also tend to hold on to them the longest; 'Molten Lava' and 'Red Jewel' are two with particularly long-lasting fruits. And since birds are usually drawn by red berries first, choosing crabapples with yellow fruits—such as 'Lancelot' and 'Walters'—can increase the odds of your getting a good show through most of the winter! All of these perform well in sunny, well-drained sites in Zones 3 to 7.

Even in the depths of winter, well-chosen perennials can light up your life with evergreen foliage, interesting seedheads, and even amazingly early blooms. This is also the time to get geared up for the busy spring season: It's closer than you might think! Check out my top tips for midwinter perennial care, then go ahead and put 'em to work in your own yard.

Don't Trash Those Trees!

Want to get your garden the best winter mulch money can buy—without spending a dime? After the holidays, drive around your neighborhood and pick up the Christmas trees people have put out for the trash. Cut off the branches and lay them over frozen perennials for a perfect lightweight, but insulating, winter mulch.

Roses in the Snow

If the early bird gets the worm, what does an extra-early perennial get? Extra cold, usually—but that's not a problem for Christmas rose (*Helleborus niger*)! This pretty plant doesn't quite live up to its name—it's definitely *not* a rose, and it rarely flowers as early as Christmas—

Grandma Putt's
GREEN THUMB TIPS

My Grandma Putt always said that no man-made mulch was half as good for a garden as a thick blanket of Mother Nature's Winter Finest. But if snow is lacking in your neck of the woods, take a tip out of Grandma's gardening notebook, and plan on making regular strolls through your yard during spells of mild weather. If frost has pushed any perennials or bulbs out of the ground, press them back down into the soil, if you can; if not, then cover them up with mulch to prevent them from drying out until you can replant them properly in spring.

but it's still a beauty by anyone's standards. Its golden-centered, bright white, bowl-shaped blooms are a welcome sight during the dull days of mid- to late winter, and the leathery, evergreen leaves look great all year long. Despite its delicate beauty, Christmas rose is no fussy prima donna; it grows just fine in partial shade and average soil anywhere from Zones 4 to 9. Talk about adaptable!

Seed Starter's Checklist

If you need lots of perennials, but don't want to blow a lot of dough, it's time to start thinking about sowing some seeds indoors. Begin gathering supplies now, and you'll be all ready to go as soon as your seeds arrive!

→ Go through all those seed catalogs that arrived after the holidays, and place your orders right away!

→ Make space for seed pots on your windowsills, or invest in a few 4-foot-long, fluorescent shop lights.

→ Gather a supply of clean, plastic pots (3- and 4-inch pots work best for most seeds).

→ Whip up a batch of my Super Seed-Starting Mix, so you'll have plenty of good growing medium on hand.

MIX & FIX

SUPER SEED-STARTING MIX

Typical potting soil is way too rich for small seedlings, and it can foster a bunch of funky fungi that'll quickly wipe out whole pots of baby plants. To get your seeds up and growing safely, I suggest blendin' up a batch of my Super Seed-Starting Mix.

2 parts peat moss
1 part perlite or vermiculite
Warm water

Mix the peat moss and perlite or vermiculite in a bag or bucket. The day before sowing seeds, moisten the mix by adding warm water—a few cups at a time—and working it in with your hands until the mix feels evenly moist to the touch.

A Bounty of Bulbs

To most folks, midwinter may seem like a bad time to be thinking about bulbs, but it just ain't so! In fact, it's actually one of the *best* times—*if* you've done some advance planning! Outdoors, it's just a few short weeks until your earliest Dutch dandies make their appearance, and in the meantime, all kinds of "forced" bulbs are busting into bloom indoors. Want to learn more? Check out my Baker's Best-of-the Bunch bulb tips, and be prepared for your most flower-filled winter ever!

Check, Please

When it comes to getting tender bulbs through the winter in good shape, a little attention goes a long way! Every few weeks, root through your bags and boxes of stored bulbs to make sure everything looks okay. If you see signs of mold or rot, discard the affected bulbs, and place the remaining ones in clean, dry packing material (such as unused peat moss or sawdust). If dahlia tubers or canna rhizomes look shriveled, sprinkle them with water to plump 'em up.

Ask Jerry

Q: *I took your advice and potted up a few amaryllis (Hippeastrum) bulbs back in the fall, and they truly were spectacular! Now that they're just about done blooming, how do I take care of them?*

A: It's amazingly easy to keep your favorite amaryllis bulbs from year to year. Simply cut off the spent flower stalks and treat the bulbs as you would any other houseplant until early summer; then sink 'em (pot and all) into the soil in a sunny spot outdoors. Come fall, cut the leaves back to a couple inches above the bulb, then lift the pots out of the soil. Set them in a cool area, and keep the soil moist. Pretty soon, the bulbs will send up new growth—and they'll be back in bloom in no time at all!

310

The Pebble Beach Bunch

Some bulbs will do their thing even without being planted—in the normal way, at least! Paperwhites, a type of polyanthus daffodil (*Narcissus tazetta*) prized for its powerfully scented flowers, will grow and bloom remarkably well in just water and pebbles.

After choosing your planter (you can use anything that doesn't have drainage holes), fill it almost to the top with pebbles or aquarium gravel. Nestle the base of the bulbs into the pebbles, then add enough water to cover the pebbles and the bottom quarter of the bulbs. Check daily, and add water as needed to keep the right level.

When the stems are about 3 inches tall, it's time to move the container into curtain-filtered sunlight. Wait until you see the flower buds forming before giving the pot full sunlight. When the blooms open, enjoy your fragrant paperwhites!

MIX & FIX

HOUSEPLANT REPOTTING MIX

While you're getting bulbs ready for forcing in midwinter, take a few minutes to repot your houseplants, too. This super soil will get 'em growing up right!

1 lb. of potting soil
1 lb. of professional potting mix
¹/₄ cup of Epsom salts
¹/₄ cup of bonemeal
1 tbsp. of instant tea granules

Thoroughly mix all of the ingredients, then sprinkle it around the root mass of your plants as you replant them. <u>Don't</u> pack it in.

The Living End

Gardeners of all ages have fun watching plants grow in plain water. Besides enjoying the seldom-seen beauty of roots floating in the water, you'll be the hit of the garden club meeting when you show off a lovely bloom growing in a hyacinth glass. This special vase looks like an hourglass: The bulb sits in the top part, and plain water (or water and pebbles, if you prefer) goes in the bottom.

To get started, take a pre-cooled hyacinth bulb (see "Grandma Putt's Green Thumb Tips" at right) and remove any soil, dead skin, and shriveled roots before nestling it into the top of the glass. Fill the glass with water up to the base of the bulb, and set it in a cool, dark place until the roots reach the bottom of the glass and the top starts to grow. Then move the glass into a cool, bright room until the bulb blooms.

Grandma Putt's
GREEN THUMB TIPS

When you buy paperwhite bulbs for forcing, they've already been chilled and are ready to start growing. You can buy pre-cooled hyacinth bulbs, too, but they cost more than ordinary bulbs. Save yourself some dough with this great tip I learned from Grandma Putt, and chill 'em yourself! Buy them as soon as they hit the garden centers, then put them in the produce drawer of your refrigerator for 8 to 10 weeks. Take them out and plant them for flowers in a few weeks!

Divine Vines and Groundcovers

If your yard is covered with a blanket of snow all winter, there's not much point in worrying about groundcovers for interest this time of year. But elsewhere, evergreen groundcovers (and vines, too) can go a long way toward getting rid of your winter blues!

How Green Is My Groundcover

For carpets of color all winter long, evergreen groundcovers are where it's at! It's no surprise that the three most widely planted

312

groundcovers in the country—English ivy (*Hedera helix*), Japanese pachysandra (*Pachysandra terminalis*), and periwinkles (*Vinca*)—all offer gorgeous, rich green foliage every month of the year. But don't overlook the beauty of groundcovers in other colors, too, like the rich gold of 'Mother Lode' creeping juniper (*Juniperus horizontalis*), the icy blue needles of creeping Colorado blue spruce (*Picea pungens* 'Procumbens'), and the deep plum foliage of purple wintercreeper (*Euonymus fortunei* 'Coloratus'). Grow 'em alone as an eye-catching landscape accent, or mix 'em up for a cheerful combo.

Perfume a Room—with Flowers!

Of all the flowering groundcovers there are to choose from, lily-of-the-valley (*Convallaria majalis*) has to be one of my favorites. But if you've ever grown it yourself, you know that it can spread like nobody's business. Well, here's a great way to make use of some of the extras: Force them for indoor bloom! Here's how:

Step 1: During a midwinter thaw, dig up a half-dozen or so plants, and cut their roots back to about 3 inches.

Step 2: Soak the plants in warm water for a few hours, then pot them up in a 6-inch container, with their tips just above the soil surface.

Step 3: Set the pot in a cool place, and keep it evenly moist. Once new growth begins, move it to a warm, bright spot. You'll be enjoying fragrant blooms in just a week or two!

Ask Jerry

Q: *After years of watching my kids take a shortcut through my groundcovers, I finally laid down a nice stepping-stone path to keep them from trampling on the plants. But now I'm noticing that the stones have shifted around, making them difficult to walk on. Any suggestions?*

A: The freeze-and-thaw cycles that can push your plants out of the ground can do the same to brick or stone walkways. To keep 'em in place, try mulching over them with 6 inches or so of chopped leaves or straw as soon as the ground freezes. When spring returns, you can quickly gather up the material and add it to your compost pile, or else use it to mulch some other part of your yard.

Spotlight on . . .

Heaths and Heathers

Back when I was boy, I remember heaths (*Erica*) and heathers (*Calluna*) growing in just about everybody's yard. Nowadays, though, you seldom see them—*except* where smart year-round gardeners have done their homework! If you've got the acidic soil and ample sunlight these plants love, you can enjoy the evergreen foliage and cheery blooms of these tough little plants every month of the year.

Most heaths and heathers grow anywhere from 6 inches to 3 feet tall, and they look great planted in groups, so they're tailor-made for use as groundcovers. Besides coming in all shades of green, their leaves can be gold, orange, red, and silvery gray, while the flowers are typically white, pink, or purple. Heathers usually bloom in mid- to late summer, while heaths can flower any time from early winter to early spring, depending on which ones you choose.

There are dozens of varieties to choose from, so I suggest that you see them for yourself at your local garden center to get the ideal plants for your particular needs. When you get them home, be sure to give them perfect drainage. Work some peat moss into the soil before planting, too—that'll get 'em growin' like gangbusters!

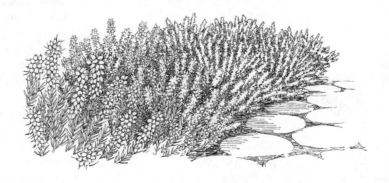

Jerry's Best Bets for...
The Big Chill

When Jack Frost is nipping at your nose and Ol' Man Winter is freezin' your toes, it's time to enjoy your year-round yard from the indoors looking out. Fill it with lots of evergreen foliage, and you'll always have something worth seeing—even when the snow is flying!

Evergreen Trees

American arborvitae
   (*Thuja occidentalis*)
American holly
   (*Ilex opaca*)
Austrian pine
   (*Pinus nigra*)
Bristlecone pine
   (*Pinus aristata*)
Canada hemlock
   (*Tsuga canadensis*)
Carolina hemlock
   (*Tsuga caroliniana*)
Chinese juniper
   (*Juniperus chinensis*)
Colorado spruce
   (*Picea pungens*)
Douglas fir
   (*Pseudotsuga menziesii*)
Eastern red cedar
   (*Juniperus virginiana*)
Eastern white pine
   (*Pinus strobus*)
Foster holly
   (*Ilex* x *attenuata*)

Fraser fir (*Abies fraseri*)
Japanese cryptomeria
   (*Cryptomeria japonica*)
Japanese red pine
   (*Pinus densiflora*)
Lacebark pine
   (*Pinus bungeana*)
Leyland cypress
   (x *Cupressocyparis
   leylandii*)
Limber pine
   (*Pinus flexilis*)
Nootka false cypress
   (*Chamaecyparis
   nootkatensis*)
Norway spruce (*Picea abies*)
Oriental spruce
   (*Picea orientalis*)
Pinyon pine (*Pinus edulis*)
Ponderosa pine
   (*Pinus ponderosa*)
Rocky Mountain juniper
   (*Juniperus scopulorum*)
Scots pine
   (*Pinus sylvestris*)
Serbian spruce
   (*Picea omorika*)
Southern magnolia
   (*Magnolia grandiflora*)
Western red cedar
   (*Thuja plicata*)
White fir (*Abies concolor*)
White spruce
   (*Picea glauca*)

Evergreen Shrubs

Blue holly (*Ilex* x *meserveae*)
'Boulevard' false cypress
   (*Chamaecyparis pisifera*
   'Boulevard')
Carolina rhododendron
   (*Rhododendron
   carolinianum*)
Cherry laurel
   (*Prunus laurocerasus*)
Chinese holly
   (*Ilex cornuta*)

Chinese juniper
   (*Juniperus chinensis*)
Common boxwood
   (*Buxus sempervirens*)
Common camellia
   (*Camellia japonica*)
Dwarf Alberta spruce
   (*Picea glauca* 'Conica')
English yew
   (*Taxus baccata*)
False hollies
   (*Osmanthus*)
Fountain leucothoe
   (*Leucothoe fontanesiana*)

Golden thread-leaved false
cypress (*Chamaecyparis
pisifera* 'Filifera Aurea')
Grape hollies
(*Mahonia*)
Hinoki false cypress
(*Chamaecyparis obtusa*)
Hybrid yew
(*Taxus* x *media*)
Inkberry (*Ilex glabra*)
Japanese aucuba
(*Aucuba japonica*)
Japanese pieris
(*Pieris japonica*)
Japanese yew
(*Taxus cuspidata*)
Little-leaved boxwood
(*Buxus microphylla*)
Mountain laurel
(*Kalmia latifolia*)
Mugo pine
(*Pinus mugo*)
'P.J.M.' rhododendron
(*Rhododendron* 'P.J.M.')
Red-tip photinia
(*Photinia* x *fraseri*)
Sasanqua camellia
(*Camellia sasanqua*)
Winter daphne
(*Daphne odora*)
Yaku rhododendron
(*Rhododendron
yakushimanum*)

Evergreen Perennials
Basket-of-gold
(*Aurinia saxatilis*)
Coral bells (*Heuchera*)
Gladwyn iris
(*Iris foetidissima*)
Heart-leaved bergenia
(*Bergenia cordifolia*)
Hellebores
(*Helleborus*)
Hens-and-chicks
(*Sempervivum*)
Italian arum
(*Arum italicum*)
Perennial candytuft
(*Iberis sempervirens*)
Pinks (*Dianthus*)
Purple wood spurge
(*Euphorbia
amygdaloides* 'Purpurea')
Stokes' aster
(*Stokesia laevis*)
Thrifts (*Armeria*)
Wall rock cresses (*Arabis*)
Yuccas (*Yucca*)

Evergreen Vines and Groundcovers
Ajugas (*Ajuga*)
Bearberry
(*Arctostaphylos uva-ursi*)
Colchican ivy
(*Hedera colchica*)
Creeping juniper
(*Juniperus horizontalis*)
English ivy
(*Hedera helix*)
European wild ginger
(*Asarum europaeum*)
Giant periwinkle
(*Vinca major*)
Hardy ice plants
(*Delosperma*)
Heathers (*Calluna*)

Heaths (*Erica*)
Japanese pachysandra
(*Pachysandra terminalis*)
Lesser periwinkle
(*Vinca minor*)
Liriopes (*Liriope*)
Mondo grasses
(*Ophiopogon*)
Moss phlox
(*Phlox subulata*)
Mother-of-thyme
(*Thymus serpyllum*)
Partridgeberry
(*Mitchella repens*)
Robb's spurge
(*Euphorbia robbiae*)
Siberian carpet cypress
(*Microbiota decussata*)
Skimmias (*Skimmia*)
Snow-in-summer
(*Cerastium tomentosum*)
Two-row stonecrop
(*Sedum spurium*)
Wintercreeper
(*Euonymus fortunei*)
Wintergreen
(*Gaultheria procumbens*)

CHAPTER 15

Late Winter: Gearing Up for Spring

O nce you've been bitten by the gardening bug, it seems like you can positively *feel* when spring's right around the corner. So shake off those winter doldrums, and check out all the tips and tricks I've packed into this chapter. Then, get ready to have the most *amazing* year-round yard you've ever imagined!

The days are finally getting longer, and pretty soon, winter's chill will be a thing of the past. If you start taking care of spring chores now, you won't get overwhelmed by the rush when the growing season kicks into high gear!

- Finish cleaning up your yard

- Prune dormant roses in mild-winter climates

- Bring branches of early-blooming trees indoors to force them into flowering

- Order seeds and plants from mail-order sources

- Root-prune trees and shrubs you plan to move later

- Sow annual and perennial seeds indoors

- Weed flower beds and borders as the weather permits

- Watch out for pests and diseases on new growth in warm climates

- Check on stored bulbs, and discard any that show signs of rot

- Cut down ornamental grasses before new growth appears

Who says you have to wait until spring for beautiful bloomers? Check out these terrific trees and super shrubs for livening up your late-winter landscape. Their bright blooms and pleasing perfumes are enough to send Ol' Man Winter scurryin' in a hurry!

This Cherry's a Real Peach

To my mind, nothing says "Welcome, spring!" like the pretty blooms of flowering cherries (*Prunus*). And if you want to give spring an extra-early welcome in your yard, you can't do better than the extra-early flowers of 'Okame' cherry (*P.* 'Okame'). It bursts into bloom soon after the first mild days of late winter, with abundant clusters of clear pink blossoms that are guaranteed to brighten your day. As an added bonus, 'Okame' cherry provides a spectacular show of fall color in glowing shades of orange and red. That's sure a lot of impact from one easy-to-grow small tree!

Go Crazy with Quince

By far, the greatest majority of early-blooming trees and shrubs come in a palette of pastel colors: mainly yellows, pale pinks, and white. So where do you turn if you're looking for a

Ask Jerry

Q: Hey, Jer—I'd swear I just saw the biggest forsythia bush in my life! I know they can get pretty large, but this one looked more like a small tree. It's blooming a few weeks earlier than other forsythias, too. Is it some special variety?

A: Dollars to doughnuts, what you saw wasn't a forsythia at all, but a cornelian cherry (*Cornus mas*). This dogwood relative is prized for its bright yellow, late-winter to early-spring blooms, which are followed by cherry-red fruits in midsummer. (The fruits are edible, by the way, but most don't have much flavor. So I usually leave 'em for the birds to feast on!)

real jolt of color to kick off the growing season with a bang? Try flowering quinces (*Chaenomeles*)! Their bold blooms pack enough punch to satisfy the most color-starved gardener, in shocking shades of sizzling scarlet, dazzling orange, and glowing coral as well as softer peach and white. The only downside is that the shrubs themselves aren't much to look at for the other 50 weeks of the year. But if you have room to tuck one among your other shrubs, you'll sure enjoy the show while it lasts!

ROOT PRUNING TONIC

Help your trees and shrubs spring back quickly after root pruning with this nourishing tonic.

1 can of beer
4 tbsp. of instant tea granules
1 tbsp. of shampoo
1 tbsp. of ammonia
1 tbsp. of hydrogen peroxide
1 tbsp. of whiskey
2 gal. of very warm water

Mix all of the ingredients together. Then pour a quart of the elixir into the soil at the spots where you've cut your shrubs' roots.

MIX & FIX

The Roots of the Matter

Thinking of moving an established tree or shrub within the next year? The job'll go a whole lot easier *then* if you try a trick called "root pruning" *now*! Simply dig a narrow, circular trench about 18 inches deep all the way around the plant. (The outer edge of the trench should be a few inches inside the outer limit of the branch tips.) Saw through any big roots, and cut smaller ones with clippers, then replace the soil. Scatter about $1/4$ pound of Epsom salts over the soil all around the plant, then give it a dose of my Root Pruning Tonic (at left). This'll encourage lots of new roots to form, and the transplanting process will go a whole lot easier on all concerned.

Pick the Right Site

How is growing early-blooming shrubs like selling a house? Location is everything! Common sense would tell you to site them in a warm, sheltered spot (against a south-facing wall, for example), but that can actually be a very *bad* idea! Yes, you'll get the earliest possible blooms, but those blossoms can get zapped into a mushy mess by the cold snaps that are almost inevitable in this changeable season.

So what's the answer? Plant winter bloomers in a cooler spot—against a north wall or on a north-facing slope. That'll delay the blooms a bit, but by the time they *do* open, there's much less chance of their getting nipped by frost. Or, if you have the space, why not try them in both places? You'll be guaranteed to get at least some flowers every year, and in good years, you'll get *double* the blooms with no extra effort!

Spotlight on...

Witch Hazels

When winter bloom and fabulous fragrance are high on your list of must-haves, witch hazels (*Hamamelis*) are what you're looking for! These showy shrubs or small trees are bedecked with an abundance of crinkled, ribbon-like petals that curl up on cold nights and unfurl when the air warms again. Bright yellow 'Arnold Promise' (*H.* x *intermedia*) is one of the best-known of the bunch, but it's also one of the latest to open (usually in late winter). Pale yellow 'Primavera' and vernal witch hazel (*H. vernalis*) aren't quite as showy, but they're usually open two or three weeks earlier.

Witch hazels thrive in evenly moist, but well-drained, humus-rich soil in Zones 5 to 9. They'll grow fine in partial shade, but they usually bloom best in full sun. Ample light also tends to bring out the brightest fall colors—usually flaming shades of gold and orange.

You *Can* Have It All!

Here's a sweet idea for cold-season color: plant wintersweet (*Chimonanthus praecox*)! This little-known shrub is a top-notch, off-season bloomer for milder climates (Zones 6 to 9), where it'll produce its sweet-scented, yellow-and-purple flowers for weeks at a time in mid- to late winter. Wintersweet is a slow grower, but eventually gets pretty large—anywhere from 6 to 12 feet tall and wide—so be sure to give it ample space at planting time. And if possible, site it near a door or walkway, so the beautiful blooms and pleasing perfume can lift your spirits every time you pass by!

Use a Bloomin' Calendar

If you're aiming for year-round excitement, keeping track of bloom times in your own yard is the very best way to make sure you have all the seasons covered. Try this terrific trick I picked up from Grandma Putt: Buy an extra monthly calendar at your local stationery store or bookstore (they're usually half-price by this time), and keep it with your gardening tools. Each time you go out to your yard, jot down the names of what's in bloom. Next winter, look back on your successes for the year, and plan to fill in any gaps with appropriate seasonal bloomers!

Jazz Up Your Yard with Jasmine

Looking to cover a slope with something out of the ordinary? Winter jasmine (*Jasminum nudiflorum*) might be just the thing!

Ask Jerry

Q: *I saw big bunches of pussy willow (Salix discolor) stems for sale at a flower shop today, weeks before they'll bloom outside. They were beautiful, but the price was outrageous! Is there a way to do the same thing with the pussy willows in my yard?*

A: You bet—and you'll save a bundle! Simply snip some stems in mid- to late winter, then place 'em in jars of lukewarm water in a cool, sunny room. They'll be ready to open in 7 to 10 days! This trick works with lots of other early bloomers, too, including apples, forsythias, peaches, plums, and witch hazels.

This mounding shrub grows in masses of slender, trailing, bright green branches that hold their color all year round. Sunny yellow blooms open a few at a time throughout the winter months, followed by rich green foliage that lasts all during the growing season. Winter jasmine can adapt to just about any growing conditions in Zones 6 to 10, so it's a top-notch choice for multi-season interest in those tough sites where nothing else seems to thrive!

Sweets for the Sweet

Is it a shrub, or is it a groundcover? Actually, it's both—and it's a beauty! I'm talking about sweet box (*Sarcococca hookeriana*). Even if it didn't bloom, this bushy evergreen would be worth growing for its glossy, deep green foliage alone. But when it *does* flower—well, WOW just about describes it! The greenish white blooms themselves aren't showy at all, since they're nestled under the leaves, but their sweet scent is noticeable from several feet away all through late winter and early spring. Sweet box grows about 4 feet tall and spreads gently to create a great replacement for grass under trees and taller shrubs. What a wonderful way to cut down on tedious trimming chores—*and* get all-year interest, too!

Rose Start-Up Tonic

Ready to get your rosebushes off to a rosy start? Late winter's the prime time to give 'em a taste of this fabulous tonic.

1 tbsp. of dishwashing liquid
1 tbsp. of hydrogen peroxide
1 tsp. of whiskey
1 tsp. of vitamin B$_1$ plant starter
$^1\!/_2$ gal. of warm tea

Mix all of these ingredients, then pour the liquid all around the root zone of each of your rosebushes.

Signs of Spring

Even though weather watching and predicting have theoretically become scientific and sophisticated today, the simple truth of the matter is that Mother

Nature can still give us the inside scoop on the coming weather. If you pay attention to her signs, it won't be long before you can use them to help you plan your day!

→ When the leaves on the trees turn their backs to the west, a storm is just around the corner.

→ Red sky at night, the next day is a delight.

→ Red sky at morning is a storm warning.

→ When the bees leave the flower patch, the rains are a comin'.

→ When the anthills are small, it will be a dry, hot summer.

Dependable Perennials

It's still a bit early to look for blooms from your flower gardens—but that doesn't mean it's time to rest on your laurels! There's plenty to do if you want to get a jump start on spring, so take a look at my top tips for pre-season perennial care, then get busy putting 'em to work!

Super-Easy Perennials from Seed

Contrary to popular belief, many perennials are just as easy to grow from seed as annuals. And believe it or not, some extra-speedy varieties can bloom the same year you sow them—just like annuals—then live on to flower year after year, too! To help ensure first-year blooms, give these speed demons a head start by sowing 'em indoors in late winter:

Anise hyssop (*Agastache foeniculum*)

Balloon flower (*Platycodon grandiflorus*)

Black-eyed Susans (*Rudbeckia*)

Carpathian harebell (*Campanula carpatica*)

'Foxy' foxglove (*Digitalis purpurea*)

Jupiter's beard (*Centranthus ruber*)

'Lady' lavender (*Lavandula angustifolia*)

Tree mallow (*Malva sylvestris*)

Potting's a Piece of—Pizza?

Getting ready to sow some seeds in late winter? Here's a terrific idea that'll make cleanup a breeze! Take the box from last night's take-out pizza and open it up to make a handy potting tray. When you're done, just close it up and throw it out or recycle it. No muss, no fuss!

Make a Mini-Greenhouse

You know those clear plastic, zippered covers that pillows, bedspreads, and sleeping bags are packed in? Well, don't throw them out: They make great little greenhouses for baby perennials! Set the sown seed pots in the bags, then place some kind of stake in each

SEED STARTER TONIC

Whether you start your seeds indoors or out, give them a good send-off with this terrific timely tonic.

1 cup of white vinegar
1 tbsp. of baby shampoo
   or dishwashing liquid
2 cups of warm water

Mix all of these ingredients together in a bowl, and let your seeds soak in the mixture overnight before planting them in well-prepared soil.

MIX
&
FIX

324

corner to hold the plastic away from the emerging seedlings, and zip the bag closed. When the young plants are an inch or so tall, gradually unzip the bag to let in the fresh air. After a week, remove the bag entirely, let it dry out, and save it for your next seed-starting session.

Growing Great Seedlings Is a Breeze!

Once your seedlings are up and growing, it's time to cut back on the TLC. In fact, a little tough love—or at least, a stiff breeze—can be just the thing for keeping all your seedlings short and sturdy, instead of spindly and sprawling. Once you've removed their plastic covering, set up a small fan at the lowest setting to blow across their tops. The moving air will keep your flowers growing low and bushy—and it'll put a stop to dastardly disease problems, too!

Ask Jerry

Q: How soon is it safe to take the mulch off my flower gardens?

A: Once the ground starts thawing for good, it's time to remove the protective mulch you put on last fall or winter. Leave the remains of last year's weed-suppressing mulch, though. Work carefully, so you don't damage the bright green bulb shoots that are poking up their heads now. While you're de-mulching, it's also a good time to pull out any winter-sprouting weeds, like chickweed.

Cut—And That's a Wrap!

When it's time to start cutting back and cleaning up the perennial garden, my favorite tool is a pair of hand-held hedge trimmers. They make short work of bushy plants like asters, boltonia (*Boltonia asteroides*), mums (*Chrysanthemum* x *morifolium*), and stonecrops (*Sedum*). They work okay for ornamental grasses, too, but for even quicker results, try electric hedge shears instead. Before cutting, tie up the tops of the grasses to keep them from scattering all over your yard, and make sure there are no stakes left in the clump.

A Measure of Success

Here's a neat way to kill two birds with one stone—turn your gardening tools into handy measuring devices! It's easy to do. Use a file to mark your long-handled tools inch by inch from the top to the bottom, then use stain or ink to fill in the file marks. Voilà! You've got an easy way to measure spacing when setting out perennials and bulbs.

Plan Now for Perfect Perennials Later

Your perennials will get off to a rip-roarin' start if you prepare their new bed a couple of weeks before you actually set out the plants. After you've cultivated the soil to a depth of at least 12 inches and mixed in a 4-inch blanket of organic matter, saturate the prepared bed with my Soil Soother Tonic (see page 326). Then cover it with mulch to help it mellow until planting time. You won't believe the results!

A Rosy Idea for Late Winter

Want to enjoy some of the earliest blooms on your block? Lenten

Grandma Putt's
GREEN THUMB TIPS

When you're busy getting your yard ready for its spring fling, it's easy to misplace your trowels, clippers, and other small tools in the rush. Well, my Grandma Putt came up with a super solution, and it's still a great one for forgetful gardeners: Simply mount an old mailbox (or a new one, if you want) on a post in one of your flower beds, and use it to store small tools, string, seed packets, and all those other little items that are so easy to lose track of. Besides providing a practical storage area, the mailbox makes a nice decorative accent, too!

roses (*Helleborus* x *hybridus*) are just the ticket! These beauties are prized for their delicate-looking, bowl- or bell-shaped blooms, usually in shades of red, pink, or white, which appear from late winter through early spring—just when you're desperate for flowers after a long, dull winter. The show doesn't end there, though: In midspring, Lenten roses send up glossy, deep green leaves that last all the way until bloom time the following year! Planted in groups, the 1-foot-tall clumps make a fantastic groundcover for shady sites—even those tough-to-dig, root-filled areas under trees and shrubs that send lesser plants to an early grave.

MIX
&
FIX

SOIL SOOTHER TONIC

Get your soil in super shape with a generous dose of this elixir.

1 can of beer
1 can of regular cola (not diet)
¹/₂ cup of dishwashing liquid
¹/₂ cup of tobacco tea*

Mix all of the ingredients together in a bucket, then apply with a 20 gallon hose-end sprayer to the point of run-off.

*Place half a handful of chewing tobacco in an old nylon stocking, and soak it in a gallon of hot water until the mixture is dark brown.

A Bounty of Bulbs

Get ready, my fellow bulb lovers—our time has come! As soon as the soil starts thawing, a bunch of extra-early bulbs will be ready to stick their noses out of the cold ground and start growin' like gangbusters. Interested in learning more about your options for these bountiful bloomers? Check out this collection of my top tips—then make a note to add them to your yard at planting time next fall!

You'll Like Aconites

There's just something about seeing winter aconites (*Eranthis hyemalis*) that puts a big smile on my face—and I'll bet my bottom dollar that they'll do the same for you! Maybe it's those bright, buttercup yellow flowers that peek up right through the snow, or that funny green ruff that's snugged up tight against the base of each blossom. Or maybe it's just that the sight of these short-but-sturdy bloomers is a sure sign that spring's right around the corner!

Winter aconites grow in full sun or partial shade, and unlike many bulbs, they appreciate soil that stays moist through the summer. The bulbs you buy in fall tend to be dried out, so remember to soak 'em in warm water overnight before planting—then be prepared to enjoy them this time next year!

Go Daffy for This Daffodil

Want to start the daffodil season off with a bang? You can enjoy those gorgeous golden blooms several weeks earlier than all of your neighbors—*if* you grow the little beauty known as *Narcissus asturiensis*! You're not likely to find it for sale at your local garden center, but some mail-order suppliers offer it, and it's definitely worth hunting out. Unlike most daffodils, which appreciate some summer moisture, this little gem thrives in the same conditions that tulips love: a full-sun site that gets hot and dry during the summer. It will even self-sow, creating clumps of can't-miss color that are sure to brighten even the dreariest late-winter day.

Grandma Putt's
GREEN THUMB TIPS

Daffodils need a bit of extra attention when you cut and bring them inside, so do what Grandma Putt did: Stand them in an inch of cold water and place them in the refrigerator for a few hours after you first bring them in. Later, when you arrange them in a vase, make sure you don't put the daffodils in with any other cut flowers—their stems excrete sap that is harmful to any other blooms standing in a vase with them.

A Quick Bulb Snack Trick

Do what professional bulb growers swear by—give your bulbs a light snack in late winter or early spring—and you'll be *amazed* at the results. Once you see their noses sticking out of the ground, spread a handful of garden food (4-12-4 or 5-10-5 formulation) over the soil.

Spotlight on . . .

Crocuses

There's no doubt about it: A winter garden simply isn't complete without crocuses! Inexpensive to buy and easy to plant, crocus corms are small enough to tuck in just about anywhere—among perennials in beds and borders, in grassy areas for a spring meadow effect, or tucked into groundcovers for spots of welcome color.

For the first crocuses on your block each year, pick a site against a south-facing wall, where the soil will be warmed by the winter sun. Then fill that spot with the earliest-blooming crocuses, including snow crocus (*Crocus chrysanthus*), cloth-of-gold crocus (*C. angustifolius*), and Thomasini's crocus (*C. tommasinianus*). To extend the crocus season through midspring, include some later-blooming Scotch crocus (*C. biflorus*) and Dutch crocus (*C. vernus*), too.

Hardy in Zones 3 to 8, crocuses need full sun and grow fine in poor to average, well-drained soil. They look best in groups of at least a dozen corms, so to get the best show, buy as many as you can afford. Plant them 3 to 4 inches deep, and about 3 inches apart, in fall.

Try These Three!

Don't let those long-winter blues get you down—celebrate them instead with these true-blue, late-winter bloomers! All three grow about 6 inches tall and appreciate a well-drained site with full sun to partial shade. Try 'em in large groupings under witch hazels (*Hamamelis*), cornelian cherry (*Cornus mas*), or forsythias for an eye-catching blue-and-gold combo.

Glory-of-the-snow (*Chionodoxa luciliae*): Starry, lavender-blue blooms with near-white centers. Zones 3 to 9.

Siberian squill (*Scilla siberica*): Nodding blooms in a rich, pure blue. Zones 3 to 8.

Striped squill (*Puschkinia scilloides*): Very similar to Siberian squill, but the blooms are pale blue with darker blue stripes. Zones 3 to 9.

On the Straight and Narrow

Tired of having your cut-flower tulips turning every which way? To straighten up curvy stems, wrap the tulips in newspaper, covering the flower heads, but not the lower third of the stems. Then recut the stems, and place the wrapped bunch upright in a container of cold water for an hour or two.

Ask Jerry

Q: *After my indoor-grown bulbs have finished blooming, can I plant them outside?*

A: Well, you *can*, but I don't recommend it for most bulbs. The results are usually disappointing and not worth the effort.

Jerry's Best Bets for...
Cold-Weather Color

After a rough winter, spring can't come nearly soon enough—so why wait? Include a selection of these excellent early bloomers, and you'll enjoy fabulous flowers and pleasing perfumes long before the calendar proclaims the official first day of spring. Just remember that winter-blooming plants tend to be much less showy than their later-flowering counterparts, so keep 'em close at hand: near a door or walkway that you use every day, or right outside a window you look out of often!

Trees

Chinese witch hazel
   (*Hamamelis mollis*)
Cornelian cherry
   (*Cornus mas*)
Fall-flowering cherry
   (*Prunus* x *subhirtella*
   'Autumnalis')
Hybrid witch hazel
   (*Hamamelis* x
   intermedia)
Japanese flowering
  apricot
   (*Prunus mume*)
'Okame' cherry
   (*Prunus* 'Okame')
Persian ironwood
   (*Parrotia persica*)
Star magnolia
   (*Magnolia stellata*)

Vernal witch hazel
   (*Hamamelis vernalis*)
Yulan magnolia
   (*Magnolia denudata*)

Shrubs

Black pussy willow
   (*Salix gracilistyla*
   'Melanostachys')
Buttercup winter hazel
   (*Corylopsis*
   pauciflora)
Common camellia
   (*Camellia*
   japonica)
February daphne
   (*Daphne*
   mezereum)
Flowering quince
   (*Chaenomeles*
   speciosa)

Fragrant viburnum
   (*Viburnum farreri*)
Japanese flowering quince
   (*Chaenomeles*
   japonica)
Laurustinus
   (*Viburnum tinus*)
Pussy willow
   (*Salix discolor*)
Sasanqua camellia
   (*Camellia sasanqua*)
Spicebush
   (*Lindera benzoin*)
Spike winter hazel
   (*Corylopsis spicata*)
Sweet box
   (*Sarcococca*
   hookeriana)
Winter daphne
   (*Daphne odora*)
Winter honeysuckle
   (*Lonicera*
   fragrantissima)
Winter jasmine
   (*Jasminum*
   nudiflorum)
Wintersweet
   (*Chimonanthus*
   praecox)

Perennials

Amur adonis
(*Adonis amurensis*)

Bearsfoot hellebore
(*Helleborus foetidus*)

Christmas rose
(*Helleborus niger*)

Corsican hellebore
(*Helleborus argutifolius*)

Lenten rose
(*Helleborus* x *hybridus*)

Virginia bluebell
(*Mertensia virginica*)

Bulbs

Baker iris
(*Iris bakeriana*)

Common snowdrop
(*Galanthus nivalis*)

Cyclamen daffodil
(*Narcissus Cyclamineus* types)

Danford iris
(*Iris danfordiae*)

Giant snowdrop
(*Galanthus elwesii*)

Glory-of-the-snow
(*Chionodoxa luciliae*)

Golden bunch crocus
(*Crocus ancyrensis*)

Grecian windflower
(*Anemone blanda*)

Hardy cyclamen
(*Cyclamen coum*)

Hoop-petticoat daffodil
(*Narcissus bulbocodium*)

Iris (*Iris histrioides*)

Narcissus asturiensis

Netted iris
(*Iris reticulata*)

Poppy anemone
(*Anemone coronaria*)

Siberian squill
(*Scilla siberica*)

Sieber crocus
(*Crocus sieberi*)

Snow crocus
(*Crocus chrysanthus*)

Spring starflower
(*Ipheion uniflorum*)

Striped squill
(*Puschkinia scilloides*)

Thomasini's crocus
(*Crocus tommasinianus*)

Tubergen squill
(*Scilla tubergeniana*)

Two-leaved squill
(*Scilla bifolia*)

Winter aconite
(*Eranthis hyemalis*)

Winter iris
(*Iris unguicularis*)

Vines

Clematis
(Clematis cirrhosa)

Groundcovers

Leather-leaved bergenia
(*Bergenia crassifolia*)

Lungworts
(*Pulmonaria*)

Winter heaths
(*Erica*)

Year-Round Tonics

Now that you've read my advice for gardening throughout the year, you know how much I rely on my time-tested mixers, fixers, and elixirs—and you should, too! So to help you find 'em fast, I've gathered them all together right here, starting at A and running through Z.

All-Around Disease Defense

Wet, rainy weather can foster funky fungi in your yard, especially in spring. But don't let the dreary days get you down—keep all of your plants happy and healthy with this excellent elixir.

1 cup of chamomile tea
1 tsp. of dishwashing liquid
½ tsp. of vegetable oil
½ tsp. of peppermint oil
1 gal. of warm water

Mix all of the ingredients together in a bucket. Mist-spray your plants every week or so before the really hot weather (75°F or higher) sets in. This elixir is strong stuff, so test it on a few leaves and wait two or three days to make sure there's no damage before spraying any plant. (For related text, see page 129.)

All-Purpose Bug/Thug Spray

To kill flower garden insects and diseases in one fell swoop, whip up a batch of my all-purpose spray. Apply in early spring, just as the bugs and thugs are waking up from their long winter's nap.

3 tbsp. of baking soda
2 tbsp. of Murphy's Oil Soap®
2 tbsp. of canola oil
2 tbsp. of vinegar
2 gal. of warm water

Mix all of the ingredients together, and mist-spray your perennials to the point of run-off. (For related text, see page 57.)

All-Purpose Varmint Repellent

Are hungry critters making your winter gardens into their own private salad bar? Grandma Putt swore by this stuff for getting rid of just about any kind of nasty critter that came down the pike—and it still works like a charm for me!

2 eggs
2 cloves of garlic
2 tbsp. of hot chili powder
2 tbsp. of ammonia
2 cups of hot water

Mix all of these ingredients in a bucket, let the mixture sit for three or four days, and then paint it on fences, trellises, and wherever else unwanted varmints are venturing. (For related text, see page 297.)

All-Season Clean-Up Tonic

To keep all of your plants in tip-top shape, apply this tonic in early evening every two weeks during the growing season.

1 cup of dishwashing liquid
1 cup of tobacco tea*
1 cup of antiseptic mouthwash
Warm water

Mix the dishwashing liquid, tobacco tea, and mouthwash in a 20 gallon hose-end sprayer, filling the balance of the jar with warm water. Liberally apply this mixture to groundcovers, vines, shrubs, trees, perennials, and other plants to discourage insects and prevent disease throughout the growing season. (For related text, see page 162.)

All-Season Green-Up Tonic

If your landscape is looking a bit peaked, give your plants a taste of this sweet treat; they'll green up in a jiffy!

1 can of beer
1 cup of ammonia
1/2 cup of dishwashing liquid
1/2 cup of liquid lawn food
1/2 cup of molasses or clear
  corn syrup

Mix all of the ingredients together in a large bucket, then pour into a 20 gallon hose-end sprayer. Saturate your lawn, trees, shrubs, and flowers with this tonic every three weeks throughout the growing season. (For related text, see page 37.)

Animal Pest Prevention Potion

Tired of pesky critters digging up your newly planted bulbs? Send 'em scurryin' with a whiff of this potion.

1 cup of ammonia
1/2 cup of dishwashing liquid
1/2 cup of urine
1/4 cup of castor oil

Mix all of these ingredients in a 20 gallon hose-end sprayer, and thoroughly saturate all of the animal runs and burrows you can find. (For related text, see page 238.)

Annual Abundance Elixir

Ready for the best-looking flower beds on the block? Give your annuals a generous dose of this tonic every few weeks, then stand back!

1 cup of beer
2 tbsp. of fish emulsion
2 tbsp. of dishwashing liquid
2 tbsp. of ammonia
2 tbsp. of whiskey
1 tbsp. of corn syrup
1 tbsp. of instant tea granules

Mix all of these ingredients with 2 gallons of warm water in a watering can. Drench your annuals every three weeks during the growing season to keep them blooming all summer long. (For related text, see page 157.)

*Place half a handful of chewing tobacco in an old nylon stocking, and soak it in a gallon of hot water until the mixture is dark brown.

Anti-Earwig Elixir

Earwigs—those long, dark, beetle-like pests with wicked-looking pincers on their nether end—love to chew holes in dahlias, mums, and other fall flowers. Chase 'em away with this simple spray.

1 whole head of garlic, chopped
2 drops of dishwashing liquid
Water

Place 1 cup of water and the garlic in a blender, and purée until smooth. Strain, then add the dishwashing liquid to the remaining liquid. Add enough water to make 1 quart of spray. Apply to earwig-infested flowers with a hand-held sprayer to send these pests a-packin'. (For related text, see page 240.)

Aphid Antidote

To keep aphids and other pests off your favorite flowers, mix up a batch of this amazing antidote.

1 small onion, chopped fine
2 medium cloves of garlic,
    chopped fine
1 tbsp. of dishwashing liquid
2 cups of water

Put all of the ingredients in a blender, blend on high, and then strain out the pulp through cheesecloth or pantyhose. Pour the liquid into a hand-held sprayer, and douse your flowers at the first sign of aphid trouble. (For related text, see page 202.)

Bed Builder Mix

If you have a site that you'd like to fill with flowering beauties someday, it's never too soon to start the soil-building process.

Scrape off the weeds and grass with a sharp spade, then add a dose of my super-duper Bed Builder Mix.

40 lbs. of bagged topsoil
10 lbs. of compost
5 lbs. of bonemeal
1 lb. of Epsom salts

Mix all of these ingredients in a wheelbarrow or garden cart, spread a 2- to 3-inch layer over the entire site, and then top the bed with mulch. Add the plants whenever you're ready! (For related text, see page 4.)

Bedding Plant Booster

Don't let your bedding plants go hungry! While they are still in their six-packs, treat them to this nutritious mixture.

2 tsp. of fish emulsion
2 tsp. of dishwashing liquid
1 tsp. of whiskey
1 qt. of water

Mix all of these ingredients, and feed the brew to your adopted seedlings every other time you water them. Also, give them a good soak with it just before you plant them out in your garden. (For related text, see page 95.)

Bedtime Snack

Fall is a fine time to break new ground, because the soil has all winter to digest slow-acting amendments. This rich mixture works miracles in heavy clay!

25 lbs. of gypsum
10 lbs. of natural organic garden
    food (either 4-12-4 or 5-10-5)
5 lbs. of bonemeal
2 lbs. of Epsom salts

Mix all of these ingredients together, then apply them to every 100 sq. ft. of soil with your hand-held broadcast spreader. Work them into the soil and cover with a thick blanket of leaves, straw, or other organic mulch. (For related text, see page 255.)

Beetle Juice

This stuff will stop any kind of pesky beetle dead in its tracks!

¹/₂ cup of beetles (alive or dead)
2 cups of water

Collect the beetles and whirl 'em up with the water in an old blender (one you'll *never* again use for food preparation). Strain the liquid through cheesecloth. Pour ¹/₄ cup into a 1 gallon hand-held sprayer, and fill the rest of the jar with water. Drench the soil around new plants to keep beetles from getting started. If they're already on the scene, spray your shrubs and roses from top to bottom, and make sure you coat both sides of the leaves. Always wear gloves when handling this mixture. (For related text, see page 142.)

Black Spot Remover Tonic

Stop those pesky black spots from messing up your roses with this tomatoey tonic.

15 tomato leaves
2 small onions
¹/₄ cup of rubbing alcohol

Chop the tomato leaves and onions into tiny pieces, and steep them in the alcohol overnight. Use a small, sponge-type paint-brush to apply the brew to both the tops and the bottoms of any affected rose leaves. (For related text, see page 177.)

Bug-Be-Gone Spray

Perennial pests can really get out of hand in areas with long, hot summers, so be prepared with this potent spray.

1 cup of Murphy's Oil Soap®
1 cup of antiseptic mouthwash
1 cup of tobacco tea*

Mix all of the ingredients together in a 20 gallon hose-end sprayer, and soak your plants to the point of run-off. (For related text, see page 151.)

Bulb Bath

To keep your bulbs bug-free, treat them to a nice warm bath before putting them into their planting bed.

2 tsp. of baby shampoo
1 tsp. of antiseptic mouthwash
¹/₄ tsp. of instant tea granules
2 gal. of warm water

Mix all of the ingredients in a bucket, then carefully place your bulbs into the mixture. Stir gently, then remove the bulbs one at a time, and plant them. When you're done, don't throw the bath water out with the babies. Your trees, shrubs, and evergreens would love a little taste, so don't let it go to waste. (For related text, see page 263.)

*Place half a handful of chewing tobacco in an old nylon stocking, and soak it in a gallon of hot water until the mixture is dark brown.

Bulb Booster

Give your bulb beds a boost each year with a taste of this miracle mix!

2 lbs. of bonemeal
2 lbs. of wood ashes
1 lb. of Epsom salts

Sprinkle this mixture on top of flower beds where bulbs are growing in early spring, just as the foliage starts to peek out of the ground. (For related text, see page 67.)

Bulb Breakfast

Don't spend a fortune buying special bagged fertilizer for your bulbs! Just whip up a batch of this marvelous mix.

10 lbs. of compost
5 lbs. of bonemeal
2 lbs. of bloodmeal
1 lb. of Epsom salts

Blend all of the ingredients together in a wheelbarrow. Before setting out your bulbs, work this hearty breakfast into every 100 sq. ft. of soil in your bulb beds and borders. Or drop 1 tablespoon of this mixture into the bottom of each planting hole. Store leftover Bulb Breakfast in an airtight container to keep it nice and dry. (For related text, see page 259.)

Bulb Cleaning Tonic

When you remove your bulbs, corms, and tubers from the ground in fall, wash them with this tonic.

2 tbsp. of baby shampoo
1 tsp. of hydrogen peroxide
1 qt. of warm water

Mix these ingredients in a bucket, and give your bulbs a bath. Just be sure to let them dry thoroughly before you put them away for the winter—otherwise, they'll rot. (For related text, see page 260.)

Bulb Soak

Get all your bulbs off to a great start by treating them to a sip of this super solution.

1 can of beer
2 tbsp. of dishwashing liquid
1/4 tsp. of instant tea granules
2 gal. of water

Mix all of the ingredients together in a large bucket, and carefully dip the bulbs in the mix before planting. (For related text, see page 98.)

Bye-Bye Birdie Brew

This timely tonic will keep pesky birds from eating the berries on your shrubs and trees before you have time to enjoy them!

1 tbsp. of baby shampoo
1 tbsp. of ammonia
1 gal. of water

Mix these ingredients together, and spray the potion on your trees and shrubs when they are full of berries. Reapply after each rain. (For related text, see page 288.)

Caterpillar Killer Tonic

To keep caterpillars in check and away from your shrubs, brew up a batch of this aromatic elixir.

**¹/₂ lb. of wormwood
    (*Artemisia*) leaves
2 tbsp. of Murphy's Oil Soap®
4 cups of warm water**

Simmer the wormwood leaves in 2 cups of warm water for 30 minutes or so. Strain out the leaves, then add the liquid and the Murphy's Oil Soap® to 2 more cups of warm water. Apply with a 6 gallon hose-end sprayer to the point of run-off. Repeat as necessary until the caterpillars are history! This tonic will protect flowers, too. (For related text, see page 174.)

Chamomile Mildew Chaser

If your flowering plants are looking gray and dusty, there's a good chance they've got powdery mildew. To send these funky fungi fleeing, apply this elixir at the first sign of trouble.

**4 chamomile tea bags
2 tbsp. of Murphy's Oil Soap®
1 qt. of boiling water**

Make a strong batch of tea by letting the tea bags steep in the boiling water for an hour or so. Once the tea cools, mix with the Murphy's Oil Soap®. Apply once a week with a 6 gallon hose-end sprayer. (For related text, see page 186.)

Clematis Chow

If you want a really fine clematis vine, I've got just the ticket—a secret family recipe developed by my Grandma Putt.

**5 gal. of well-cured horse or
    cow manure
¹/₂ cup of lime
¹/₂ cup of bonemeal**

Mix the ingredients together in a wheelbarrow and spread over the root zone of your clematis, first thing in the spring. Your clematis will be as happy as a clam! (For related text, see page 72.)

Compost Booster Tonic

Whether you use it as a mulch or dig it into the soil to help hold water, you can never have too much compost! To keep your pile cookin' and the compost a comin', try the following formula.

**1 can of beer
1 can of regular cola (not diet)
1 cup of ammonia
¹/₂ cup of weak tea water*
2 tbsp. of baby shampoo**

Mix all of the ingredients together and pour into a 20 gallon hose-end sprayer. Saturate your compost pile every time you add a new, foot-deep layer of ingredients to it. (For related text, see page 194.)

---

*Soak a used tea bag and 1 teaspoon of dishwashing liquid in a gallon of warm water until the mix is light brown.

Compost Tea

Compost tea is the most healthful drink any bulb or flower could ask for. It delivers a balanced supply of important nutrients—major *and* minor—and fends off diseases at the same time.

1½ gal. of fresh compost
4½ gal. of warm water

Pour the water into a 5-gallon bucket. Scoop the compost into a cotton, burlap, or pantyhose sack, tie it closed, and put it into the water. Cover the bucket and let it steep for three to seven days. Pour the solution into a watering can or hand-held sprayer, and give your plants a good spritzing with it every two to three weeks throughout the growing season. Dump the solids back into your compost pile. (For related text, see page 28.)

Container Plant Food

To give your container gardens a real boost, make this marvelous master mix of fortified water.

1 tbsp. of 15-30-15 plant food
½ tsp. of gelatin
½ tsp. of dishwashing liquid
½ tsp. of corn syrup
½ tsp. of whiskey
¼ tsp. of instant tea granules

Mix all of these ingredients in a 1-gallon milk jug, filling the balance of the jug with water. Then add ½ cup of this mixture to every gallon of water you use to water all of your container plants. (For related text, see page 167.)

Crazy Daisy Spray

If you grow painted daisy (*Tanacetum coccineum*)—also called pyrethrum daisy—its early-summer blooms give you the makings for a great homemade pest spray.

⅛ cup of 70% isopropyl alcohol
1 cup of packed, fresh painted
    daisy flower heads

Pour the alcohol over the flower heads and let it sit overnight. Strain out the flowers, then store the extract in a labeled and sealed container. When you need it, mix the extract with three quarts of water and apply with a hand-held sprayer to control a wide range of garden pests. (For related text, see page 152.)

Damping-Off Prevention Tonic

You can foil the fungi that cause damping-off disease by dosing your seedlings with this terrific tonic.

4 tsp. of chamomile tea
1 tsp. of dishwashing liquid
1 qt. of boiling water

Mix these ingredients and let them steep for at least an hour (the stronger, the better). Strain, then cool. Mist-spray your seedlings with this tonic as soon as their little heads appear above the soil. (For related text, see page 65.)

Dandy Division Tonic

When dividing perennials, soak the best-rooted pieces in this tonic for about 10 minutes just before replanting them.

1 can of beer
¼ cup of instant tea granules
2 tbsp. of dishwashing liquid
2 gal. of water

When you're finished planting, dribble any leftover tonic around the newly set divisions. (For related text, see page 234.)

Deer Buster Egg Brew

If you notice that deer are starting to nibble on your winter landscape, protect the plants with this potent brew.

2 eggs
2 cloves of garlic
2 tbsp. of Tabasco® sauce
2 tbsp. of cayenne pepper
2 cups of water

Put all of the ingredients in a blender and purée. Allow the mixture to sit for two days, then pour or spray it all over and around the plants you need to protect. Reapply every other week or so, or after a rain, to keep the odor fresh. (For related text, see page 304.)

Dog-Be-Gone

Digging dogs can destroy a good-looking groundcover patch quick as a wink. To keep Fido away from his favorite digging spots, liberally apply this mix to the soil.

2 cloves of garlic
2 small onions
1 jalapeño pepper
1 tbsp. of cayenne pepper
1 tbsp. of Tabasco® sauce
1 tbsp. of chili powder
1 qt. of warm water

Chop the garlic, onions, and jalapeño pepper finely, then combine with all of the remaining ingredients. Let the mix sit for 24 hours, then sprinkle it on any areas where dogs are a problem. (For related text, see page 244.)

Double-Punch Garlic Tea

Thrips can really do a number on white- and pale-petaled flowers, causing discolored streaks and deformed blooms. Send 'em packing with a dose of this excellent elixir.

5 unpeeled cloves of garlic,
coarsely chopped
2 cups of boiling water
½ cup of tobacco tea*
1 tsp. of instant tea granules
1 tsp. of baby shampoo

Place the chopped garlic in a heatproof bowl, and pour the boiling water over it. Let it steep overnight. Then strain it through a coffee filter, mix it with the other ingredients in a hand-held sprayer, and thoroughly drench your plants. (For related text, see page 11.)

*Place half a handful of chewing tobacco in an old nylon stocking, and soak it in a gallon of hot water until the mixture is dark brown.

Elephant's Ears Elixir

To grow the biggest elephant's ears on the block, give 'em a regular taste of this power-packed tonic!

1 can of beer
1 cup of all-purpose plant food
¼ cup of ammonia

Mix the ingredients together, and pour them into a 20 gallon hose-end sprayer. Fill the balance of the sprayer with water. Every three weeks, spray the plants until the liquid runs off the leaves. (For related text, see page 126.)

Fabulous Foliar Formula

For big, bright, shiny leaves in even the toughest soil, feed your foliage plants this fantastic formula every three weeks.

1 can of beer
½ cup of fish emulsion
½ cup of ammonia
¼ cup of blackstrap molasses
¼ cup of instant tea granules

Mix all of the ingredients together in a 20 gallon hose-end sprayer and apply thoroughly until it starts running off the leaves. This formula works best on plants that aren't blooming; if yours are in flower, aim the spray at the foliage, and try to avoid wetting the blooms. (For related text, see page 43.)

Fantastic Flowering Shrub Tonic

A dose of this elixir in early spring will give your flowering shrubs the energy they need to produce a fantastic floral extravaganza!

1 tbsp. of baby shampoo
1 tsp. of hydrated lime
1 tsp. of iron sulfate
1 gal. of water

Mix all of these ingredients together. For an extra "kicker," add 1 tablespoon of Liquid Iron to the mixture. Then spray the elixir on all of your flowering shrubs to the point of run-off. (For related text, see page 50.)

Fern Food

To keep all of your outdoor ferns looking lush, give them a dose of this milky brew.

2 cups of milk
2 tbsp. of Epsom salts

Combine the milk and Epsom salts in your 20 gallon hose-end sprayer, and give your ferns a generous drink until they are saturated. (For related text, see page 212.)

Flower Bed Bonanza

After fall cleanup, spray all of your perennial beds with this mixture.

1 can of beer
1 can of regular cola (not diet)
½ cup of dishwashing liquid
½ cup of tobacco tea*

Mix all of the ingredients together in a

---

*Place half a handful of chewing tobacco in an old nylon stocking, and soak it in a gallon of hot water until the mixture is dark brown.

bucket, then apply liberally with your 20 gallon hose-end sprayer. (For related text, see page 277.)

Flower Feeder

Use this all-purpose food to keep your flowers flourishing.

1 can of beer
2 tbsp. of fish emulsion
2 tbsp. of dishwashing liquid
2 tbsp. of ammonia
2 tbsp. of hydrogen peroxide
2 tbsp. of whiskey
1 tbsp. of clear corn syrup
1 tbsp. of unflavored gelatin
4 tsp. of instant tea granules
2 gal. of warm water

Mix all of the ingredients together, and water all of your flowering plants every two weeks in the morning. (For related text, see page 119.)

Flower Flea Fluid

"Flower fleas" was Grandma Putt's name for leafhoppers. When she spotted any of these feisty little guys bugging her best bloomers, she'd let 'em have it with this powerful stuff.

1 cup of tobacco tea*
1 tbsp. of baby shampoo or dish-
   washing liquid
1 qt. of water

Mix all of these ingredients together in a hand-held sprayer, and apply liberally to leaves until they are dripping wet on both sides. (For related text, see page 242.)

Flower-Power Prep Mix

Here's a flower-power mixture that'll really energize your beds and produce a bounty of bright, beautiful blooms.

4 cups of bonemeal
2 cups of gypsum
2 cups of Epsom salts
1 cup of wood ashes
1 cup of lime
4 tbsp. of medicated baby powder
1 tbsp. of baking powder

Combine all of these ingredients in a bucket, and work the mixture into the soil before you plant to get all your flowers off to a rip-roarin' start! (For related text, see page 121.)

Flowering Shrub Elixir

Don't waste your hard-earned dough on fancy, pre-packaged shrub fertilizers from your local garden center! Instead, just whip up a batch of this terrific tonic, and you'll have the best-looking flowering shrubs on the block.

1/2 can of beer
1/2 cup of fish emulsion
1/2 cup of ammonia
1/4 cup of baby shampoo
2 tbsp. of hydrogen peroxide

Mix all of the ingredients together, and pour into your 20 gallon hose-end sprayer. Then every three weeks during the spring and summer, spray your shrubs until the tonic starts dripping off their leaves. That'll get 'em growin' like gangbusters! (For related text, see page 19.)

*Place half a handful of chewing tobacco in an old nylon stocking, and soak it in a gallon of hot water until the mixture is dark brown.

Foundation Food

High-visibility beds around the foundation of your house are perfect for four-season flowers, but the soil there is often awful. Whip up the following mix to fortify your beds and make 'em burst with blooms—with a minimum of work!

10 parts compost
3 parts bonemeal
2 parts bloodmeal
1 part kelp meal

Mix the ingredients in a garden cart or wheelbarrow. Spread a thin layer (about a half-inch or so) over the entire planting area, and lightly scratch it into the soil around shrubs. Add a new layer each year. Top it with shredded bark or other mulch. (For related text, see page 8.)

Fragrant Pest Fighter

People love perfumed perennials, but pests sure don't! So the next time you're out in your flower garden, gather the ingredients for this aromatic pest-control spray.

1/2 cup of fresh tansy (*Tanacetum vulgare*) or mugwort (*Artemisia vulgaris*) leaves
1/2 cup of fresh lavender flowers and/or leaves
1/2 cup of fresh sage (*Salvia officinalis*) leaves
Boiling water
2 cups of room-temperature water
1 teaspoon of Murphy's Oil Soap®

Place the leaves and flowers in a 1-quart glass jar; fill with boiling water, cover, and let sit until cool. Add 1/8 cup of that liquid to the 2 cups of room-temperature water and the Murphy's Oil Soap®. Pour into a hand-held sprayer, and apply to all your flowers to keep pests at bay! (For related text, see page 154.)

Frozen Feed

To give your perennials a welcome winter snack and a rip-roarin' start in spring, wait until the ground freezes, then apply this mixture.

25 lbs. of garden gypsum
10 lbs. of garden fertilizer (4-2-4 or 5-10-5)
5 lbs. of bonemeal

Mix all of the ingredients together, then spread the mixture evenly over your beds and borders. This amount will cover 100 sq. ft. (For related text, see page 294.)

Fungus Fighter

Get sweet on your peonies, and give 'em a dose of molasses to keep dastardly diseases away! At the first sign of trouble, try this tonic.

1/2 cup of molasses
1/2 cup of powdered milk
1 tsp. of baking soda
1 gal. of warm water

Mix the molasses, powdered milk, and baking soda into a paste. Place the mixture into the toe of an old nylon stocking, and let it steep in the warm water for several hours. Then strain, and use the remaining liquid as a fungus-fighting spray for peonies and other perennials every two weeks throughout the growing season. I guarantee you'll have no more fungus troubles! (For related text, see page 86.)

Garlic Tea Tonic

When thrips zero in on your prize peonies, zap 'em with this elixir.

5 cloves of unpeeled garlic, coarsely chopped
2 cups of boiling water
1 tsp. of baby shampoo

Place the chopped garlic in a heat-proof bowl, and pour the boiling water over it. Steep overnight. Strain through a coffee filter, and pour the liquid into a hand-held sprayer along with the baby shampoo. Spray of affected plants, then store the rest at room temperature. (For related text, see page 148.)

Get-Up-and-Grow Iris Tonic

For the most eye-catching bearded irises on the block, feed your plants a dose of this magical mix.

6 parts hydrated lime
4 parts bonemeal

Mix the ingredients together and sprinkle around established plants in early spring. Your irises will get off to a flying start! (For related text, see page 70.)

Gopher-Go Tonic

Having problems with gophers getting after your bulbs? I've had amazing results with this tonic, and so have others who've tried it!

4 tbsp. of castor oil
4 tbsp. of dishwashing liquid
4 tbsp. of urine
Warm water

Combine the castor oil, dishwashing liquid, and urine in $1/2$ cup of warm water, then stir them into 2 gallons of warm water. Pour the mix over the infested areas. (For related text, see page 264.)

Groundcover Chow

Give your groundcovers a taste of this mix in spring, then stand back, and watch 'em grow!

3 parts bonemeal
3 parts greensand or wood ashes
1 part bloodmeal

Mix the ingredients together. Scatter 2 tablespoons around each clump of plants, and scratch into the soil surface. (For related text, see page 30.)

Groundcover Starter Mix

Get new groundcovers growing like gang-busters with this power-packed punch.

3 parts of bonemeal
1 part Epsom salts
1 part gypsum

Mix all of the ingredients together and scatter in the planting hole and on the soil surface, too. (For related text, see page 74.)

Handy Herbal Fertilizer

Why bother buying fancy commercial fertilizers? If you've got comfrey (*Symphytum officinale*) in your yard, you have the fixin's for a nutrient-rich brew *all* of your year-round bloomers will love.

5 to 10 comfrey leaves
1 qt. of water
Dishwashing liquid

Pack the comfrey leaves in a large flowerpot with at least one drain hole. Set another flowerpot—upside down this time—into a 5-gallon bucket. Place the leaf-filled pot on top of the upside-down pot, then set a brick on top of the leaves. As the leaves decompose, a brown liquid will appear in the bottom of the bucket. Add 1 tablespoon of this liquid to 1 quart of water, toss in a few drops of dishwashing liquid, and pour this around any plant that needs a quick nutrient boost. (For related text, see page 188.)

Herb Soil Booster Tonic

Want to liven up your year-round landscape with fragrant herbs? Then get 'em off on the right root with this super soil booster mix!

5 lbs. of lime
5 lbs. of gypsum
1 lb. of 5-10-5 garden food
1/2 cup of Epsom salts

Work this mix into each 50 sq. ft. of herb garden area to a depth of 12 to 18 inches, and then let it sit for 7 to 10 days before planting. (For related text, see page 117.)

Hot Bite Spray

Want to keep pesky squirrels from nipping off the buds of your prized tulips? This spicy mixture'll make 'em think twice about taking a bite!

3 tbsp. of cayenne pepper
1 tbsp. of Tabasco® sauce
1 tbsp. of ammonia
1 tbsp. of baby shampoo
2 cups of hot water

Mix the cayenne pepper with the hot water in a bottle, and shake well. Let the mixture sit overnight, then pour off the liquid without disturbing the sediment. Mix the liquid with the other ingredients in a hand-held sprayer. Keep a batch on hand as long as new tulip buds are forming, and spritz the flower stems as often as you can to keep 'em hot, hot, hot! It's strong medicine, so make sure you wear rubber gloves while you're handling this brew. (For related text, see page 68.)

Hot Bug Brew

Want to get all of those bad bugs out of your flower beds—*pronto*? Give 'em a shot of this spicy solution!

3 hot green peppers (canned
    or fresh)
3 medium cloves of garlic
1 small onion
1 tbsp. of dishwashing liquid
3 cups of water

Purée the peppers, garlic, and onion in a blender. Pour the purée into a jar, and add the dishwashing liquid and water. Let stand for 24 hours, then strain out the pulp with cheesecloth or pantyhose. Use a hand-held sprayer to apply the remaining liquid to bug-infested bulbs and perennials. (For related text, see page 161.)

Houseplant Repotting Mix

While you're getting bulbs ready for forcing in midwinter, take a few minutes to repot your houseplants, too. This super soil will get 'em growing up right!

1 lb. of potting soil
1 lb. of professional potting mix
¼ cup of Epsom salts
¼ cup of bonemeal
1 tbsp. of instant tea granules

Thoroughly mix all of the ingredients, then sprinkle it around the root mass of your plants as you replant them. *Don't* pack it in. (For related text, see page 310.)

Hummingbird Nectar

Hummers will visit a feeder all summer long, once they get the idea it's filled with nectar. You can buy packets of nectar mix, but making your own is easy and inexpensive.

1 part white sugar (not honey,
which hosts bacteria harmful
to hummers)
4 parts water
A few drops of red food coloring
(optional)

Boil the mix, and let it cool before filling the feeder. Once hummers start coming, decrease the solution to about 1 part sugar and 8 parts water. No, this isn't the old bait-and-switch tactic—there's a good reason for diluting the solution. Humming-

birds can sometimes suffer a fatal liver disorder if they get too much sugar. Replace the nectar every three days or so—every other day if temperatures are above 60°F. But first wash the feeder with soap and scalding water, and rinse thoroughly. Otherwise, the nectar and/or feeder can host hummingbird-harming bacteria. (For related text, see page 197.)

Iris Energizer Tonic

To get an eyeful of early-summer irises, treat your plants to this tasty tonic!

½ cup of beer
Vitamin B₁ plant starter
(mixed at 25 percent of the
recommended rate)
2 tbsp. of dishwashing liquid
1 gal. of warm water

Mix the ingredients together in a bucket and drench the soil around your irises to keep 'em growing right. (For related text, see page 146.)

Knock 'Em Dead Tonic

This tough tonic is all you need to wipe out a wide variety of garden pests.

6 cloves of garlic, chopped fine
1 small onion, chopped fine
1 tbsp. of cayenne pepper
1 tbsp. of dishwashing liquid
1 qt. of warm water

Mix all of these ingredients and let sit overnight. Strain out the solid matter, pour the liquid into a hand-held sprayer, and knock those pests for a loop. (For related text, see page 195.)

Mulch Moisturizer Tonic

When you give your trees and shrubs a fresh layer of organic mulch in early summer, overspray it with this super tonic to give it a little extra kick.

1 can of regular cola (not diet)
1/2 cup of ammonia
1/2 cup of antiseptic mouthwash
1/2 cup of baby shampoo

Mix all of these ingredients in your 20 gallon hose-end sprayer, and give the mulch a long, cool drink. (For related text, see page 139.)

No-Jive Chive Spray

Scale insects form tiny bumps on twigs as they suck the plant's sap, causing weak or stunted growth. If you spot these pests on your young trees and shrubs, scrape off as many as you can with your fingernail or a plastic spoon, then drench the affected parts with this simple spray.

1/4 cup of dried chives
Water
Liquid soap

Pour 2 cups of boiling water over the chives and let them sit for one hour. Strain out the leaves, then mix 1 part of the liquid with 2 parts water. Add a few drops of liquid soap. Pour into a hand-held sprayer, shake, and apply to the point of run-off. (For related text, see page 17.)

Nutrient Boost for Neglected Soil

If you have a site with poor, dry soil or seem to have lots of yellowed, sick-looking plants, try this surefire pick-me-up!

6 parts greensand or wood ashes
3 parts cottonseed meal
3 parts bonemeal

Mix the ingredients together. Add 2 cups of gypsum and 1 cup of limestone per gallon of blend. Apply 5 pounds per 100 sq. ft. a few weeks before planting, or work the mix around the bases of established plants. (For related text, see page 44.)

Organic Bulb Snack

No matter when you plant, your bulbs will thank you for a taste of this all-natural nutrient boost.

10 lbs. of compost
5 lbs. of bonemeal
1 lb. of Epsom salts

Mix the ingredients, then drop 1 tablespoon of the mixture into the bottom of each planting hole. Store any leftover Organic Bulb Snack in an airtight container to keep it nice and dry. (For related text, see page 219.)

Ornamental Grass Chow

Here's a fantastic formula for feeding your ornamental grasses that'll give 'em plenty of growing power.

2 lbs. of dry oatmeal
2 lbs. of crushed dry dog food
1 handful of human hair

Work a handful of this mixture into the soil, and then plant to your heart's content! (For related text, see page 101.)

Perennial Pick-Me-Up

Give your just-divided perennials a taste of the following tonic to get 'em growin' like gangbusters!

1 can of beer
1 cup of all-purpose plant food
¹/₄ cup of ammonia

Mix the ingredients together, and pour them into a 20 gallon hose-end sprayer. Fill the balance of the sprayer jar with water, then saturate the ground around the perennials. Repeat one week later. (For related text, see page 62.)

Perennial Planting Potion

To make sure your flowers get growing on the right root, be sure to feed them this magical mixture.

¹/₂ can of beer
¹/₂ cup of ammonia
2 tbsp. of hydrogen peroxide
1 tbsp. of dishwashing liquid
2 gal. of warm water

Mix all of the ingredients together, and soak the soil around each transplant. You can also sprinkle it over your blooming beauties throughout the summer. (For related text, see page 114.)

Perennial Potting Mix

Here's how to make the perfect growing mix for all of your potted perennial plants and seedlings.

1 part sharp sand
1 part clay loam
1 part organic matter or professional planter mix

Per cubic foot of soil mixture, add:

1¹/₂ cups of Epsom salts
³/₄ cup of coffee grounds (rinsed)
12 eggshells (dried and crushed to a powder)

Blend all of the ingredients together, and use the mixture to make your perennials feel comfy and cozy in their new home. (For related text, see page 182.)

Perfect Potting Soil

If you've got a lot of flowers to pot up, you'll need plenty of potting soil. So mix up a big batch of this simple blend, and keep it handy!

1 part topsoil
1 part peat moss
1 part vermiculite
1 part compost

Mix all of the ingredients together and use for potting up all kinds of annuals, perennials, and bulbs—shrubs, too! (For related text, see page 169.)

Potted Plant Picnic

Container plants need lots of energy to stay chock-full of flowers, so whatever you do, don't skimp on the fertilizer! Here's a meal your potted plants are sure to appreciate.

2 tbsp. of brewed black coffee
2 tbsp. of whiskey
1 tsp. of fish emulsion
¹/₂ tsp. of unflavored gelatin
¹/₂ tsp. of baby shampoo
¹/₂ tsp. of ammonia
1 gal. of water

Mix all of the ingredients together and feed to each of your potted plants once a week. (For related text, see page 222.)

Powdery Mildew Control

Late summer's prime time for your phlox to shine, so don't let messy mildew spoil the show! Try this terrific tonic instead.

4 tbsp. of baking soda
2 tbsp. of Murphy's Oil Soap®
1 gal. of warm water

Mix all of the ingredients together. Pour into a hand-held mist sprayer, and apply liberally, as soon as you see the telltale white spots on your phlox. (For related text, see page 214.)

Quassia Slug Spray

There's no getting around it: Slugs love perennials, and hostas in particular. But don't despair—here's a magical mixer that'll really knock those slimy slitherers for a loop.

4 oz. of quassia chips (available at health food stores)
1 gal. of water

Crush, grind, or chop the chips, add them to the water in a bucket, and let steep for 12 to 24 hours. Strain through cheese-cloth, then spray the liquid on hostas and other slug-prone plants. (For related text, see page 180.)

Repotting Booster Tonic

When your rooted cuttings are ready for transplanting, a dose of this terrific tonic will help 'em adjust to their new homes in a jiffy.

¹/₂ cup of weak tea water*
¹/₂ tsp. of all-purpose plant food
¹/₂ tsp. of vitamin B₁ plant starter
1 gal. of warm water

Mix all of the ingredients together, and gently pour the tonic through the soil of your repotted plants. Allow the pots to drain for 15 minutes or so, then pour off any excess in the tray, and treat your trees and shrubs to the leftovers! (For related text, see page 175.)

*Soak a used tea bag and 1 teaspoon of dishwashing liquid in a gallon of warm water until the mix is light brown.

Rhubarb Pest Repellent Tonic

Are bad bugs getting the best of your fall flowers? Here's a potent plant tonic that'll say "Scram!" to just about any kind of pest you can think of.

3 medium-size rhubarb leaves
1/4 cup of dishwashing liquid
1 gal. of water

Chop up the rhubarb leaves, put the pieces in the water, and bring it to a boil. Let the mixture cool, then strain it through cheesecloth to filter out the leaf bits. Mix in the dishwashing liquid. Apply this terrific tonic to your plants with a small hand-held sprayer, and kiss your pest problems good-bye! (For related text, see page 235.)

Rise-'n'-Shine Clean-Up Tonic

Want to start the growing season with a bang? This tonic will rouse your yard out of its slumber in spring, nailing any wayward bugs and thugs that spent the winter in your garden.

1 cup of Murphy's Oil Soap®
1 cup of tobacco tea*
1 cup of antiseptic mouthwash
1/4 cup of Tabasco® sauce

Mix all of these ingredients in a 20 gallon hose-end sprayer, filling the balance of the sprayer jar with warm water. Apply to everything in your yard to the point of run-off. (For related text, see page 10.)

Robust Rose Food

Feed your established rosebushes first thing in the spring with this fabulous food. They'll love you for it!

5 lbs. of garden food
2 cups of bonemeal
1 cup of Epsom salts
1 cup of sugar
4 pulverized (dried) banana peels

Mix all of these ingredients together, and sprinkle a handful or two around the base of each plant. (For related text, see page 53.)

Root Pruning Tonic

Help your trees and shrubs spring back quickly after root pruning with this terrific tonic.

1 can of beer
4 tbsp. of instant tea granules
1 tbsp. of shampoo
1 tbsp. of ammonia
1 tbsp. of hydrogen peroxide
1 tbsp. of whiskey
2 gal. of very warm water

Mix all of the ingredients together. Then pour a quart of the elixir into the soil at the spots where you've cut your shrubs' roots. (For related text, see page 318.)

*Place half a handful of chewing tobacco in an old nylon stocking, and soak it in a gallon of hot water until the mixture is dark brown.

Root Revival Tonic

Use this terrific tonic to give your bare-root perennials a bit of refreshment before they go into the garden.

¼ cup of brewed tea
1 tbsp. of dishwashing liquid
1 tbsp. of Epsom salts
1 gal. of water

Let the plants sit in this tonic for up to 24 hours. (For related text, see page 59.)

Rose Ambrosia Tonic

If your roses could talk, they would have great things to say about this grand elixir, which gives them just what they need to grow strong and bloom like gangbusters.

1 cup of beer
2 tsp. of instant tea granules
1 tsp. of flower food
    5-10-5 or 5-10-10
1 tsp. of fish emulsion
1 tsp. of hydrogen peroxide
1 tsp. of dishwashing liquid

Mix all of these ingredients in 2 gallons of warm water, and give each of your roses 1 pint every three weeks throughout the growing season. Dribble it into the soil after you've watered, so it will penetrate deep into the root zone. (For related text, see page 111.)

Rose Aphid Antidote

Keep pesky pests off your prized roses with this simple citrus solution.

1 lemon or orange peel, coarsely
    chopped
1 tbsp. of baby shampoo
2 cups of water

Put these ingredients into a blender, and blend on high for 10 to 15 seconds. Use a coffee filter to strain out the pulp. Pour the liquid into a hand-held sprayer. Before applying this tonic, blast your roses with a strong spray of water from your garden hose to dislodge some of the aphids. About 10 minutes later, thoroughly spray buds and young stems with this mix. Repeat after four days. (For related text, see page 144.)

Rose Revival Tonics

This dynamic duo will get your bare-root roses off and growing like champs. First, wash your newly purchased bare-root rosebushes, roots and all, in a bucket of warm water with the following added.

1 tbsp. of dishwashing liquid
¼ tsp. of liquid bleach

Then before planting, soak your bare-root rosebushes for about half an hour in a clean bucket filled with 1 gallon of warm water with the following added to it.

2 tbsp. of clear corn syrup
1 tsp. of dishwashing liquid
1 tsp. of ammonia

(For related text, see page 52.)

Rose Rousin' Elixir

To get bare-root roses off to a rip-roarin' start, give 'em a taste of this magical mixer before you plant.

1 tbsp. of 5-8-5 or 5-10-5
    garden fertilizer
1 tbsp. of baby shampoo
1 tbsp. of corn syrup
1 gal. of warm water

Mix these ingredients together in a small bucket, and soak the roots in the solution overnight. When you're done, sprinkle this mixture around all your other rosebushes, too—they'll love you for it! (For related text, see page 274.)

Rose Start-Up Tonic

Ready to get your rosebushes off to a rosy start? Late winter's the prime time to give 'em a taste of this terrific tonic.

1 tbsp. of dishwashing liquid
1 tbsp. of hydrogen peroxide
1 tsp. of whiskey
1 tsp. of vitamin B_1 plant starter
$1/2$ gal. of warm tea

Mix all of these ingredients, then pour the liquid all around the root zone of each of your rosebushes. (For related text, see page 321.)

Rosy Clean-Up Elixir

Late fall to early winter is the best time to get a jump on the insects and diseases that like to plague roses. So after your bushes have shed their leaves, but before you mulch them for the winter, spray 'em thoroughly with this terrific tonic.

1 cup of baby shampoo
1 cup of antiseptic mouthwash
1 cup of tobacco tea*

Place all of these ingredients in a 20 gallon hose-end sprayer and douse each rose-bush from top to bottom. (For related text, see page 290.)

Rosy Feeding Regime

Believe you me, roses are the hardest-working flowering plants in your garden. These beauties bloom only for the sake of showing off, as much as they can, for as long as they can. But all this hard work takes lots of energy—and that's where you come in! Follow this simple feeding routine, and your roses will have all the food they need to keep those blooms comin' along! Start with a dose of this elixir in mid- to late spring.

4 cups of bonemeal
1 cup of 5-10-5 garden fertilizer
1 cup of Epsom salts

Mix these ingredients together in a bucket, then give each bush 1 heaping tablespoon, or work in 4 pounds per 100 sq. ft. of rose bed. Then every three weeks after that, give 'em a drink of this terrific tonic.

1 cup of beer
2 tsp. of instant tea granules
1 tsp. of 5-10-5 fertilizer
1 tsp. of fish emulsion
1 tsp. of hydrogen peroxide
1 tsp. of dishwashing liquid
2 gal. of warm water

Mix the ingredients together, then water each plant with 1 pint of the solution in the morning. Stop feeding by July 15 in the North, and August 15 in the South. (For related text, see page 85.)

*Place half a handful of chewing tobacco in an old nylon stocking, and soak it in a gallon of hot water until the mixture is dark brown.

Scat Cat Tonic

Cats can be great pets, but they can also be real pests if they dig around or roll on tender vine shoots. Try this spicy solution to keep them away from your prized plantings.

5 tbsp. of flour
4 tbsp. of powdered mustard
3 tbsp. of cayenne pepper
2 tbsp. of chili powder
2 qts. of warm water

Mix all of the ingredients together. Sprinkle the solution around the areas you want to protect by keeping kitty away. (For related text, see page 127.)

Seed and Soil Energizer Tonic

This potion will get your seeds off to a rip-roaring start!

1 tsp. of dishwashing liquid
1 tsp. of ammonia
1 tsp. of whiskey
1 qt. of weak tea

Mix all of these ingredients together, pour into a hand-held sprayer, and shake gently. Then once a day, mist the surface of your seedbeds. (For related text, see page 149.)

Seed Starter Tonic

Whether you start your seeds indoors or out, give them a good send-off with this timely tonic.

1 cup of white vinegar
1 tbsp. of baby shampoo or
   dishwashing liquid
2 cups of warm water

Mix all of these ingredients together in a bowl, and let your seeds soak in the mixture overnight before planting them in well-prepared soil. (For related text, see page 323.)

Seedling Starter Tonic

Give annual seedlings a break on moving day by serving them a sip of this starter tonic. This helps them recover quickly from transplanting shock.

1 tbsp. of fish emulsion
1 tbsp. of ammonia
1 tbsp. of Murphy's Oil Soap®
1 tsp. of instant tea granules
1 qt. of warm water

Mix all of the ingredients in the warm water. Pour into a hand-held sprayer, and mist the young plants several times a day until they're back on their feet and growing again. (For related text, see page 25.)

Shrub Pest Preventer

Fend off funky fungi and other wintertime nasties with this truly excellent elixir.

1 cup of baby shampoo
1 cup of antiseptic mouthwash
1 cup of tobacco tea*
1 cup of chamomile tea
Warm water

Mix the shampoo, mouthwash, and teas in a bucket, and then add 2 cups of it to a 20 gallon hose-end sprayer, filling the balance of the sprayer jar with warm water. Over-

*Place half a handful of chewing tobacco in an old nylon stocking, and soak it in a gallon of hot water until the mixture is dark brown.

spray your shrubs until they are dripping wet whenever the temperature is above 50°F. (For related text, see page 251.)

Shrub Stimulator Tonic

Nothing can get your shrubs off to a super start like this powerful potion!

4 tbsp. of instant tea granules
4 tbsp. of bourbon, or ½ can of beer
2 tbsp. of dishwashing liquid
2 gal. of warm water

Mix all of these ingredients together, and sprinkle the mixture over all of your shrubs in late spring. (For related text, see page 109.)

Simple Soap-and-Oil Spray

Are pesky pests taking a bite out of your pretty perennials? Then send them packing with this surefire spray!

1 cup of vegetable oil
1 tbsp. of dishwashing liquid
1 cup of water

Mix the vegetable oil and dishwashing liquid. Add 1 or 2 teaspoons of the soap-and-oil mixture to the water in a hand-held sprayer. Shake to mix, then spray on plants to control aphids, whiteflies, and spider mites. (For related text, see page 116.)

Sleepytime Mulch Tonic

When Old Man Winter is just around the corner, you should tuck your beds in with a thick blanket of mulch. This mixture feeds the mulch that slowly feeds your garden.

1 can of beer
1 can of regular cola (not diet)
1 cup of baby shampoo
½ cup of ammonia
¼ cup of instant tea granules

Mix all of these ingredients in a bucket, pour the mixture into a 20 gallon hose-end sprayer, and saturate the mulch in flower beds, around shrubs, and beneath trees. (For related text, see page 293.)

Slug-It-Out Tonic

Slimy slugs can really do a number of tender annual seedlings, sometimes eating them whole! Send those slithering pests packing with a dose of this beery brew!

1 can of beer
1 tbsp. of sugar
1 tsp. of baker's yeast

Mix these ingredients in a bowl, and let 'em sit for 24 hours. Then pour the mixture into shallow aluminum pie pans, and set the pans so the rims are just at ground level in various areas of your garden. You'll catch lots and lots of slugs, and you'll know they died very happy! (For related text, see page 159.)

Slugweiser

Shady sites make ideal hangouts for slugs and snails, so be prepared to take control! To drown your slug sorrows, try this sure cure.

1 lb. of brown sugar
1/2 pkg. (1 1/2 tsp.) of dry yeast
Warm water

Pour the sugar and yeast into a 1-gallon plastic jug, fill it with warm water, and let it sit for two days, uncovered. Then pour it into your slug traps, and let the good times roll! (For related text, see page 35.)

Soil Energizer Elixir

Whatever kind of garden you're planning, you'll get great results if you perk up the soil before planting with this energizing elixir!

1 can of beer
1 cup of regular cola (not diet)
1 cup of dishwashing liquid
1 cup of antiseptic mouthwash
1/4 tsp. of instant tea granules

Mix these ingredients in a bucket or container, and fill a 20 gallon hose-end sprayer. Overspray the soil in your garden to the point of run-off (or until small puddles start to form), then let it sit at least two weeks. This recipe makes enough to cover 100 sq. ft. of garden area. (For related text, see page 63.)

Soil Soother Tonic

Get your soil in super shape with a generous dose of this elixir.

1 can of beer
1 can of regular cola (not diet)
1/2 cup of dishwashing liquid
1/2 cup of tobacco tea*

Mix all of the ingredients together in a bucket, then apply with a 20 gallon hose-end sprayer to the point of run-off. (For related text, see page 326.)

Spring Shrub Restorer

This elixir is just the ticket for perking up tired, old shrubs and getting them started on their way to a robust, new life.

1 can of beer
1 cup of ammonia
1/2 cup of dishwashing liquid
1/2 cup of molasses or clear
   corn syrup

Mix all of these ingredients in a 20 gallon hose-end sprayer. Drench shrubs thoroughly, including the undersides of the leaves. If you have any left over, spray it on your trees, too! (For related text, see page 83.)

*Place half a handful of chewing tobacco in an old nylon stocking, and soak it in a gallon of hot water until the mixture is dark brown.

Squeaky Clean Tonic

No matter what bad-guy bugs are buggin' your plants, this tough tonic'll stop 'em in their tracks.

1 cup of antiseptic mouthwash
1 cup of tobacco tea*
1 cup of chamomile tea
1 cup of urine
1/2 cup of Murphy's Oil Soap®
1/2 cup of lemon-scented
dishwashing liquid

Mix all of these ingredients in a large bucket, then pour into a 20 gallon hose-end sprayer, and apply to the point of run-off. (For related text, see page 208.)

Summer Rejuvenating Tonic

Whenever Grandma Putt's carefully planned annual gardens started to look a little tired in late summer, she'd give 'em a good drink of this potent pick-me-up.

1/4 cup of beer
1 tbsp. of corn syrup
1 tbsp. of baby shampoo
1 tbsp. of 15-30-15 fertilizer
1 gal. of water

Mix all of these ingredients, then slowly dribble the solution onto the soil around your annuals. Within two weeks, they'll be real comeback kids! (For related text, see page 216.)

Super Seed-Starting Mix

Typical potting soil is way too rich for small seedlings, and it can foster a bunch of funky fungi that'll quickly wipe out whole pots of baby plants. To get your seeds up and growing safely, I suggest blendin' up a batch of my Super Seed-Starting Mix.

2 parts peat moss
1 part perlite or vermiculite
Warm water

Mix the peat moss and perlite or vermiculite in a bag or bucket. The day before sowing seeds, moisten the mix by adding warm water—a few cups at a time—and working it in with your hands until the mix feels evenly moist to the touch. (For related text, see page 308.)

Super Shrub Soil Mix

Get your new shrubs off to a spectacular start with a dose of this magical mix!

2 bushels of compost
1/2 cup of Epsom salts
1/2 cup of bonemeal
1 tbsp. of medicated baby powder

Mix all of these ingredients together in a container, and work about a cup into each hole when you plant your shrubs. (For related text, see page 82.)

*Place half a handful of chewing tobacco in an old nylon stocking, and soak it in a gallon of hot water until the mixture is dark brown.

Super Spider Mite Mix

Spider mites are tiny, all right, but they get up to mite-y BIG mischief in your garden! When they show up, send 'em scurryin' with this floury remedy.

4 cups of wheat flour
1/2 cup of buttermilk (not fat-free)
5 gal. of water

Mix all of the ingredients together, and mist-spray your plants to the point of run-off. This mix will suffocate the little buggers without harming your flowers. (For related text, see page 203.)

Surefire Slug Spray

This simple spray'll zap these slimy pests in a flash!

1 1/2 cups of ammonia
1 tbsp. of Murphy's Oil Soap®
1 1/2 cups of water

Mix these ingredients in a hand-held sprayer, and spray any areas where you see signs of slug activity. (For related text, see page 93.)

Terrific Tree Chow

Give established trees a taste of this mix in spring, and they'll be rarin' to grow!

25 lbs. of garden food (5-10-5
    is fine)
1 lb. of sugar
1/2 lb. of Epsom salts

Feed your trees by drilling holes in the ground out at the weep line (at the tip of the farthest branch), 8 to 10 inches deep and 18 to 24 inches apart. Fill the holes

with 2 tablespoons of the above mixture, and sprinkle the remainder over the soil. (For related text, see page 79.)

Timely Tree Tonic

A couple of times during the growing season, treat your trees to a dose of this tonic to keep 'em in top shape.

1 cup of beer
4 1/2 tbsp. of instant tea granules
1 tbsp. of baby shampoo
1 tbsp. of ammonia
1 tbsp. of whiskey
1 tbsp. of hydrogen peroxide
1 tbsp. of gelatin
2 gal. of warm water

Mix all of these ingredients in a bucket, and give each tree up to a quart of this tonic about once a month from late spring through summer. (For related text, see page 108.)

Transplant Tonic

This terrific tonic is perfect for getting your transplants off to a super-fast start!

1/2 can of beer
1 tbsp. of ammonia
1 tbsp. of instant tea
1 tbsp. of baby shampoo
1 gal. of water

Mix all of the ingredients together. Use 1 cup of the tonic to water each transplant. (For related text, see page 122.)

Tree Transplanting Tonic

Energize your soil with this amazing mix to help it hold moisture and encourage good drainage.

¹/₃ cup of hydrogen peroxide
¹/₄ cup of instant tea granules
¹/₄ cup of whiskey
¹/₄ cup of baby shampoo
2 tbsp. of fish emulsion
1 gal. of warm water

Mix all of these ingredients in a bucket, and pour it into the hole when you transplant a tree or shrub. (For related text, see page 55.)

Ultra-Light Potting Soil

To keep your really big pots and planters from being back-breakers, use this lightweight potting mix.

4 parts perlite, moistened
4 parts compost
1 part potting soil
¹/₂ part cow manure

Mix all of these ingredients together, then fill your containers. This mix dries out

very quickly, particularly in the hot summer sun, so be sure to keep an eye on your flowers, and water them as needed. (For related text, see page 133.)

Winter Walkway Protection Tonic

To keep the grass and groundcovers around your walks and driveways in good shape during the winter, first sprinkle the areas liberally with gypsum. Then apply this tonic.

1 cup of dishwashing liquid
¹/₂ cup of ammonia
¹/₂ cup of beer

Mix all of these ingredients in a 20 gallon hose-end sprayer, and then apply the mixture over the gypsum. (For related text, see page 280.)

Winterizing Tonic

To head off trouble next spring, zap cutworms and other bad bugs with this tonic.

1 cup of Murphy's Oil Soap®
1 cup of tobacco tea*
1 cup of antiseptic mouthwash
Warm water

Mix the Murphy's Oil Soap®, tobacco tea, and mouthwash in a 20 gallon hose-end sprayer, filling the balance with warm water. Saturate your lawn and garden, and they'll be rarin' to grow come spring! (For related text, see page 266.)

*Place half a handful of chewing tobacco in an old nylon stocking, and soak it in a gallon of hot water until the mixture is dark brown.

Wonderful Weed Killer

Nothing spoils the look of a formal garden quicker than weed-filled paths. Use this tonic to kill weeds in gravel walks, or in cracks between bricks or stones in walkways.

1 gal. of white vinegar
1 cup of table salt
1 tbsp. of dishwashing liquid

Mix all of the ingredients together until the salt has dissolved. Spray the solution on weeds, or pour it along cracks to kill weeds. Don't spray it on plants that you want to keep, and don't pour it on soil that you want to be able to garden in someday! (For related text, see page 200.)

Year-Round Refresher

Use this elixir every three weeks from spring through fall to keep your potted plants healthy and happy. (In warm climates, you can use it year-round.)

1 cup of beer
1 cup of baby shampoo
1 cup of liquid lawn food
1/2 cup of molasses
2 tbsp. of fish emulsion
Ammonia

Mix the beer, shampoo, lawn food, molasses, and fish emulsion in a 20 gallon hose-end sprayer. Fill the balance of the sprayer jar with ammonia, then spray away! (For related text, see page 166.)

Yellow Jacket Trap

Are pesky yellow jackets spoiling your summer flower fun? Lure them to their doom with this sweet brew.

1 banana peel
1 cup of sugar
1 cup of vinegar
Water

Cut the banana peel into pieces and slip them into a 2-liter, plastic soda bottle. Combine the sugar and vinegar in a separate container, then pour the mixture into the soda bottle. Add enough water to fill the bottle to within a few inches of the top, then hang it from a sturdy tree branch. Yellow jackets will fly in, but they won't get out! (For related text, see page 184.)

Zinnia Spot Spray

If you're seeing gray spots on your zinnia leaves, whip up a batch of this simple solution.

2 tbsp. of baby shampoo
1 tbsp. of baking soda
1 gal. of warm water

Mix these ingredients together, and mist-spray your plants lightly once a week to keep funky fungi from zapping your zinnias! (For related text, see page 192.)

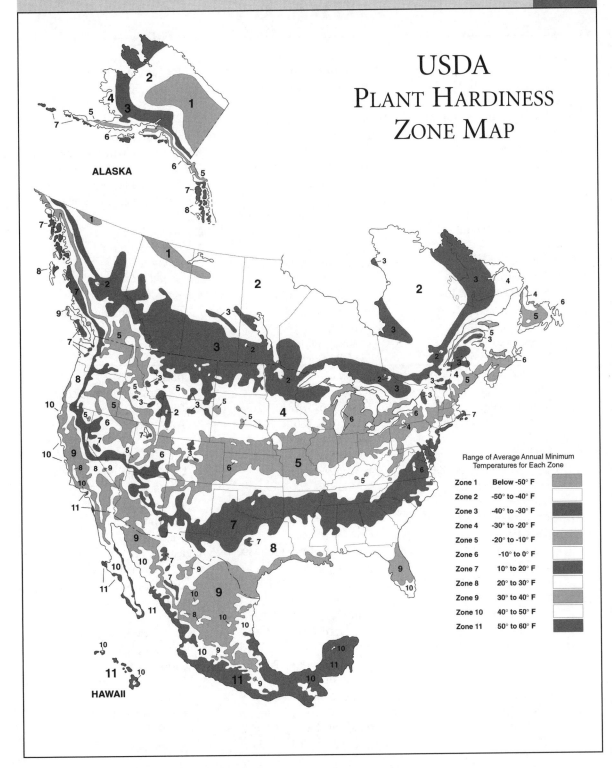

USDA
PLANT HARDINESS
ZONE MAP

ALASKA

HAWAII

Range of Average Annual Minimum
Temperatures for Each Zone

Zone 1	Below -50° F
Zone 2	-50° to -40° F
Zone 3	-40° to -30° F
Zone 4	-30° to -20° F
Zone 5	-20° to -10° F
Zone 6	-10° to 0° F
Zone 7	10° to 20° F
Zone 8	20° to 30° F
Zone 9	30° to 40° F
Zone 10	40° to 50° F
Zone 11	50° to 60° F

Index